Praise for
Relentless

"*Relentless* will stir your passion for the things of God and strengthen your resolve to stand firm in faith and pursue the destiny that God has laid out for you."

—JOYCE MEYER, best-selling author and Bible teacher

"John Bevere has a mandate on his life to serve the body of Christ. His desire to see everyone find and flourish in their God-given destiny is evident in his teachings. His love for Christ and deep revelation of the Word of God will have you pursuing the cause of Christ, relentlessly."

—BRIAN AND BOBBIE HOUSTON, senior pastors, Hillsong Church

"It's one thing to write on a subject; it's another thing to be a living demonstration of what you share. In word and in his life, John Bevere reveals the powerful effect that the relentless pursuit of God's purpose produces. He inspires readers to move from spiritual passivity to a passionate pursuit of God's will...a challenge worth embracing!"

—JAMES ROBISON, president, LIFE Outreach International,
    Fort Worth, Texas

"John Bevere captures the premiere criteria for navigating through the vicissitudes of this life. He challenges every believer to go beyond the goal of stability into the much needed attribute of becoming *Relentless*. People who achieve great goals in life did it in part because they were relentless. I encourage you to take the time to read carefully this necessary word."

—BISHOP T. D. JAKES, The Potter's House

"There are far too many one-hit wonders in the church. So few finish faithfully. But it doesn't have to be that way. John Bevere, one of the most inspiring men in the body of Christ today, compellingly challenges us to believe that our lives are not destined to be cautionary tales of what could have been. Your faith and passion don't have to flame out or fizzle. You can be *Relentless*."

—STEVEN FURTICK, lead pastor, Elevation Church and author
    of *Sun Stand Still*

"Each book John Bevere writes is a worthy contribution to building a solid, healthy, and fruitful life in Christ and for Him! Thanks John, for another brick!"

—JACK W. HAYFORD

"*Relentless* is what the enemy is toward us. It is time we were likewise, relentless in both our faith and actions. God is raising up a tenacious people who will not rest until His will is done. This book is an invaluable tool in this pursuit."

—CHRISTINE CAINE, director, Equip & Empower Ministries, and founder, The A21 Campaign

"A few years ago I was given a bracelet with the words RELENTLESS on it… and I have worn the bracelet ever since, to remind my heart about my pursuit of Christ and His purpose for my life. This book, by the awesome John Bevere, continues to tell the great unfolding story of our passion and pursuit of Jesus and His incredibly great love for us. I *know* that this teaching will open the space of your heart that yearns for more."

—DARLENE ZSCHECH, worship leader and singer/songwriter

"*Relentless* is one of the most spiritually provoking books I've read. John compels us to go beyond just enduring in life to overcoming with God's authority in every area of our lives. It is a timely message of empowerment for the body of Christ that will propel you into the call of God on your life in a fierce and bold way. If you truly have a desire to finish strong and live relentlessly in every area of life God is calling you to, you've got to read this book."

—STOVALL WEEMS, lead pastor, Celebration Church, Jacksonville, Florida, and author of *Awakening*

"John Bevere's new book *Relentless* is a must read for those who have experienced a stumbling block of adversity. *Relentless* will walk you through God's grace as He uses the valleys and storms in life to equip us for His destined purpose. John reminds us that God never gives up on us and we should never give up on Him."

—JENTEZEN FRANKLIN, senior pastor, Free Chapel, and *New York Times* best-selling author

THE POWER YOU NEED TO NEVER GIVE UP

RELENTLESS

JOHN BEVERE

BEST-SELLING AUTHOR OF *THE BAIT OF SATAN*

WATERBROOK
PRESS

RELENTLESS
PUBLISHED BY WATERBROOK PRESS
12265 Oracle Boulevard, Suite 200
Colorado Springs, Colorado 80921

ISBN 978-0-307-45775-2
ISBN 978-0-307-45777-6 (electronic)

Copyright © 2011 by John P. Bevere Jr.

Cover design by Kristopher Orr; cover photo by Tim Flach, Getty Images

Published in the United States by WaterBrook Multnomah, an imprint of the Crown Publishing Group, a division of Random House Inc., New York.

WATERBROOK and its deer colophon are registered trademarks of Random House Inc.

Library of Congress Cataloging-in-Publication Data
Bevere, John.
    Relentless : the power you need to never give up / John Bevere.—1st ed.
        p. cm.
    ISBN 978-0-307-45775-2—ISBN 978-0-307-45777-6 (electronic) 1. Success—Religious aspects—Christianity. 2. Perseverance (Ethics) 3. Persistence. I. Title.
    BV4598.3.B48 2011
    248.4—dc23

                                        2011026747

Printed in the United States of America
2012

10 9 8 7

Special Sales
Most WaterBrook Multnomah books are available at special quantity discounts when purchased in bulk by corporations, organizations, and special-interest groups. Custom imprinting or excerpting can also be done to fit special needs. For information, please e-mail SpecialMarkets@WaterBrook-Multnomah.com or call 1-800-603-7051.

I dedicate this book to my son...

Alec Bevere

You have overcome obstacles and risen above adversity.
Already your life is a testimony of God's favor and grace.
I am so proud of you and will love you forever.

CONTENTS

INTRODUCTION

Shortly after I began writing this book, I watched a movie that vividly illustrates the importance of being relentless. *The Ghost and the Darkness* stars Michael Douglas and Val Kilmer, and it is based on an event that took place in the late 1800s.

A brilliant military engineer named Patterson (Val Kilmer) is hired to oversee the building of a railway bridge to span the Tsavo River of Uganda and thus increase the reach of the British East African Railway. The project is already behind schedule when Patterson arrives on site.

He soon learns why. Workmen have been disappearing. They vanish under the cover of night, never to be seen again. Patterson quickly learns that two man-eating lions have been stalking the work campsites. To stop their killing rampage he sets traps and tries various different methods, but the deadly duo seem to anticipate Patterson's moves and escape his snares.

When the death count reaches thirty, the railroad enlists the help of American hunter Charles Remington (Michael Douglas). His tracking and hunting abilities are renown, yet the lions continue to kill at will. Night after night they wreak death until the workers come to believe the lions are evil spirits that cannot be stopped. As the death toll passes 130, panic and fear grip the men of the work camp and Patterson and Remington watch helplessly as the entire work force flees by jumping onto a train as it rolls through Tsavo.

It's this life-defining moment that stirred me. The lines are clearly drawn. On one side you have a cowardly supervisor who feeds the fear of his men while inciting them to abandon the work they agreed to finish. On the other side you have three men—Remington, Patterson, and Patterson's aide—who refuse to shirk their duties or allow fear to drive them to defeat.

The three men are left to face the cunning monsters on their own. They try and fail to kill them multiple times. The task before them is daunting and extremely dangerous. It could cost them their lives, but they are determined to stop the opposition and finish the bridge. They are armed with superior weapons. Remington and Patterson are convinced that they will ultimately win if they are wise, alert, determined…and *refuse to give up.*

Space and time here doesn't allow for many more details, but this you must know: the man-eating lions are finally stopped. But victory comes at great cost.

The workmen return, and now they see their project engineer, Patterson, quite differently. He is the one who faced death and did not yield. The men hold him in such high regard that they rally behind his cause and accomplish the seemingly impossible. The bridge is completed on time!

As ambassadors of God, we too build bridges. Ours don't cross rivers; they span the gap between heaven and earth. Likewise, we face opposition, and the Scriptures depict our adversary as a lion seeking to devour. But, just as with the lions of Tsavo, our enemy doesn't possess weapons…we do. He's been disarmed, and we have been armed with the most powerful weapons available to men and women.

There are battles to be won and strongholds to overcome. Often these are rooted in mind-sets, modes of operation, and patterns the enemy has instilled in the people of this world. Our opposition is formidable, but "in Christ" we are more powerful.

So we face a very important question: *Will we be like the frightened workmen who fled adversity to save their lives, or will we be courageous and relentless as we pursue heaven's mandate?* I believe within this message are truths that have the potential to forge within you a relentless stance. Not only will these truths strengthen you to stand strong, but they will equip you with the power to overcome and make a positive difference.

It's essential that you be grounded in this knowledge. For far too long God's people have gone into captivity and been destroyed for a lack of it (see Isaiah 5:13; Hosea 4:6). Correct knowledge weaves a foundation of faith, and by faith we effect change in a lost and dark world.

You were created to make a difference in your world of influence. Together, let's prayerfully accept the challenge as we discover the relentless power to never give up!

1

RELENTLESS

Finishing is better than starting.

ECCLESIASTES 7:8 (NLT)

I imagine you agree with me on this: *how we "finish" is more important than how we "begin."*

In the Christian life, the ultimate finish will be having our Lord say to us at the end, "Well done, My good and faithful servant!"

What will it take for you and me to hear those remarkable words from the One who means everything to us?

To finish life well requires that we live life well. This certainly includes knowing how to "never give up." It means having a *relentless* spirit.

How do we acquire that? And why is it so important?

❧

Honestly, I am concerned that many believers are not going to finish well. God once gave me a sobering vision that relates to the theme of this book.[1]

A man was rowing a boat against the river's strong current. He was straining hard to advance against the flow of the water—a tough task, but doable.

Other boats, bigger and luxurious and containing parties of people,

---

1. I briefly shared this vision in a previous book, *A Heart Ablaze* (Nashville: Thomas Nelson, 1999). I now feel such an urgency to retell this story and elaborate upon it in more detail.

frequently passed him flowing downstream. The people on these boats were laughing, drinking, and at ease. Occasionally they would look over at the man battling the current and mock him. He had to fight for every inch of progress while they did very little to absolutely nothing for theirs.

After a while the man grew weary of pressing against the current. Tired and discouraged, he put up the oars. For a few moments he continued to drift upstream from the momentum, but soon came to a standstill. Then something sad and terrible happened: though still pointed upstream, his rowboat began to drift downstream with the current.

Soon the man noticed another party boat. This one was different from the other party boats for—like his own rowboat—this party boat also was pointed upstream, yet was flowing downstream with the current. This boat also carried people who were laughing, socializing, and at ease. Since it was pointed upstream—the direction the man had wanted to go—he decided to hop on and join with them. They now became a close-knit group. Unlike the other party boats that faced and traveled downstream, this boat pointed upstream. But, sadly, it continued flowing downstream with the current.

What is the interpretation of this vision? The river represents the world and the rowboat is our human body that enables us to live and function in this world. The man in the rowboat is a believer; his oars symbolize God's unmerited grace. The party boats depict those joined in one purpose, and the river's current represents the flow of this world, which is under the sway of the evil one.

By the oars of grace, the man has the ability to resist the current and move upstream to his destiny in advancing the kingdom of God. His physical strength represents his faith. Sadly, his strength wanes and he grows weary of the fight. He doesn't think he has what it takes, when in reality he does. Consequently, he eventually runs out of steam and quits.

Once the man quits rowing, the boat continues moving forward (upstream) for a short time due to sheer momentum. And this is where deception moves in. He still sees some fruit in his life, even though what produced it no longer propels him. He erroneously thinks he can live at ease—no longer alert and vigilant—and still lead a successful Christian life.

Finally, the boat comes to a standstill, and then it begins to drift backward (downstream)—slowly at first, but eventually at the same speed as the current.

Here's the telling part of the vision: while his boat is still pointed upstream, he drifts backward with the current. He now has the appearance of Christianity—knows the talk, the songs, and the mannerisms of the kingdom—but in reality he is conforming to the ways of the world (see 1 John 2:15–17).

Eventually our protagonist spots another boat, a party of other "believers" like him. They all consider themselves part of the church because they, too, are pointed upstream. They know the talk, the songs, and the mannerisms. However, they are at ease because they've settled for a fruitless "Christian" life and are under the sway of the evil one who controls the current.

Those in this "Christianity boat" are no longer persecuted or mocked by the nonbelieving world. In fact, they are accepted and sometimes hailed by the world's influencers. They no longer press, press, press forward as the apostle Paul encouraged every Christian to do: "I press toward the goal for the prize of the upward call of God in Christ Jesus" (Philippians 3:14). In fact, these drifting believers have little or no resistance to the ways of the world.

Consider what the apostle John wrote:

> Practically everything that goes on in the world—wanting your own way, wanting everything for yourself, wanting to appear important—has nothing to do with the Father. It just isolates you from him. The world and all its wanting, wanting, wanting is on the way out—but whoever does what God wants is set for eternity. (1 John 2:16–17, MSG)

The vision I've described for you depicts three types of people: the *believer*, the *unbeliever*, and the *deceived*.

- The *unbeliever* just flows with the current, oblivious to the reality of wanting, wanting, wanting.
- The *believer* must press, press, press in the fight of faith to attain kingdom advancement.
- The *deceived* hides his or her motive of wanting, wanting, wanting through "Christian appearance" and the misuse of Scripture.

I know this vision presents a disturbing view of people of faith today, but it forces each of us to ask a vitally important question: "Which person do *I* resemble?" After all, God's Word commands us to...

> Test yourselves to make sure you are solid in the faith. Don't drift along taking everything for granted. Give yourselves regular checkups. You need firsthand evidence, not mere hearsay, that Jesus Christ is in you. Test it out. If you fail the test, do something about it. (2 Corinthians 13:5, MSG)

After seeing this vision and becoming aware of its interpretation, I became even more convicted by these words written to the Hebrew Christians:

> Lift up your tired hands, then, and strengthen your trembling knees! Keep walking on straight paths.... Guard against turning back from the grace of God. (Hebrews 12:12–13, 15, TEV)

As children of God, we should desperately want to finish well for His glory. You and I should never want to turn back from God's grace by growing weary, putting up our oars, and drifting with the current of this world's system.

We need look no further than Scripture to find examples of what happens when people do or do not finish well. Consider Solomon, son of David and the wisest, richest, most powerful man of his time. He achieved heights that no human being for generations before or many afterward even came close to. However, he faltered—put up his oars—in the latter part of his reign, turning his heart from God to align with the world's system.

Because Solomon had many foreign wives, more than likely he experienced tremendous conflict within his household over being single-minded in his allegiance and obedience to Jehovah. In order to keep peace, he did not remain loyal to Jehovah, but rather built altars for and even worshiped his favored wives' foreign gods.

Solomon suffered greatly from his folly, but his children and grandchildren were affected even more profoundly. The kingdom that was entrusted to him, one that was strong from his father David's faithfulness and grew even stronger with Solomon's excellent start, suffered, was divided, and eventually withered from his failure to finish well. Israel's history would have been significantly different if Solomon had remained *relentless*.

Now let's compare Solomon with John the Baptist. John was resolute and held fast to truth, valiantly living and proclaiming it. He, like Solomon, was faced with adversity, but John's potential consequences were far worse, for it wasn't a wife or several but the king of Judea who didn't embrace the truth John proclaimed. Solomon faced a conflicted household, but John faced jail, torture, and possibly even death. Yet in the face of such cruel and extreme consequences, John remained immovable in his stance for truth, both in how he lived and the message he proclaimed. The result: John's legacy is superior to Solomon's.

Not only did John and Solomon face adversity—a rapid river's current—but so do you and I. We are in a serious battle against the world's vain, shallow values. Its influence is powerful. Deceptive. Alluring. It's far too easy to grow weary, to think it's okay to cease our perseverance, give in, and drift with the prevailing currents. But the only way for you and me to finish strong is to be relentless in our faith. In doing so we will become something to be reckoned with, a genuine threat to the kingdom of darkness.

A RELENTLESS SPIRIT

What does it mean to be relentless? The term describes an attitude or posture that is resolute, persistent, and unyielding. Simply put, it does not relent. To relent is to become more lenient, to slacken, or even to concede. Some of the synonyms that help define *relentless* are "adamant, rigorous, severe, uncompromising, unstoppable, tenacious," and even "dogged." Other descriptions include "constant, gritty, single-minded, steadfast, persistent," and "stringent."

Relentlessness can apply to an evil, unyielding force, but for our discussion we're going to consider it in a positive, godly sense. Therefore, we'll apply the term to one who is valiant, courageous, and determined to complete the task at hand. Whether for the short-term or the long-term, a relentless heart is in it to finish according to the desired end. Nothing will deter him or her from the completed goal.

As we contemplate the relentless believer, we're talking about one who is absolutely unyielding in faith, hope, and obedience to God—no matter what the adversity. The relentless believer, committed in every way to finishing well, is a history maker in the truest sense and will forever be known by heaven as one who warranted the Master's hearty "Well done."

These words on being relentless have not always described a man I know well—*me*! In fact, instead of having a relentless spirit, I had a "give-up" spirit. To be blunt, I was a quitter.

I became a child of God in 1979 while attending Purdue University. At the completion of that semester I returned home brimming with such enthusiasm that I immediately shared my newfound faith with my Catholic parents. My mother's reply? "John, this is one of your new fads. You'll quit this just like you've quit everything else."

The piercing sting of her comment wasn't her negative words or what seemed like a degrading indictment. No, it was quite the opposite because she was painfully right: I had a history of quitting almost everything.

> The relentless believer...is a history maker in the truest sense.

I recall fighting the fear, as a single man, that I would never be able to have a lasting marriage. I typically stopped seeing girls past the second or third date. They were attractive and gifted and possessed great personalities, but I grew tired of them. Other guys would later date these same girls and form lasting relationships. Yet my pattern was to go from one girl to the next.

And it wasn't just in dating that I was a quitter. I began piano lessons but begged to quit after six months. My parents wouldn't let me. Finally I became so apathetic that my piano teacher pleaded with my mom and dad to let me give up piano. In all her years of teaching piano, I was the only student she ever had encouraged to stop!

Later, I talked my parents into letting me take guitar lessons. We purchased an expensive guitar and I started strumming with passion, but it lasted only a few months.

In sports, same result. I played baseball and quit after a couple of years. Then it was basketball, which lasted only one season. Next came golf; again, one season. Track and field: same result.

The list continues. I'd start reading books but never finish. In high school I read only one book in its entirety—Ernest Hemingway's *The Old Man and the Sea*. It was required reading, and since the book was short and I enjoyed fishing, I finished it.

I joined clubs only to quit a short time later. I turned to special interests and bought expensive equipment, only to allow it to sit in the closet or rust from lack of use after a strong and enthusiastic start.

In short, my mom was accurate in her assessment. Would I repeat my established pattern? Would I quit Christianity, my newfound faith in God, my new passion? Would my Bibles and study books end up in the closet with all my other short-lived interests?

The good news is that this former quitter has been passionate about Jesus Christ now for more than thirty years. I'm as committed today—yes, even more so—as I was when I came home and told my parents about my new faith. God Almighty, my Father, changed me from one who quickly conceded or tired. Through His Holy Spirit, He built within me the virtue of a relentless spirit.

God made me a *relentless believer.*

If you have received Jesus Christ as your Lord, that same virtue is available to you. But it has to be developed. That's the purpose of this book—to reveal how you can increase and enhance this ability that God has freely given you so you can live well and finish strong.

GOD WROTE A BOOK ABOUT YOU

Do you realize who you are and how much God needs you—to fulfill your destiny in advancing His cause here on earth? Does it surprise you that the heavenly Father is depending on you?

God has specifically designed a life-course for you! Your entire life was mapped out prior to your birth. The psalmist declares:

You saw me before I was born.
    Every day of my life was recorded in your book.
Every moment was laid out
    before a single day had passed. (Psalm 139:16, NLT)

God wrote a book about you before your parents even thought of having you—*before a single day had passed.* Celebrities and rulers aren't the only ones with books containing their life story. No, yours is recorded too, but the amazing reality is this: it was mapped out and penned by God before you were born.

You may protest, "John, you have no idea who you're talking to! My life has had bumps, bruises, and even wrecks due to my bad choices. Did God author that?"

No, a thousand times, no! God mapped out our lives, and it is up to us to make the right choices in order to walk in the exhilarating path He created for us. Wrong choices can detour us, but genuine repentance can right the ship.

You may again question, "But I've had terrible things happen that were not the result of bad choices. Life has dealt me some hard blows. Did God author those disappointments and hardships?"

Again, no! We live in a fallen world. Consequently, Jesus said we would have tribulation and would suffer adversity. The good news is that because God knew what manner of evil would try to overtake you before you were born, in His wisdom He made paths to escape and even come out triumphant. This is why in His Word He calls relentless believers "overcomers."

Hebrews 12:1 exhorts each of us, "Let us run with endurance the race that is set before us." God has set a race before you, me, and each of His children. For you to finish the race well means you'll have to run with endurance, or *relentlessness.* It cannot be completed any other way. It's interesting to note that this is the single virtue highlighted in this passage. The writer doesn't say "Let us run with happiness" or "Let us run with purpose" or "Let us run with seriousness." Don't get me wrong—happiness, purpose, and seriousness, as well as other virtues, are all important to the Christian walk. But the key virtue is relentlessness.

It takes a *relentless* spirit to finish well. Finishing well requires persistence and endurance. I love The Message Bible's rendition of Hebrews 12:1: "Strip down, start running—and never quit!" Completing our course is crucial not only for us but also for those we are called to influence. It's important not to turn back or veer from the path that God has put before us. If you are a child of God, you have what it takes! God has placed that enabling power, the Holy Spirit, within you. If you remain steadfast, you will be able to declare with the apostle Paul, "I have finished the race, and I have remained faithful" (2 Timothy 4:7, NLT).

You may be facing adversity in your marriage, family, employment, business, school, finances, health, or elsewhere. Your situation may seem utterly hopeless and without solution—intimidating, exhausting currents trying to force you to give up and drift downstream. The good news is, "With men it is impossible, but not with God; for with God all things are possible" (Mark 10:27). No matter how tough your circumstances, they are not impossible to God. But Jesus did place an important qualifier on this promise. *"If you can believe,"* He said, "all things are possible to him who *believes*" (Mark 9:23). It takes a *relentless believer* to see the impossible become possible. That's what this message is all about: facing what is beyond your human ability and, by God's strength and grace, seeing the impossible made possible.

Hear me! God desires to call you "great in His sight" (Luke 1:15). He is *for you,* and no one wants your success in life more than God Himself. He's prepared for you a fabulous life and foresees a great finish in which you leave a legacy of faith, significance, and greatness to the benefit of others. But it's all contingent on you being a *relentless* believer.

> No one wants your success in life more than God.

You may be thinking, *But, John, honestly, I'm not exactly a resolute type of person. I don't have a history of sticking it out through tough times.*

If that describes you, there's more good news. Your history doesn't matter. Because of the grace of Jesus Christ, you're not doomed to repeat the past. It's indeed possible for you to become a *relentless believer* and to finish well. You're a candidate for great joy in seeing a desirable end. Whether it is for a short-term chapter of your life or your full lifetime, you are destined to be great in the sight of God. This is His promise!

There's no escaping the adversity waiting for each of us if we follow the path of Jesus. The stakes are high and the eternal rewards priceless. You have a vicious enemy who, to put it bluntly, wants to destroy your influence and wreck your God-assigned mission. As far as Satan's concerned, you are a threat and need to be stopped—indeed, he will be happy when you are "dead." But because of what happened at the cross, Satan is a defeated foe! Every battle we face against him is already won! But we still have to fight him, his cohorts, and their influence—*relentlessly.* Together we will learn how.

You were created to make a difference in this world. You are a child of the King, destined to rule on His behalf. The keys to the kingdom are in your pocket! As you walk closely with Him and commit to being relentless in your faith, He will give you all the strength and guidance you need to overcome the strong currents that flow against you.

Before we move on, let's commit this journey together to the Lord:

> *Dear God, as I read this book may Your Holy Spirit teach and enlighten me. I want more than mere information or inspiration; I want to know the richness and enormity of the calling You've placed upon my life. I want to know the power You've placed within me to accomplish my destiny.*
>
> *Through this message, strengthen me to stand firm in truth and relentless in battle against any adversity that arises to hinder what You want accomplished through me. You've brought me forth for such a time as this; I pray that the message of* Relentless *would equip me to help fulfill Your divine plan while bringing glory to Your name and joy to Your heart. It's in the name of Jesus Christ that I make this request. Amen.*

2

RULING IN LIFE

For the word of God is living and powerful.

HEBREWS 4:12

If we were to read the Word of God exactly as it is, most of us would be dramatically different from what we are.

Sometimes our greatest challenge is to simply believe His Word over our existing conditions. If your state of affairs is not favorable at the moment, you know that it can be changed—that your circumstances are not final. The only thing that is absolutely never changing is the Word of God. Jesus Christ stated years ago, "Heaven and earth will disappear, but my words will remain forever" (Luke 21:33, NLT). Look upward and observe the sun that has given light and warmth to our planet as long as man has been here. It will pass away before the Word of God proves untrue. The Word of God stands forever!

Our Almighty Father declares, "I am ready to perform My word" (Jeremiah 1:12). Notice that He is ready. When will He perform it? The simple answer is, when someone believes Him. Jesus affirms that "all things are possible to him who believes" (Mark 9:23). So let's relentlessly believe!

WE ARE TO RULE IN THIS LIFE

In the next four chapters we're going to explore and develop an extremely important truth—a truth that's vital to our quest to finish well as relentless believers. I'll alert you that it *may* appear that we're veering a bit off subject, but stay with me. I assure you that it all comes together to help us complete our journey.

With this in mind, let's examine one of the most potent scriptures in the New Testament:

> All who receive God's abundant grace and are freely put right with him will rule in life through Christ. (Romans 5:17, TEV)

Look carefully at the phrase *rule in life*. The New International Version translates it "reign in life"; Weymouth rephrases it "reign as kings in life." You and I, as God's children, are to rule as kings or queens! These words are not merely man's words, for we know that "all Scripture is given by inspiration of God" (2 Timothy 3:16). Therefore, God is literally stating that we will *rule in life* through the power of His Son. Notice He doesn't say, "You will rule in heaven one day" or "You will rule in the next life." No, He clearly decrees that we are to rule in *this* life as kings or queens through Christ.

One of my dictionary's primary definitions of a king or queen is "one that is supreme or preeminent in a particular sphere." The word *reign* is defined as "dominance or widespread influence." To reign as a king or queen is to have supreme dominance and influence over a particular sphere. In what sphere are we to be unsurpassed or paramount? The sphere of life.

In other words, life on this earth is not to surpass us; we are to govern it. This is the Word of God, His promise to you! I encourage you to firmly settle this in your heart.

DEFAULT STATEMENT

Consider the default statement we've all heard uttered for years. When situations become difficult, unfavorable, damaging, and even life-threatening, well-meaning people often default to the assurance that "God is in control." This statement implies that there's no reason to fight opposition because God, out of His loving and good nature, will somehow turn all adversity around for ultimate good since He's the One controlling everything.

The truth is, *God put us in control*. Now before you throw this book down, please hear me out.

In the Psalms we read, "The heavens are the Lord's heavens, but the earth has He given to the children of men" (Psalm 115:16, AMP). The Message states it this way: "The heaven of heavens is for GOD, but *he put us in charge* of the earth."

Who is in charge of the earth? We are!

Almighty God is the Sovereign Creator, and He made a sovereign choice to give man rulership over the earth and how affairs are run on it. If God had retained control of the earth as many believe, then when Adam began lifting the forbidden fruit toward his mouth, God would have intervened and slapped it from his hand. "What's up with you, Adam?" God would have exclaimed. "Don't you realize the consequences of what you're about to do? Don't you realize all the pain, suffering, sickness, disease, famine, hunger, poverty, murder, theft, and more that will come on you and your descendants? Not to mention the earthquakes, tornadoes, hurricanes, pestilence, drought, and danger from wild animals? Do you not understand that all of nature will go into a corruptive state? And, most importantly, that I will have to send My only Son to suffer a terrible death in order to redeem mankind back to Me?"

But God didn't hold Adam back, because He had bequeathed the earth to mankind. Our loving Creator God is not like so many who give authority and then revoke it if they don't like the way it's being handled. When God gives something, it's a permanent gift. We have His Word on it: "For God's gifts and his call can never be withdrawn" (Romans 11:29, NLT).

Someone may counter, "But the Bible states that 'The earth is the Lord's, and all its fullness'" (Psalm 24:1). In reply, let me relate something that has transpired with my family over the past few years.

Awhile back Lisa's mother, Shirley, who is in her seventies, was living alone in a Florida apartment with no kin nearby. Lisa and I really wanted to have her close to our family, and one day Lisa noticed some great townhomes for sale not more than five minutes from our house. They were perfect! So we approached Shirley with an offer to purchase one of the townhomes for her to live in, inviting her to join our team at Messenger International. With joy, Mom accepted. The townhome was purchased, and in order for Mom to feel a sense of independence, we decided to

> When God gives something, it's a permanent gift.

charge her a nominal rent each month. It has been a couple of years since she moved in, and she is flourishing in every area of life.

In all that time as owner, I've not once told her how she is to decorate her home or arrange her furniture. I haven't told her how to run her household; what she is to cook for breakfast, lunch, or dinner; or what appliances to buy. Lisa's mom is in charge of the day-to-day operations. I own that townhouse—I have the title deed—but I have leased it to her and she is to run the affairs of that property as she desires. She can ask for my help anytime, but I'm not going to interfere unless she does.

In the same way, the earth is the Lord's. He is the owner, but He has leased it to mankind. Listen to what He said when He created us and gave us the "townhome" of earth:

> God created human beings, making them to be like himself. He created
> them male and female, blessed them, and said, "Have many children, so
> that your descendants will live all over the earth and *bring it under their*
> *control. I am putting you in charge.*" (Genesis 1:27–28, TEV)

God put us in charge of His big townhome. You and I, not God, are in control of how life is run on this planet.

A NEW LANDLORD

The huge problem arose in the Garden of Eden when the devil entered the serpent's body and convinced Adam and Eve to disobey God's Word and embrace his lie. Once mankind did this we gave ourselves over to a new landlord whose name is Satan. Not only did we give ourselves, but we also gave all that was under our domain. All of mankind's descendants, as well as nature itself, now was under the sway of the wicked one.

This quantum shift to the new landlord explains the encounter that came later between Satan and Jesus. The devil took Jesus up to a high mountain and showed Him all the kingdoms of the world. Satan offered, "To You I will give all this power and authority and their glory (all their magnificence, excellence, preeminence, dignity, and grace), *for it has been turned over to me,* and I give it to whomever I will" (Luke 4:6, AMP).

When were all the kingdoms of the world "turned over" to the devil? It happened in the Garden of Eden thousands of years earlier when Adam gave up the right to rule the earth God had entrusted to him. What God had given to man was now in the hands of His archenemy. This is why the Scriptures tell us, "We know [positively] that we are of God, and the whole world [around us] is under the power of the evil one" (1 John 5:19, AMP).

THE TAKE-BACK PLAN

God desired to get back into the hands of mankind what Adam had relinquished. However, He couldn't come in the form of deity and just snatch it back, because God doesn't retract the authority He gives and Adam had officially relinquished it. A man lost it, so a Man would have to restore it. This is why Jesus had to come as the "Son of Man." He was born of a woman, making Him 100 percent man. He was fathered by the Holy Spirit, making Him 100 percent God (and thus free from the curse of sin). However, we are clearly told that "When the time came, he [Jesus] set aside the privileges of deity and took on the status of a slave, became human!" (Philippians 2:7, MSG). Even though He is God, He set aside His deity and walked the earth as a man.

Jesus lived perfectly obedient to the Father. Because of His innocence and willful embrace of the cross, He was able to purchase back with His own blood what Adam had lost. Scripture says He "disarmed principalities and powers, He made a public spectacle of them, triumphing over them in it" (Colossians 2:15). Now He alone possesses the authority Adam relinquished. This is why He clearly states, "All authority [all power of rule] has been given to Me in heaven and on earth" (Matthew 28:18).

One day He will return and restore all of nature as it was before the fall of Adam in the Garden of Eden. As the apostle Paul wrote,

> For the creation (nature) was subjected to frailty (to futility, condemned to frustration), not because of some intentional fault on its

part, but...will be set free from its bondage to decay and corruption [and gain an entrance] into the glorious freedom of God's children. (Romans 8:20–21, AMP)

Nature is still subject to frailty: our physical bodies still grow old and die, the physical world is still corrupt and decays, wild beasts still hunt and eat weaker animals, snakes still possess vile venom, disease still runs rampant, and hurricanes and tornadoes still destroy. However, there is One who has authority over it all and can turn it around, and that One is Christ.

WHO IS CHRIST?

So the question now becomes, Who is *Christ*? This is where an unrenewed mind once again steals from the children of God. When many think of Christ, they think of only Jesus Christ, almost as if *Christ* is His last name. These dear people don't think of anyone else other than our Great King who died on the cross and was resurrected. Yes, the name *Christ* does refer to our Lord and Savior, but let's see what God's Word says.

Paul tells us, "Now all of you together are Christ's body, and each one of you is a separate and necessary part of it" (1 Corinthians 12:27, NLT). We believers, together, are Christ's body. Each of us is a vital "body part." Jesus is the head, we are the body; it's that simple!

Individually, you have a head on top of your shoulders, but you also possess two hands, two feet, two knees, two arms, a chest, a stomach, a liver, two kidneys, and so on. When you think of yourself, do you think of your head as being separate from or different from your body? Would you call your head by one proper name and your body by a different proper name? Of course not. You are one being—one person. If you saw my head, you would refer to it as John Bevere. If my head was momentarily concealed, and you saw only my body, you would still refer to it as John Bevere. My head and body are one.

In the same way, Christ's head and His body are one. Jesus is the head, and we are different parts of His body, so we are one in Christ. So when you read *Christ* in the New Testament, you need to see not just the One who died on the cross but also yourself. This is why Scripture states, "For both He who sanctifies and those who are being sanctified are all of one" (Hebrews 2:11). Jesus himself prayed, "I do not pray for these alone, but also for those who will believe in Me through their word; that they all may be one, as You, Father, are in Me, and I in You; that they also may be *one in Us*" (John 17:20–21).

You are one with Jesus. Literally, *one*!

Just so you can rest assured that I'm not pulling a single scripture or two out of context, allow me to quickly share some others that will affirm your faith and understanding of this exciting principle. I ask that you read carefully and ponder these scriptures as if you've never read or heard them before:

- Peter writes that we have been reborn by the Word of God so that we might be "partakers of the divine nature" (1 Peter 1:23; 2 Peter 1:4). The word *nature* is defined as "the innate or essential qualities or character of a person." You and I have the same essential qualities as Jesus, just as my hand is the same genetic makeup as my head because I am *one* human being, not *two*.

- John the apostle writes, "Of His *fullness* we have all received" (John 1:16). Did you hear the word *fullness*? When we join John's words to Peter's, we find that we've received the *fullness* of Christ's essential qualities or spiritual genetic makeup.

- Later, in his first epistle, John writes, "As He [Jesus] is, so are we in this world" (1 John 4:17). He is not referring to the next life in this passage. No, he writes in the present tense: As Jesus *is*, so are *we*. Exactly as Jesus is, so also are we—right now, today!

- Paul writes, "Do you not know that your bodies are members of Christ?" (1 Corinthians 6:15). The manner in which he states this implies that this knowledge should be basic. Are you missing this elementary reality? Do we as a church truly believe these words?

CHRIST'S AUTHORITY

Now that we know we're included when we hear the word *Christ,* let's see what this revelation means to the level of power and authority we have in Him. In his letter to the Ephesians, Paul prayed passionately that every follower of Christ might comprehend "what is the immeasurable and unlimited and surpassing greatness of His power" (Ephesians 1:19, AMP).

What descriptive words! What magnitude implied! Would you agree that the Lord of glory has immeasurable, unlimited power? Would you affirm that His power far surpasses any greatness, any other authority, and any other power in the universe? I'm sure you'd support this assertion without hesitation.

However, would you say the very same thing about *yourself*? More importantly, would you really believe it? If not, you've inadvertently separated yourself from Christ. Are you part of a different body? Are you not part of Christ, a member of His body? You may be thinking, *John Bevere, now you're getting too far out on a limb!* But am I? To see that I'm not, continue with the next phrase of the above scripture: "what is the immeasurable and unlimited and surpassing greatness of His power *in and for us who believe*" (Ephesians 1:19, AMP).

Paul was referencing us all along. Why? As a believer in Jesus Christ, you are part of Christ. Therefore, the exact power Christ has, you have! "As He is, so are we in this world." Are you allowing this to soak into your heart?

Staying with the Amplified Bible translation, let's continue to unpack Paul's prayer for us in Ephesians:

> …as demonstrated in the working of His mighty strength, which
> He exerted in Christ when He raised Him from the dead and seated
> Him at His [own] right hand in the heavenly [places]. (Ephesians
> 1:19–20)

Do you believe that the Lord Jesus Christ was crucified, died, buried, raised up from the dead, and is now seated in the highest place of authority? If you are an authentic Christian, you certainly do. But do you believe all of this in regard to *yourself*? Chances are, most believers do not see themselves in this light. Yet Paul writes,

> Or do you not know that as many of us as were baptized [immersed]
> into Christ Jesus were baptized [immersed] into His death? Therefore we
> were buried with Him through baptism [immersion] into death, that just

as Christ was raised from the dead by the glory of the Father, even so we
also should walk in newness of life. (Romans 6:3–4)

Note that this passage isn't referring to the act of water baptism, but to our
"immersion" into Christ's body by the Spirit of God when we were born again
(see 1 Corinthians 12:13). We are Christ's body; therefore, the moment we were
immersed into Him, our history changed. We died with Him, were buried with
Him, were raised with Him, and, as brand-new beings, we live as He does!
Again, "As He is, so are we in this world." We are in Christ! We *are* Christ!

Please don't get hung up on the statement "we are Christ." To illustrate this
truth, let me share an example. Let's say you and your friend Jim are at the beach.
Jim decides to go in the water and wades out far enough so that he's submerged
from his shoulders down. If another friend came by at that moment and asked,
"Where is Jim?" you wouldn't respond, "Jim's body is in the ocean." No, you'd say,
"Jim is in the ocean." You'd say this because, even
though his head is not under the water, Jim's head
and body are all one.

Well, "we are Christ" in the earth. He is the
Head, and we are His body! We are one with Him!

According to Ephesians 1:20, because we are
part of Christ we are now seated in a ruling place. In
fact, it's the highest place of authority in the uni-
verse, other than that of God the Father. Jesus said, "All authority [all power of
rule] has been given to Me in heaven and on earth" (Matthew 28:18). Paul
continues,

> Far above all rule and authority and power and dominion and every
> name that is named [above every title that can be conferred], not only in
> this age and in this world, but also in the age and the world which are to
> come. (Ephesians 1:21, AMP)

Do you believe the Lord Jesus is seated far above all rule, authority, and
power in this world and in the universe? As a Christian, of course you do. But I
ask again: Do you believe this in regard to *yourself* ? You may not see yourself

> Because we are
> part of Christ we are
> now seated in a
> ruling place.

in this light. Chances are even better you don't believe this reality. If so, you've again separated yourself from Christ in your thinking or in what you believe. Are you part of a different body? No, you are part of Christ! We all are in Christ. We *are* Christ. We are His body! Listen carefully as Paul confirms this:

> And He has put all things under His feet and has appointed Him the universal and supreme Head of the church [a headship exercised throughout the church], which is His body, the fullness of Him Who fills all in all [for in that body lives the full measure of Him Who makes everything complete, and Who fills everything everywhere with Himself]. (Ephesians 1:22–23, AMP)

We are His body, the full measure of Jesus Christ, completely one with Him. Paul states that *all things* have been put under His feet. If you are the part of Christ's body who happens to be a toe, you are still far above—not just a little above—all rule, power, and dominion in this earth and under the earth. In Christ, your authority has been restored and even made greater than what Adam lost.

It's a good possibility that God foresaw we would have difficulty grasping the magnitude of this reality, so He inspired Paul to make it crystal clear in the second chapter of Ephesians. He would leave no doubts. Remember that the chapters and verses were added later—this is one letter, one continuing thought:

> And He raised us up together with Him and made us sit down together [giving us joint seating with Him] in the heavenly sphere [by virtue of our being] in Christ Jesus. (Ephesians 2:6, AMP)

The head is not cut off from the body. We are all together, seated in a place of rulership, authority, and power in the heavenly sphere. In other words, we are in a sphere that is above any forces of this earth—in fact, *far above*!

There is not one demon spirit, fallen angel, or even Satan himself who has power or authority over us. We reign supreme because of our position and authority in Christ!

Hallelujah!

RULE IN LIFE

In light of what we've highlighted, let's look back at the verse of scripture noted early in this chapter.

> All who receive God's abundant grace and are freely put right with him
> will *rule in life* through Christ. (Romans 5:17, TEV)

Focus for a moment on the phrase "rule in life through Christ." As members of Christ's body, we are to rule over and against all opposition to life and godliness. Since we are the ones who are to govern here on earth, if things go wrong and stay wrong, is it because we are relinquishing or not executing our authority?

Many years ago my pastor announced to our large congregation that I would be entering into the preaching ministry. A few days later, an older minister approached my wife and said, "Lisa, I have a word from God for your husband."

We were very young and desperate to grow and learn (as we still are). Lisa responded, "Tell me the word and I'll pass it along to John."

The older minister said, "Tell John that if he doesn't walk in his God-given authority, someone else will take it away from him and use it against him."

When Lisa passed those words on to me, they pierced my being like a light-saber cutting into my heart. And I've witnessed over the years just how true his words were—not just for me, but for anyone who is in Christ. I have grieved often as I watch many who truly love God but are bound to, and controlled by, opposing forces and situations. Our Lord Jesus paid such an enormous price to set them free, yet they still are in bondage. Adverse weather, natural disaster, sickness, disease, demonic influence, circumstances of opposition—the list is endless. These forces control and dominate good people who are actually kings and queens in this life but who are ignorant of who they are in Christ.

If you are one of these who has been ruled rather than ruling, then I've got good news. If you'll take to heart the Word of God that we've unearthed in this chapter, your life will begin to change. You now know the power and authority you possess to help those who are ignorant or helpless; you can now bring the good life of the kingdom to those in need.

The apostle John made a strong statement to all of us who are part of Christ's body: "Those who say they live in God should live their lives as Christ did" (1 John 2:6, NLT).

Jesus had already asserted this when He said, "As the Father has sent Me, I also send you" (John 20:21). As Jesus ruled, so He wants us to rule. When the storm came to destroy Jesus and His staff, He spoke to the wind and the sea, and they obeyed Him. When He needed food for the masses in the wilderness, He multiplied the little they had and fed thousands, with more food left over than when they started. When He had no boat and needed to cross the sea, He walked on the water. When the wine supply ran out at the wedding, He turned water into wine. He caused a fig tree to shrivel up and die with the spoken words of His mouth. He put an ear back on an assailant who'd lost it by the edge of a sword. He cleansed those who were diseased, made the blind see, the deaf hear, and the lame walk. None of these earthly challenges were a match for the One who *ruled in life*.

Demon-inspired men didn't intimidate Him; He had an answer to stop their opposing words in every confrontation. Evil rulers couldn't catch him. Angry crowds couldn't push Him off the brow of a hill; He just walked right through their midst. Demon-possessed people didn't scare Him; He just freed them. The list is almost endless, for as John summarized at the close of his account of Jesus' life, "Truly Jesus did many other signs in the presence of His disciples, which are not written in this book.... If they were written one by one, I suppose that even the world itself could not contain the books that would be written" (John 20:30; 21:25).

Jesus Christ ruled in life. He ruled over opposition and adversity. He brought heaven to earth. He set the bar for us to follow. And He expects us to do even more: "The truth is, anyone who believes in me will do the same works I have done, and even greater works" (John 14:12, NLT).

Which brings us to the next logical questions. *How* do we rule in life? Where does the power come from?

3

THE POWER SOURCE

All who receive God's abundant grace and are freely
put right with him will rule in life through Christ.

ROMANS 5:17 (TEV)

s we have discovered, we know we are to rule in life as kings and
queens. Life on this earth is not to rule us; we are to rule it.

The next logical question to ask is, *Do I have the power or ability*
to do it?

Well, consider the Chihuahua and the grizzly bear.

Chihuahuas are small, yappy dogs. They can be persistent and even relentless. Have you ever encountered a Chihuahua with an attitude? He will yap and
bark nonstop to get you out of his assumed territory. He may even bite at your
ankle. If you gently push him away, he'll relentlessly continue his quest to dominate you. However, if you become tired of the dog's behavior, all you have to do
is give him one good kick and a strong shout and the Chihuahua will scurry
away, intimidated and shamefully defeated. Why? That little dog has no power
over a full-grown human being.

On the other hand, if an adult grizzly bear has the same determination to
take you out and you don't happen to have a powerful rifle, you're in huge
trouble. The bear could easily overpower you and take your life.

As we know so well, there are forces that do not want us to finish well. As
we fight them, how do we know we have power over these forces? When it
comes to battling these supernatural foes, are we like the Chihuahua or the grizzly bear? Where does the power come from to rule?

The answer is also found in Romans 5:17: We are able to rule because of "God's abundant *grace*." (My book *Extraordinary* offers a detailed explanation of the full meaning of grace, so here I will discuss only the most critical points.)

THE GREAT DISCONNECT

It's on the subject of "abundant grace" that a huge—and I mean *huge*—disconnect occurs among America's evangelical Christians.

In 2009 our ministry conducted a survey across America that questioned thousands of born-again, Bible-believing, Sunday-morning church-attending Christ followers from various denominations and independent congregations. The survey asked people to "give three or more definitions or descriptions of the grace of God." An overwhelming majority of the responders defined God's grace as (1) salvation; (2) an unmerited gift; and (3) forgiveness of sins.

I'm so glad American Christians understand that we are saved by grace and only by grace. Salvation doesn't come by being sprinkled with water, attending a certain church, keeping religious laws, or doing enough good works to outweigh our bad. Ephesians 2:8–9 clearly states, "For *by grace* you have been saved through faith, and that not of yourselves; *it is the gift of God,* not of works, lest anyone should boast." It's reassuring to know that evangelical Christians are firmly established in the knowledge that God's grace cannot be earned or merited but received only through faith in Jesus Christ's redemptive work at Calvary.

> It's a tragedy to see well-meaning people try to earn God's favor.

It's a tragedy to see well-meaning people try to *earn* God's favor. I've witnessed too many heartbreaking situations in which men and women depend on their own works or behavior to try to bring themselves into right standing with God.

No matter how good society says you are, Ephesians 2:8–9 instructs that you can never save yourself by your own efforts from the impending judgment due to mankind. Salvation is received only by faith, for it is God's gift to us through the death and resurrection of His Son.

It's also tragic to observe those who have received, by faith, God's gift of eternal salvation, but who then proceed to live as though they can earn His ongoing grace through their works. These believers feel they must pray longer, fast more often, and perform more charitable deeds or other related Christian works. The apostle Paul had to reprimand the Galatian church for this very misstep: "I suspect you would never intend this, but this is what happens. When you attempt to live by your own religious plans and projects, you are cut off from Christ, you fall out of grace" (Galatians 5:4, MSG). It's sad to see so many well-intentioned Christians falling into this same trap today.

The survey also revealed that, in general, U.S. Christians know it is by the grace of God that our sins have been eradicated. Ephesians 1:7 confirms this wonderful truth: "In Him we have redemption through His blood, the forgiveness of sins, according to the riches of His grace." It is God's free gift that remits our sins forever and ever. Thank God!

So most American believers seem well established in the foundational truths that God's grace includes salvation, it is an unmerited gift, and it is forgiveness of sins. Ministers of the gospel seem to have done a good job emphasizing these important areas, and I believe God is well pleased on this account.

But then comes the tragedy that the survey uncovered. Only 2 percent of the thousands surveyed believed that "grace is God's empowerment." Yet this is exactly how God describes His grace:

My grace is all you need, for *my power* is greatest when you are weak. (2 Corinthians 12:9, TEV)

If you look up this verse in a red-letter edition of the Bible, where all words spoken by Jesus are in red and all others are in black, you'll see that the words above are not black. They're red. So although these words are reported by the apostle Paul, they are not his words—they are straight from the Lord Himself. God defines His grace as His empowerment. Yet, according to the survey, only 2 percent of U.S. Christians know and understand this. (The actual figure was 1.9 percent. That's less than two of every 100 believers! Our omnipotent, Almighty God defines His grace as His empowerment, yet less than two of every 100 Christians know it. How alarming!)

GRACE-EMPOWERMENT

The word *weak*, as it's used in the 2 Corinthians 12:9 passage, means "inability." God is saying, "My grace (power) is optimum when you face situations that are beyond your ability to handle." This is seen in Paul's comments regarding the Macedonian believers: "We make known to you the *grace of God* bestowed on the churches of Macedonia.... For I bear witness that according to *their ability,* yes, and *beyond their ability*" (2 Corinthians 8:1, 3). God's grace had made it possible for the Macedonian Christians to go beyond their own ability. That's grace—it is God's empowerment.

Earlier, Paul had written to the same audience, "Our relations with you, have been ruled by God-given frankness and sincerity, by the *power of God's grace* and not by human wisdom" (2 Corinthians 1:12, TEV). Again grace is represented as God's empowerment.

Peter defines the grace of God in the same way. "Grace and peace be multiplied to you...as His divine power [*grace*] has given to us all things that pertain to life and godliness" (2 Peter 1:2–3). Again *grace* is referred to as "His divine power." Peter is saying that everything needed for us to live as God intends is available through the empowerment of His grace, which we have received by faith.

Let's take it further by going to the Greek. The Greek word most frequently used for *grace* in the New Testament is *charis,* defined by James Strong in his highly respected *Exhaustive Concordance of the Bible* as "gift," "benefit," "favor," "gracious," and "liberality." If you couple this initial definition with selected scriptures from the books of Romans, Galatians, and Ephesians, you clearly see the aspect of grace the majority of American Christians are familiar with. However, Strong doesn't stop there. He goes on to define *grace* as "the divine influence upon the heart, and its reflection in the life."

From this definition we can see that there is an *outward reflection* of what is done in the heart, which underscores the empowerment of grace. The Bible tells us that when Barnabas arrived at the church of Antioch "and *saw the evidence* of the grace of God, he was glad" (Acts 11:23, NIV). He didn't hear about grace, he saw the evidence of it. He saw the empowerment of heart that was reflected in how the people lived their lives.

This is why James writes, "Show me your faith [grace] without your works, and I will show you my faith [grace] by my works" (James 2:18). I inserted the word *grace* for *faith* because it is by faith that we access the grace of God (see Romans 5:2). James is saying, "Let me see the evidence of the empowerment, which is the true indicator that you've really received grace through believing."

Zondervan's *Encyclopedia of Bible Words* states this about *charis:* "This grace is a dynamic force that does more than affect our standing with God by crediting us with righteousness. Grace affects our experience as well. Grace is marked always by God's enabling work within us to overcome our helplessness."

After careful reading of every verse in the New Testament concerning grace, after hours of studying every Greek dictionary I can get my hands on, and after speaking to fluent Greek-speaking individuals, my personal summary-definition of *grace* goes like this:

> Grace is God's free empowerment that gives us the ability
> to go beyond our natural ability.

WHY SO TRAGIC?

Why is it such a tragedy that only 2 percent of Christians in the U.S. understand the empowerment of God's grace? Let me illustrate with a hypothetical scenario.

Let's say we did some research and discovered a small tribe living in the bush near the equator in Africa. We've learned that this tribe has to walk two miles every day to get fresh water from the closest spring. Then they must carry this heavy water back to their camp to provide fresh water to their people.

When the villagers need food, animals don't just walk through their camp and say, "I'm your dinner; spear me." No, tribesmen have to go out to where the animals are and hunt them. Sometimes after killing the wildebeest or antelope they have to carry that dead, heavy animal eight to ten miles back to their little camp.

Whenever they need supplies that they can't find in the bush, they have to walk more than thirty-five miles to the nearest village, purchase or trade for the supplies, and carry them the same distance back to their camp.

After learning all this we decide to give them a gift. Yes, we are going to *favor* them by being *gracious* and *liberally benefitting* them (these are all the definitions of *grace* listed by Strong). We decide to buy them a brand-new Land Rover.

We purchase the vehicle, ship it to the coast of Africa, and then personally drive it to their area. After parking it nearby, we go into the bush, get the chief and small tribe, and walk them out to show off the Land Rover. With big smiles we declare, "This is our gift to you!"

We invite the chief to sit in the front passenger seat. One of us gets in behind the steering wheel and starts the vehicle. We happily exclaim, "Chief, this Land Rover is amazing! It has air conditioning! So if it's 108 degrees Fahrenheit outside, all you need to do is push this button and dial this knob to 72, and you'll experience a comfortable 72 degrees even though it's blazing hot outside."

Then we announce to him, "Also, this Land Rover has a heater in it. So if it's cold outside, push this button and turn the knob to 75, and you'll experience a cozy 75 degrees inside even though it's below 40 degrees outside.

"We also put an XM Satellite Radio in this Land Rover. Do you know what that means? You can hear live broadcasts from all over the world while you're inside this vehicle." You tune in to a live broadcast from the BBC in England— the chief is amazed.

"But that's not all, Chief," you continue. "We also have a DVD player in this Land Rover." We whip out some DVDs. We insert one, hit Play, and the chief is amazed when he sees the beautiful full-color screen projecting the movie.

"But there's more! This Land Rover also has a CD player." We insert a worship CD, and the chief is astounded as the vehicle is filled with beautiful worship music.

We both get out of the Land Rover, and the chief asks, "What are we to give you for this great gift?"

"Nothing," we reassure him. "You could never buy this from us. It is our free gift to you and your tribe. We love you all!"

The chief and his tribe are so thankful. We leave. But months later, we learn that the tribe is still hiking four miles round trip every day for water. They are still walking miles to their hunting grounds and carrying their heavy kills back to their camp, and they're still hiking thirty-five miles to get supplies at the nearest village. Why? Because we neglected to tell them that the primary functional definition of that Land Rover is *transportation*. We pointed out everything to the chief except for one of the most important features: this Land Rover will transport you wherever you need to go and will carry your load for you.

In the same manner, many in Christian leadership have neglected to tell Western Christians that the primary functional definition of the grace of God is *His empowerment*.

PRIMARY FUNCTIONAL DEFINITION

You may challenge me: "The primary functional definition of *grace* is God's empowerment? How can you make such a statement?"

Recently as I was in prayer, I sensed the Lord asking me a thought-provoking question: *Son, how did I introduce grace in My book, the New Testament?* Since I have authored more than a dozen books, that question really meant something to me. Whenever I introduce a new term in a book, one that most readers may not be familiar with, I give the primary definition. Later in the book I can give secondary definitions, but it's important up front to list the principal definition.

For example, if I were to write a letter to the chief to inform him of the Land Rover, I would announce in the first paragraph,

> *Chief, we are giving you a brand-new Land Rover. Its primary function is transportation. Now your people will no longer have to carry heavy water on their backs for miles during their daily round trip; someone in the tribe can drive the vehicle there and haul the water back. Now your people will no longer have to carry for miles back to the camp the heavy game you hunt; someone can just drive the vehicle to the spot of the kill and haul the game back. Furthermore, your people will not have to walk thirty-five miles to get supplies from the nearest village; just drive there and haul the supplies back in a tenth of the time.*

It would be important to give the primary purpose of the Land Rover up front because the chief and his people have never seen a vehicle before.

Then, in the second paragraph of the letter, I might tell him about the air conditioner and heater. I could devote the third paragraph to the XM Satellite Radio, and the fourth paragraph to the DVD and CD players. Then conclude the letter by informing him that it is a gift. But I would give him the primary functional definition of that vehicle in the first paragraph.

With that in mind, let's return to the Lord's question to me: *How did I introduce grace in My book, the New Testament?*

I responded, "I don't know." I went to my computer, opened the Bible concordance, and found out how God introduces grace in the New Testament. He does it in John 1:16: "Of His [Jesus'] fullness we have all received, and grace for grace."

Notice that John writes "grace for grace." I have a Greek friend who lives in Athens. He's a minister who not only speaks Greek as his primary language but also has studied ancient Greek. He's my go-to person when it comes to the Greek language. He shared with me that in this verse, John is actually stating that God has given us "the richest abundance of grace." In other words, the apostle is telling us that the overflow—or abundance—of what grace does is that it gives us the fullness of Jesus Christ! Did you hear that? The fullness of Jesus Christ Himself! That speaks of ability and power.

I want to be sure you comprehend what is being said here. Suppose I approach an average tennis player. He's only a C-level player in his local club. I say to him, "We now have scientific means of being able to give you the fullness—the full ability—of Roger Federer." (If you're not into pro tennis, Federer is among the greatest players in the history of the sport.) What do you think this C-level player's response would be? He'd say, "Absolutely! Give it to me right away! What do we need to do?" And once we gave him the fullness of Roger Federer, what would happen? You guessed it: He'd win his club championship, then qualify for the U.S. Open and win it, then win a few Wimbledon tournaments as well.

Suppose I approach a freshman architecture student at a state university. I say, "We now have a new scientific means of being able to put on you the fullness—the full ability—of Frank Lloyd Wright." What do you think this young student's response would be? He'd exclaim, "Wow, put it on me right now!" And once we did, what would this student do? He'd leave his school and launch his award-winning career.

One more example to drive this home. Suppose I approach a struggling businessman by saying, "We have a new scientific means of being able to give you the fullness—the full ability—of Bill Gates." What do you think the struggling businessman's response would be? He'd cry out, "I want it! Let's do it!" What would he do after receiving Bill Gates's full ability? He'd start thinking of ways to design new products and make business investments that he'd never thought of before.

Well, grace hasn't given any of us the fullness of Roger Federer, Frank Lloyd Wright, or Bill Gates. That would be a grace far too small. No, God's grace has given us the fullness of Jesus Christ Himself! Do you comprehend this? That's ability! That's power!

So God doesn't introduce grace in the New Testament as a free gift, although I'm forever grateful that it's His free gift. Nor does He introduce it as remittance for our sins, although again I'm forever grateful His grace does take away our sins. No, He introduces grace as the empowerment that gives us the fullness of Jesus Christ.

> **God's grace has given us the fullness of Jesus Christ Himself!**

As you'll recall from the previous chapter, Peter writes that God's grace makes us "partakers of the divine nature" (2 Peter 1:2–4). The word *nature* describes the essential qualities or characteristics of a person. Therefore, God's grace freely gives us the fullness of the essential qualities and characteristics of Jesus Himself! And this is why John states, "As He is, so are we in this world" (1 John 4:17). Do you comprehend the magnitude of these words?

This underscores our empowerment and potential to rule in life! God's grace has re-created us to be exactly as Jesus is; it has empowered us to live as He lived. We are literally in Christ. We're His body. We are Christ in the earth. We are Christians. And this is why John so boldly writes, "Whoever claims to live in him must walk as Jesus did" (1 John 2:6, NIV).

Let these words sink into your heart: we are to live just as Jesus lived on this earth. This is not a biblical suggestion; it's a biblical command!

4

HOW JESUS WALKED

Whoever claims to live in him must walk as Jesus did.

1 JOHN 2:6 (NIV)

f we are to walk as Jesus did, we must ask, "How did He walk?"

First, He walked in amazing godliness and purity. The lusts of this world did not govern Him; He ruled over unnatural and ungodly desires. In the same manner, the apostle Paul informs us of the acceptable way to serve God:

> Let us *purify ourselves* from *everything* that makes body or soul unclean,
> and let us be *completely holy.* (2 Corinthians 7:1, TEV)

Do you hear his words "purify ourselves"? It's interesting that he doesn't say "God is going to purify you." Let me clarify. The blood of Jesus cleanses all our sin away—that's redemption's benefit. However, the apostle is speaking of our sanctification here; in other words, living out what was already freely done for us. To put it simply, it's about how we are expected to live and conduct ourselves as believers. He's speaking of the outward transformation that should take place resulting from our redemption.

Did you also notice the word *everything* in that verse? We're not to purify ourselves from *some things* or even *most things* that make body or soul unclean, but from *everything.* We are expected to purify ourselves so that we are *completely* holy. Peter affirms this by writing, "Be holy in all that you do, just as God who called you is holy" (1 Peter 1:15, TEV). If we take these words seriously and don't water them down (as some do and teach), then the acceptable way to serve God is to walk in the same manner of godliness Jesus did. How are we supposed to do that? Through the grace of God.

Let me illustrate. When I was in high school I was a very effective sinner. What does that mean? Well, my nature was to sin, and I did it quite effectively.

In my early teens my dad asked my kid sister and me if we wanted to go to the town theater to see a movie called *The Ten Commandments* starring Charlton Heston. In my hometown of three thousand people, our theater didn't show fifteen movies simultaneously; it showed only one at a time. We didn't have Xbox or Wii games or large flat-screen TVs or all the other forms of media readily available today—just primitive, small-screen color TVs. So if anyone offered to pay for me to see any movie on the big screen, I was all over it. I enthusiastically agreed to go.

We're sitting in the theater watching this movie, and suddenly there's the scene where the earth opens up and swallows Dathan and all his evil buddies who had opposed Moses. Swallowed them alive, straight down into hell. As a very effective sinner beholding this on the massive screen, I started repenting like crazy. I began sequentially going through all my evil and lustful behavior, asking forgiveness and promising God I would never do any of those things again. I left that theater a completely changed young man! But it lasted for only a week, and then I was back into all my sinful behavior. Why? I'd had *repentance* but no *grace*.

Years later in college, one of my fraternity brothers presented Campus Crusade's Four Spiritual Laws. After reading the fourth law, I received Jesus Christ as my Lord, and He became my Savior. At that moment I became a child of God. But the truth is, I kept living in the same sinful way I had lived before I received Christ. This was due to a lack of teaching and Bible knowledge, for I didn't know the power that was now available to me.

A few years passed. Then a verse of scripture, which I had read several times before, seemed to jump off the page: "Pursue…holiness, without which no one will see the Lord" (Hebrews 12:14). These words hit me like a ton of bricks. *Wow,* I thought, *I want to see God, and this says in order to do so I must live a holy life!* Unfortunately, I didn't get this right either: I became a legalist. I began to beat up those around me with my legalistic reasoning. I'd charge them to "live holy," but I couldn't empower them to do it. I still based holy living on human ability and willpower, not God's enabling power. I managed to make my wife, friends, and everyone else who got close to me very uncomfortable.

Sometime later, the Lord spoke to me as I was praying: *Son, holiness is not a work of your flesh; it is a product of My grace.* That was it! That's what was missing. I came to understand that grace is God's empowering presence in my life and it gives me the ability to do what I otherwise couldn't accomplish in my own ability: cleanse myself from everything that makes body or soul unclean and be completely holy. This is the acceptable way to serve God. This is why the writer of Hebrews goes on to say,

> Let us have *grace*, by which we may serve God *acceptably*. (Hebrews 12:28)

Grace empowers us to serve God acceptably; it empowers us to purify ourselves from what we couldn't purify ourselves from in our own ability.

According to the national survey we've been examining, we can infer that as high as 98 percent of the Christians in the U.S. are trying to live godly lives in their own ability! Only 2 percent know that grace is God's empowerment, which means it is impossible for the 98 percent to partake of this empowerment because they are unaware of its availability. We receive from God by faith, and you cannot have faith in what you don't know. As Paul states, "How can they believe if they have not heard the message? (Romans 10:14, TEV). We can benefit only from what we know we possess.

Returning to our African tribe example, if the tribe doesn't know that the Land Rover's main function is transportation, they won't drive it. They'll keep jumping inside and enjoying the AC, heater, DVD player, radio, and CD player, but they'll never consider driving the vehicle.

Once I purchased a very nice camera. I opened the packaging, took out the camera, and immediately began to do with it what I had always done with previous cameras: I just pointed and shot my desired photos. Frankly, I think this is what most people do when they purchase a camera.

After several years of owning my fine camera, one day I became curious as to why a friend was able to take such amazing night, landscape, action, and close-up pictures. I asked and found out why; I discovered my camera had all the capabilities that my friend's camera possessed. I pulled out the owner's manual and started learning how to use all of my camera's features. Soon I was taking much better photos! I had been ignorant of what I had, and therefore couldn't enjoy the benefits.

The same is true for the unfortunate 98 percent. They haven't gotten into the Manual of Life, the Bible, to discover what grace has provided for them. They've merely imitated what they've seen the majority model and teach. They don't know the potential they possess and are limited.

What happens if we try to live a holy or sanctified life in our own ability? One of two things: either we become hypocritical legalists (talking one strict way but living inwardly and secretly in a different manner), or we continue our loose lifestyles while holding firm to the unbiblical belief that "grace covers all the sin I've chosen to continue practicing." So we view "living like Jesus" as a nice goal but one that is unrealistic.

From this mind-set, some believers and teachers have invented a crazy doctrine: "Jesus Christ's redemption makes us God's children; however, we're all still sinners, bound to our humanity." We incorrectly think we're bound to live no differently than the rest of lost humanity, and thus our ungodly and lustful behavior is excused and covered. It leads to a false sense of peace.

But this is not at all what the gospel proclaims in the New Testament. The good news is that Jesus not only paid the price to free us from the *penalty* of sin, but He also equally paid the price to free us from the *power* of sin! This is clear in Paul's words: "For sin shall not have dominion over you, for you are not under law but under grace" (Romans 6:14). The law could only restrain people. Grace, on the other hand, is the empowerment that frees us from what we couldn't free ourselves from in our own ability—sin. This is why Paul exhorted the Christians in Corinth, "We beg you who have received God's grace not to let it be wasted" (2 Corinthians 6:1, TEV).

Paul is not speaking of wasting the type of grace that has been taught in many of our Western churches. That kind of grace goes something like this: "I know I'm not living like I should, but that's okay because I'm saved and covered by the grace of God." In many cases it has gone even further as some believers think or say, "I can do what I desire because my salvation is based not on my performance but on what Jesus did for me. I'm covered by grace." So now there is virtually no conviction to live a godly life. Can we waste this grace? The reality is, we can't. This mind-set is a gross misrepresentation of the purpose and power of God's grace.

However, when we understand that grace is God's empowering presence that gives us the ability to do what we otherwise couldn't do in our own ability—cleanse ourselves from everything that makes body or soul unclean and to be completely holy—then we might understand how we could waste it.

Say we decide ten years later to go and check on that small tribe in Africa. We travel to the same area where we delivered the Land Rover, and strangely enough, the vehicle is still parked in the exact same spot. Dust and dirt covers the vehicle, and grass has grown up all around it. We force the door open, and upon inspecting the instruments we discover that the odometer reads exactly what it read the day we delivered it a decade earlier. Would we not say to one another, "They wasted the gift we gave them ten years ago!"

This tribe may have written songs about the "free gift" of the Land Rover or even proclaimed compelling messages to each other about it. They may have even hopped inside the vehicle when the rains came and written songs and taught compelling messages about how they were covered by the vehicle. But the fact remains, they didn't drive it. They wasted the gift!

Likewise, Paul doesn't want you or me to miss out on the primary blessing and benefit of God's incredible grace:

> We beg you who have received God's grace not to let it be wasted.... So then, let us purify ourselves from everything that makes body or soul unclean, and let us be completely holy. (2 Corinthians 6:1; 7:1, TEV)

How much clearer can it be? My question is, Why has this not been taught and emphasized more clearly in our churches?

JESUS MET THE NEEDS OF MANKIND

A few pages back, we saw the biblical imperative that "Whoever claims to live in him must walk as Jesus did," as John wrote in his first epistle (verse 2:6, NIV).

Notice the word *must*. As we observed earlier, this verse is not a suggestion but a command. God *expects* us to walk as Jesus did. So let's further ask, How else did Jesus walk?

It's clear from the Gospels that Jesus met the needs of mankind. He healed the sick, cleansed the diseased, delivered people from bondage, opened blind eyes and deaf ears, made the mute speak and the crippled walk, multiplied food to feed the hungry, and even raised the dead. Then He charged us, "As the Father has sent Me, I also send you" (John 20:21).

How are we supposed to do these things? Through the free gift of God's grace! The Bible records of the early church, "And with *great power* the apostles gave witness to the resurrection of the Lord Jesus. And *great grace* was upon them all" (Acts 4:33).

Why does God associate *great power* with *great grace*? Because *grace* is God's *power*!

You may be thinking, *Well, John, this speaks of the apostles, and I'm not an apostle or pastor.* Then let me tell you about a "regular" person. The church in Jerusalem had a restaurant, and one of the men who worked the tables was a guy named Stephen. He was not an apostle, prophet, evangelist, pastor, or teacher. No, he waited tables for older women. Yet the Bible declares: "Stephen, a man full of God's grace…performed amazing miracles and signs among the people" (Acts 6:8, NLT).

How did he perform the amazing miracles if he wasn't an apostle or pastor? Through the power of God's grace! He did just what Jesus did, meeting the needs of mankind through the power of the free gift of grace.

This same free gift is made available to every believer. It's yours and it's mine. For this reason, Jesus commanded us to "Go throughout the whole world and preach the gospel to all people.… Believers will be given the power to perform miracles…they will place their hands on sick people, and these will get well" (Mark 16:15, 17–18, TEV). Jesus did *not* say "Only apostles will be given power [grace] to perform miracles," and He didn't say "Only apostles will be given grace [power] to become children of God." No, God's Word clearly states, "But as many as received him, to them gave he *power* to become the sons [and daughters] of God" (John 1:12, KJV). We have no problem believing this, right? Well, the same Bible tells us, "Believers [not just apostles] will be given the power [the free gift of grace] to perform miracles" so that we can walk just as Jesus walked! In God's power, we can rule over sickness, disease, and any other adversity life may bring against those we love.

WISDOM, UNDERSTANDING, INSIGHT, INGENUITY, CREATIVITY

How else did Jesus walk? He walked in amazing wisdom, understanding, insight, ingenuity, and creativity. His wisdom astounded even the most educated people. Where did His wisdom come from?

> "The Child [Jesus] grew and became strong in spirit, filled with wisdom; and the grace of God was upon Him." (Luke 2:40)

Grace is why Jesus had extraordinary wisdom.

Which brings up a good question. If (as many Christians have been taught) God's grace is only for forgiveness of sins and entrance into heaven, then why would Jesus need grace? He never committed sin, so He was never in need of forgiveness. Well, we know that although Jesus is the Son of God, He was birthed and walked our earth as a man. He stripped himself of all the divine privileges of being God (see Philippians 2:7). Therefore He needed grace's empowerment to walk in the wisdom, understanding, insight, ingenuity, and creativity that so embodied His character.

I love the creativity of His wisdom, ingenuity, and discretion. It literally saved one woman's life. John chapter 8 tells how some religious zealots caught a woman in the act of adultery. They dragged her into the temple square and threw her down in front of Jesus. (I'd like to know why they didn't do the same with the man who committed adultery with her.) They questioned, "Moses commanded that such a woman must be stoned to death. But what do You say?"

In such a confrontation, creative wisdom is needed. Jesus stooped down and began writing on the ground. (I personally believe He was listing the names of these leaders' secret lovers. Perhaps He was writing *Hannah, Rachel, Isabel*.) When the leaders kept pressing their question, the Master looked up from his writing and said, "Okay, boys, whoever among you has committed no sin, let him be the first to throw a stone at her." Then he continued writing in the dirt.

I like to imagine that these sanctimonious leaders now saw the names of the women with whom they'd had affairs. But whether for this reason or because Jesus had posed a very convicting ultimatum, they all dropped the rocks they were holding and got away from the scene quickly. The Bible tells us, "When they heard this, they all left, one by one, the older ones first" (John 8:9, TEV). Jesus was left there alone with the woman.

Then He stood up and asked the lady, "Where are they? Is there no one left to condemn you?" She acknowledged that all of her accusers were gone. Jesus then said, "I do not condemn you either. Go, but do not sin again" (verses 10–11, TEV).

His wisdom and creativity saved her life. Notice that Jesus did not condemn her. He was the only one without sin, so mercy spoke at that moment. He didn't pronounce the judgment she deserved according to the law. However, He said, "Go, but do not sin again." Now grace spoke, for grace gives us what we don't deserve, whereas mercy doesn't give us what we do deserve. Mercy didn't condemn her, but God's grace empowered her to not go back into the deadly trap of adultery.

The grace of God on Jesus gave Him the wisdom to free the woman from the condemnation of the religious zealots. It also empowered her to walk free from adultery. What power grace holds!

In another situation, Jesus was near the shore of the Sea of Galilee where a professional fishing company was having the worst day of their existence. This company had not caught one fish all day. What if you owned a large retail store and didn't make one sale all day? That would qualify as your worst day ever. But one word of creative wisdom from Jesus turned it into the most successful business day of their entire career! Jesus wasn't a fisherman; He was a carpenter—but He had grace! What wisdom and power!

What power grace holds!

In other situations, Jesus knew where to find a donkey because of grace's wisdom. He didn't even have to check Craigslist or eBay. He knew how to pay His taxes without going to H&R Block—He told Peter to go catch a fish and when he opened the fish's mouth he'd find a coin for the exact amount. It happened just as grace revealed.

The insight Jesus had was amazing. He knew there was a devil working on His staff before Satan ever manifested his wickedness through Judas. He knew that Nathanael was a man of no deceit before they even met.

CHANGE SOCIETY

In essence, the grace of God on Jesus' life gave Him the ability to change the societies He was a part of. He went to a wedding in Cana. Weddings were not small affairs; the entire village would participate. This particular wedding was about to go down the drain because the hosts ran out of wine early. Can you imagine the shame these two families would carry for years to come? But one encounter with the grace of God on Jesus, and the wedding was elevated to a whole new level of excellence.

In another community called Nain, the government was going to have to provide for a widow who had just lost her only son to death. For the rest of her life the state was going to have to provide food, clothing, and shelter from tax-payers' money. However, one encounter with the grace of God on Jesus, and the state would never have to give her money. Her dignity was restored and her posterity would continue (see Luke 7:11–15).

In another town, Jesus met up with the leader of organized crime. We're talking about someone who today would be considered the godfather of the syndicate. One encounter with the grace of God on Jesus, and Zacchaeus made vows that would make that society become a safer, more prosperous place to live. People would no longer be conned by the tax man. Not only that, but Zacchaeus cried out, "I will give half my belongings to the poor." The town's welfare victims would benefit! And it went even further. Zacchaeus vowed to return 400 percent to everyone he'd stolen from, thus stimulating the economy of that region (see Luke 19:1–8). One encounter with God's grace accomplished all that!

In another incident, a young man who was insane—completely out of his mind—had been left alone to suffer. They didn't have state mental institutions in those days, but the government would still be burdened to care for him. They would have to use taxpayers' money to insure he was fed, clothed, and protected. It took a lot of clothing, too, because the young man kept tearing his off. Yet one encounter with the grace of God on Jesus, and this former madman was healed. He would not waste away in solitary confinement at taxpayers' expense. He would no longer need care and protection, and the funds could go to help better serve the community. And now the ten towns of the region of the Decapolis would hear about the kingdom of God through this one man who encountered God's grace (see Mark 5)!

Consider all the deaf, blind, crippled, diseased, and other physically impaired people that the government would no longer have to provide for due to the grace of God on Jesus. Not only that, but these people became productive citizens in their societies. We could go on and on—even beyond what's written in the Gospels, for as we observed earlier, John writes that the world of books couldn't contain all the miracles of grace accomplished by Jesus in His three years of public ministry.

Remember, Jesus promised that "Those who believe in me will do what I do—yes, they will do even greater things" (John 14:12, TEV). How? Through God's free, unmerited gift of grace. We are to change our societies in the same manner Jesus changed His—through the free gift of God's grace!

THE QUEST

I firmly believe that the principalities and powers of the dark world have made it one of their chief goals to keep this knowledge from us. They sigh in relief that 98 percent of Christians in America view grace only as a free, unmerited gift and the forgiveness of sins while remaining ignorant of its incredible power. This means that merely 2 percent are a real threat to their strongholds.

The enemy doesn't fear us having nice church buildings, published books, large gatherings, television programs, or satellite broadcasts as long as we are ignorant of the amazing power available to us. What the dark forces fear is that believers will discover the power that has freely been placed in us and, subsequently, the ability we have to boldly, creatively change society as Jesus did. They fear us taking our place as *rulers in this life.*

Martin Luther was on a quest when he nailed his Ninety-Five Theses to the door of the All Saints Church in Wittenberg, Germany on October 31, 1517. That act sparked the Reformation. The church has never been the same since. It was a work of God's Spirit through a man. The summation of his theses was that *the just shall live by faith.* He confronted the indulgences of the established church that kept people in bondage.

Well, I'm also on a quest. I know there are others with me. We want to enlist you. We're not pounding ninety-five theses onto an old wooden door but onto the hearts of fellow believers. Our message: *Grace is not merely a God-given cover-up of our sin. It empowers us to live like Jesus, to rule in this life by manifesting heaven's authority and power to change our world of influence.*

Let's be determined to raise that 2 percent statistic to 100 percent. When believers hear the word *grace,* may we immediately think "empowerment beyond our human ability."

5

Distinguished

*All who receive God's abundant grace and are freely
put right with him will* rule in life *through Christ.*

Romans 5:17 (tev)

The magnitude of Romans 5:17 is almost too great to be realistic. Its message is stunning. Perhaps this is the reason many have overlooked it.

Each of us who has received Jesus as Lord of our life is to govern in the realm of life. All who have freely received God's grace are empowered to be preeminent over any adversity this world can throw against them. Life on this earth is not to rule us; we are to rule in life. Through the power of God's grace we are to change our societies just as Jesus changed His. This is our mandate.

Practically Speaking

So let's venture further into what it means to rule in life by the grace of God. We are to go beyond the norm, to break out of the status quo. It means we no longer view life as an eight-to-five job in which we collect a paycheck every other week, then retire, then die and finally end up in heaven. What a pathetic outlook on life! It's definitely not how God intends for us to live. We were created for so much more!

We become influencers knowing that God has called us to be the head and not the tail; above and not beneath (see Deuteronomy 28:13). Not only are we to rise above adverse circumstances in life, but we're also to outshine those who don't have a covenant with God. We are to be leaders in the midst of an unenlightened world. The head sets the direction, course, and trends. The tail follows. We should be leaders in all aspects of our society, not followers.

If you're a public schoolteacher, then through the gift of grace you constantly come up with fresh, creative, and innovative ways to communicate knowledge and wisdom to your students that none of the other educators in your school system have thought of. You set the bar high and inspire your students in such a way that others marvel. Your fellow educators cannot help but discuss among themselves, "Where is he (or she) getting such great ideas?"

If you're in the medical field, then through the gift of grace you come up with new and more effective ways to treat sickness and disease. Your fellow workers scratch their heads and marvel, "Where is he (or she) getting such innovative ideas?"

If you're a designer, through God's gift of grace you originate the fresh and creative designs that others emulate. You set the prevailing styles and trends that society follows. You are sought out for your work and are known for your trend-setting. You're so ahead of the curve that others in your field scratch their heads and say to one another, "Where is he (or she) getting such creative ideas?"

If you're in the political arena, through the gift of grace you display wisdom for solving social issues that others have seen as impossible to rectify. You lead the way in lawmaking and are elected or promoted rapidly beyond your contemporaries. Your discretion and ingenuity cause others in your field to scratch their heads and say, "Where does he (or she) get all the wisdom and great ideas?"

If you're in law enforcement, by the gift of grace on your life you bring peace to situations in which others have struggled. Just as Jesus knew where to find the donkey, you know where to find the criminals. You pull together the needed evidence to solve the case more quickly than any other detective in your community. Your insight, ability, and wisdom are so keen that other people in your field scratch their heads and say to one another, "Where does he (or she) get such savvy?"

As a businessman or woman, through God's gift of grace you develop inventive products and sales techniques as well as keen marketing strategies that are ahead of the curve. You perceive what's profitable and what's not. You'll know when to buy and when to sell; when to get in and when to get out. Other business people scratch their heads trying to figure out why you're so successful.

These are not lofty, unrealistic examples. They model our mandate. Each of us is called to a different sector of society, but wherever we're located in life's arena we should manifest headship, leadership, and mastery. Our businesses should thrive even when others struggle. Our communities should be safe, delightful, and prosperous. Our places of employment should boom. Our music should be fresh and original—emulated by secular musicians instead of Christian music imitating theirs.

The same should be true with our graphic, video, and architectural designs. The creativity of the family of God should inspire and be sought after on every level. Our performances—whether in athletics, entertainment, the arts, media, or any other field—should stand out as exemplary. Our cities, states, and nations should flourish when the righteous govern.

Whenever and wherever believers are involved, there should be an abundance of creativity, productivity, tranquility, sensitivity, and ingenuity. We are to be light in the darkness. Through God's incredible grace in our lives, we should *distinguish ourselves* in the midst of a dark society.

DISTINGUISHING OURSELVES

We who are empowered by the grace of God should stand out and be standouts in all arenas of life. Read this testimony of Daniel carefully:

> Daniel so *distinguished himself* among the administrators and the satraps
> by his exceptional qualities that the king planned to set him over the
> whole kingdom. (Daniel 6:3, NIV)

This is remarkable. Daniel *distinguished himself.* Note that the account doesn't read, "God distinguished Daniel." Every major translation shows that this outstanding young man distinguished *himself.* The Message version of God's Word uses today's vernacular: Daniel "completely outclassed the other" leaders.

How did he do it? He had exceptional qualities because he was connected with God. Daniel was disciplined at staying in close, continual touch with the Creator. It should be no different for anyone who is in covenant with God today.

The New American Standard version reads, "Daniel began distinguishing himself…because he possessed an *extraordinary* spirit." The word *extraordinary* means "to go beyond the norm, to break out of the status quo, to exceed the common measure." Sometimes we can better comprehend a word by examining what it is not—its antonyms: *common, ordinary,* or *normal.* So living a normal life would manifest a lifestyle opposite of one possessing an extraordinary spirit.

The account tells us that Daniel's *spirit* was extraordinary, not his mind or body. If the spirit is extraordinary, then mind, body, creativity, ingenuity, wisdom, knowledge, and all other aspects of our life follow suit. It's our spirit that shapes our life. If we really know the grace given to us, we know there are no limits, for "all things are possible to him who believes" (Mark 9:23). Daniel tapped into what was available in His relationship with God. Because of his covenant with the Almighty, Daniel knew that he was to rule circumstances and not be ruled by them; he was to be the head and not the tail.

Let's think this through more thoroughly. Daniel and his three friends were taken from their tiny nation called Israel and brought into the most powerful nation of the world. If you're American and you think our nation has been great during the past fifty years, let me tell you, America is nothing compared to the power and splendor of Babylon. Babylon ruled the entire known world! They were top of the class economically, politically, militarily, socially, scientifically, in knowledge and in all other realms. However, we find that "No matter what question the king asked or what problem he raised, these four [Daniel, Hananiah, Mishael, and Azariah] knew *ten times more*" than the other leaders of the kingdom (Daniel 1:20, TEV). Other translations say these four were ten times better, ten times wiser, and understood ten times more. They suggested and implemented ideas the wise men of Babylon never thought of—and the ideas worked.

GREATER THAN DANIEL, GREATER THAN JOHN

With this in mind, read Jesus' words: "John is greater than anyone who has ever lived" (Luke 7:28, TEV). This means John the Baptist was greater than Daniel. Don't try to compare the two by what they did, for John labored in the realm of ministry and Daniel in the realm of civil government. However, Jesus clearly presents John as "greater." But He then goes on to say: "But the one who is least in the Kingdom of God is greater than John" (Luke 7:28, TEV).

Why is the one who is least in the kingdom of God greater than Daniel or John? Jesus hadn't yet gone to the cross to liberate mankind, so John didn't have a reborn spirit. He wasn't yet part of Christ's body. It couldn't be said of John, "As Jesus is, so is John the Baptist in this world." John was not raised up together with Christ and made to sit with Christ in heavenly places. Yet all these statements are true of us today. This is why the least in the kingdom is greater than John.

It's estimated that there have been approximately two billion Christians on earth since the time of Jesus' resurrection. Chances are slim, but if it so happens that you're "the least of" the two billion (i.e., if your "greatness number" lies right at the two-billion mark) you're still greater than John the Baptist! Which means you're also greater than Daniel! So the question arises: *Are you distinguishing yourself?*

Are you ten times smarter, better, and wiser, ten times more intuitive, creative, and innovative than those you work with who are not in covenant relationship with God through Jesus Christ? (Not to mention, are you ten times more patient, loving, disciplined, kind, hospitable, compassionate, and generous than those you work with?) If not, why not? Why aren't the vast majority of born-again believers ten times more proficient than the world? Could it be that only 2 percent of us understand that grace is God's empowerment, which gives us the ability to go beyond our natural abilities so we may rule in life and distinguish ourselves as Daniel did? (Note: We are told to bear the burdens of the weak in the church. However, the Bible doesn't say they are to remain weak the rest of their lives. They too should be given the vision to distinguish themselves in their world of influence.)

Jesus declares that we are "the light of the world" (see Matthew 5:14). Referring to His children as light in the midst of darkness is not just a one-time occurrence in the New Testament, for the following scriptures support Christ's metaphor: Matthew 5:14–16; Luke 12:3; John 8:12; Acts 13:47; Romans 13:12; Ephesians 5:8, 14; Colossians 1:12; Philippians 2:15; 1 Thessalonians 5:5; 1 John 1:7; 2:9–10. I think you can see that being light to our dark world is a major theme of our life in Christ.

Have you ever paused to contemplate what it means to be the light of the world? Unfortunately, many view being "light" as behaving sweetly, carrying our Bibles wherever we go, and quoting John 3:16 often. But what if Daniel had regarded being light in this way? What if his goal had been to walk into Babylon's government offices, treat people nice, and say to his fellow workers, "Hey, Babylonian leaders, Psalm 23 says, 'The Lord is my Shepherd, I shall not want...'"?

What would the satraps and governors have said to each other whenever Daniel left the office to pray at lunchtime? Can you imagine? I'm sure it would have been something like, "We're so glad the fanatic is out of the offices. Hope he prays all afternoon. He's so positively weird."

Why did they make it a law that Daniel couldn't pray (see Daniel 6:6–8)? The only logical reason is that Daniel was ten times smarter and wiser—ten times more knowledgeable, innovative, and creative than any of them. He was getting promoted over them until he was head of them all. They were baffled. I can picture them complaining among themselves, "We just don't get it. We were trained by the most knowledgeable, gifted, and wisest teachers, scientists, and leaders in the entire world. He's from this insignificant little country. So where is he getting these ideas? How is he so much better than us? It must be all the praying. He prays to his God three times a day! Let's make a law against that so he doesn't continue to outshine us!"

Daniel was a shining light amid that dark culture because he was an extraordinary individual. In their case, his contemporaries didn't like it. They were envious. However, I can imagine that many others, including the king, saw evidence of the living God in Daniel's abilities. Daniel's excellence was attractive and caused the leaders to honor the God of Daniel. It wasn't Daniel's knowledge of Scripture, or the fact that he was nice or that he prayed three times a day that caused them to take notice—it was the fact that Daniel was so much better in his field of work.

In the light of this, now hear Jesus' words to us in regard to light: "Let your light so shine before men, that they may see your good works and glorify your Father in heaven" (Matthew 5:16). Jesus specifically speaks of our works standing out to unbelievers. How is it that we reduced it to merely treating people in a nice manner and quoting scriptures?

MODERN-DAY EXAMPLES

I have a friend, Ben, who was vice president of one of the largest automotive companies in the world. Over dinner one evening he told me that before becoming vice president, he had worked on a major competitor's corporate top engineering team. "John, I was reading in the book of Daniel that he and his three friends were ten times better than their co-workers," my friend told me. "So I prayed, 'Lord, if Daniel and his friends were ten times better than their co-workers, and they were under the Old Covenant, then I should be at least ten times better than my co-workers because I'm under the New Covenant of grace.'"

My friend continued, "John, this major corporation did an annual cost savings and productivity analysis on each employee on the senior design team." In other words, this study showed the proficiency of each team member's ideas, ingenuity, and productivity. "The second-best employee on the entire team came in at thirty-five million dollars in savings and productivity that year. Do you know what I did?"

I smiled, anticipating what was coming. "What did you do?"

He responded, "I did three hundred and fifty million dollars in savings and productivity. I was ten times better than the number-two man." That explained how Ben grew to become one of the top executives in one of the largest corporations in America.

I'm thinking of a husband and wife who work on our staff at Messenger International. One summer they brought their two sons to one of my meetings where I was teaching these principles. After the service, their youngest son, Tyler, who had just turned eleven, said to his dad, "Because I have the grace of God, I should be much better than any other football player in our city league."

Rather than me telling Tyler's story of the following football season, allow me to share a letter from his father and mother:

John,
Here are Tyler's stats for his fall season (nine games including play-offs and
championship game). This is the Colorado Springs citywide league for the
11- to 12-year-olds.

Our son is 5 feet, 5 inches tall, 105 pounds, and his age is 11 years. I would say he has a typical (nothing outside the norm) build when looking at photos of him with his teammates.

At the beginning of the season, the head of his football league was watching him practice at the yearly football camp. He said, "Man, Tyler looks ten times faster than he did last year!"

Tyler had 893 yards rushing in 78 carries. The next-closest running back had 518 yards in 70 carries. He sat out of half a game because the coach thought that it was unsportsmanlike to utilize him [further]. Tyler had 17 touchdowns in 78 carries. The next closest player had 7 touchdowns in 70 carries.

About halfway through the regular season, the coaches of opponent teams started building their defenses around the plays that they saw Tyler run. During the games, we heard the coaches yelling, "Watch out for 68!" "Can somebody please stop 68?" "What are you guys doing? He'll burn you!" Number 68 was Tyler.

People Tyler didn't know would come down from the stands after the game and say "Hi" and chat with him. He was shocked and felt a little odd, but we told him the grace of God gives him influence and that he needs to continue to trust in it. We also told him to learn to use his influence correctly.

Sincerely, Jim & Kelly T.

It's amazing to me how easily many young people believe the Word of God and act accordingly. Young Tyler has set a great example for all of us!

THE GRACE IN US

Why have we simply not believed what God states in His Word? Our covenant with Him reads, "Now to Him who is *able* to do exceedingly abundantly above all that we ask or think, according to the power [grace] that works in us" (Ephesians 3:20). It is not according to the power that comes periodically from heaven; nor is it according to the power that comes from finding a man or woman who possesses a special ministry gift. No, it is according to *the power that works in us.*

Pay particular attention to the front portion of that verse: God is *able.*

Imagine that a severe famine hits a particular area of the world. However, a very generous and charitable nation in another part of the globe sends its military to the troubled area with barges and cargo planes filled with fresh vegetables, fruits, grains, meat, and fresh water. The military general releases a statement to the citizens: "We are able to give as much food as you can carry away." The first guy comes with a picnic basket and carries away a couple days' supply of food for two people. The next guy comes with a large sack and carries away enough food to feed his family for five days. However, the next guy backs in with a huge pickup truck and carries away enough food to last his family and several hungry neighbors for the next month.

The guy with the picnic basket sees the pickup truck driving past his home with more than a ton of food in the bed. "Perturbed" doesn't describe his demeanor; he's irate! He complains to the neighbors and anyone else who will listen, and finally his complaints reach the ear of the general. The general summons him and counters, "Hey, we told you we were *able* to give you as much food as you could carry away. Why did you come with such a small container? Why didn't you come with a larger container? Why didn't you back up your pickup truck into our outpost?"

What is the Christian's container when it comes to God's grace? According to Ephesians 3:20, it is what we can *ask or think*. God is saying, "My grace [power] in you can go far beyond any container you bring!" In other words, our container determines how much we will partake of the unlimited supply available. To put it bluntly, our container is the only thing that limits God. I believe God is asking you and me, "Why are you thinking of only what it takes to get by? Why are you merely thinking of you and your family? Why are you not tapping into the full potential I've placed within you and making a significant mark on everyone around you as Daniel did?"

> Our container is the only thing that limits God.

This is why Paul passionately prays that we might know and understand "what is the immeasurable and unlimited and surpassing greatness of His power *in* and *for* us who believe" (Ephesians 1:19, AMP).

Look at Paul's choice of words carefully: *immeasurable, unlimited, surpassing greatness*. When it comes to God's power for your life, what does each of those words mean to you? Notice that Paul is talking of "power *in* us," not power that we might get periodically from a chosen minister if God happens to be feeling good that day. It is also "power *for* us," empowering us to rule in this life. It is power *for* us to rise above and distinguish ourselves so that others can see the evidence of the resurrection power of Jesus Christ! It is power *for* us to shine as bright lights in this dim world.

Now we must ask: Are we living beneath that for which Jesus paid a very high price? If we're honest, our answer has to be yes. The result of our self-imposed mediocrity is a tragic shortfall of our potential to impact our world for the kingdom.

Why is it that we so often succumb to the world's faithless ways? For example, when a recession hits, why do we Christians tend to fear and falter along with everyone else? Sometimes I think we ought to just rewrite Philippians 4:19 to say, "And my God shall supply all your need according to how Wall Street, the banking system, and the economy are doing." Isn't that the way many of us behaved during the most recent global recession? But according to the truths we're exploring from God's Word, tough times are when we should shine more brightly than ever! Resources do not leave the planet during recession. Ideas aren't banned, creativity doesn't dry up, and innovation and hard work don't become extinct. Such dark hours should be when God's people step up, when His power within us invigorates the million- and billion-dollar ideas that will help people the most. A recession means only that the normal channels of financial flow have been interrupted, that what's needed are new and creative channels and fresh ideas. And you and I should be the ones coming up with these channels and ideas because our creative power source never runs dry!

Back in the 1920s, somebody should have told Aimee Semple McPherson that it wasn't possible for a woman in that era to build a five-thousand-seat auditorium in the middle of Los Angeles. They also should have told her it was impossible to sustain this facility through the Great Depression. Yet she did it. I've preached in that auditorium, and a great church meets there today. It is reported that Hollywood producers would sneak out to Aimee's Sunday night sermons to get ideas from the props she built for illustrations. They would, in turn, use these ideas for their Hollywood sets. Aimee was influencing the world, shining as a light.

I compare Aimee's ministry to a TV program I came across awhile back. A man was singing "Amazing Grace" in front of a huge audience. At the front of the audience were three people sitting at a judges' table. Once the man finished with his song, the judges started assessing his performance. I was in shock as the judges said things like, "You did okay; your inflections could have been stronger; your pitch was a little high…"

I lost strength in my legs. I cried out, "Lord, You created the universe. You created the great nebulas and supernovas, the fabulous Rocky Mountains, the amazing sea creatures. You live inside us. And we are going to *American Idol* for our inspiration!" Think of it: Aimee influenced Hollywood with her creativity, but ours is so lacking due to the dormancy of grace that we're limited to gleaning our inspiration from Hollywood.

I was overwhelmed with sadness. I thought about it long and hard. I came to the conclusion, *Of course, if all we teach is that grace forgives our sins and grants us entrance into heaven, we won't stand out as lights in this world.* It's almost as if God has permitted us to become a laughing stock in the world's eyes. In our desire to create a message that is easy and convenient, that doesn't take relentless believing or the fight of faith, God must be lamenting, *I'll permit you to suffer the embarrassment of your own wisdom.*

Why have we simply not believed His promises and His conditions? Why have we tried to make His wisdom fit into our lifestyle rather than seek the radical transformation that occurs when we confront our lives with His truth?

MY EXPERIENCE WITH GRACE

One of my worst subjects in school was English—particularly creative writing. I shivered when an assignment was given that involved any sort of writing. It normally took me three or four hours to compose a one- or two-page paper. I'd sit staring at a blank piece of paper for great lengths of time trying to figure out how to begin. (Yes, this was before personal computers and iPads!) I'd eventually compose a sentence, stare at it, think it was terrible, and throw the paper away. On the next attempt, I might get two sentences down, again conclude that they were horrible, and toss that sheet away. This process continued until I'd wasted several sheets of paper and lots of time. An hour or so later, I might have a paragraph or two that seemed to make some sense. Eventually, even though the work was good by my standards, I'd end up with a very low grade for the assignment.

I sometimes wonder if my English teachers passed me to the next grade just so they wouldn't have to put up with me the next year. You think I'm exaggerating? The truth is I scored 370 out of 800 on the verbal (English) portion of the SAT exam. That's only 46 percent, which would be considered "flunking with flying colors." Fortunately, I had ability in mathematics and science, and that led to my acceptance as an engineering major at Purdue University.

So in 1991, when God said to me in prayer, *Son, I want you to write,* I thought He was making a huge mistake. *Could it be possible,* I thought, *that God has so many children on this planet that He's confusing me with someone else?*

I'm ashamed to admit it, but what He asked seemed so ridiculous that I did nothing. At that time I lacked the knowledge of what I've been sharing with you about the incredible, empowering nature of God's grace.

Ten months later, and within just two weeks of each other, two women from two different states approached me. One was from Texas, the other from Florida. Each woman spoke the same words to me: "John Bevere, if you don't write the messages God is giving you, He'll give them to someone else and you will be judged for your disobedience."

When I heard the second woman giving the same admonition I'd heard just two weeks earlier, the fear of God struck me. *I'd better listen, and I'd better write!* But I really did think God was making a huge mistake. I couldn't compose a ten-page paper, let alone an entire book! In desperation, I wrote out a contract with God on a piece of notebook paper. *I need grace,* I wrote. *I can't do this without Your ability.* I signed the contract and dated it.

Later, I sat down to write. I didn't start with an outline, for I had no idea how to compose one or where the process would specifically take me. I just had a general subject idea. Suddenly, thoughts came to mind that I had never thought of, taught, or heard anyone else teach before. I just wrote and wrote. Eventually, I had a book-length manuscript. Later, I wrote a second book, then a third. As of today, I've authored fifteen books with total sales in the millions and published in more than sixty languages around the globe. One book, *Drawing Near,* won the annual Retailer's Choice award in 2004, and several have been bestsellers both nationally and internationally.

Do you see, based on my "natural" ability, why I could never take credit for this? It's all God's grace!

I've stood in a hockey arena in Europe with more than eight thousand people in attendance, many of whom were Christian leaders, and asked how many had read one of my books. In amazement I've watched as nearly everyone raised their hands. At an international conference in Eastern Europe, the conference host asked six thousand leaders from more than sixty nations if they had read at least one of my books published in their own language. It was overwhelming for me to see about 90 percent raise their hands. I've been told by Iranian publishers (at the time of this writing seven of my titles are in Farsi, the official language of Iran), "You are one of the most-read Christian authors in all Iran." Such reports continue to come in. But my point is, *What grace!*

Let me share with you a dream of mine: I want to find my high school English teachers and show them the fifteen books I've written by the grace of God, watch them faint, then revive them and lead them to Christ. The fruit would distinguish me in their eyes and clearly demonstrate the amazing grace of our Lord Jesus Christ!

It is for this reason Paul boldly claims, "By the grace of God I am what I am" (1 Corinthians 15:10). Listen to me, dear reader: You are not who you are because of who you were born to, what side of the tracks you grew up on, what ethnic group you are associated with, what gender you are, or where you were educated. You are who you are by the grace of God!

Early in life I was also a terrible public speaker. After Lisa and I were married, one of the first times she heard me preach the gospel she fell sound asleep within ten minutes. Her best friend, Amy, was sitting next to her and was also so deep in sleep that I could see drool from her wide-open mouth! They both remained asleep throughout my message.

A couple of years ago, Lisa found a videotape of me speaking in 1984. She played it and within seconds I cried out, "Lisa, throw it away!" She grabbed the videotape, hugged it to her chest with both hands, and laughed hysterically. "No way," she said. "This is blackmail material!"

Today, and only by God's empowering grace, I've spoken before five thousand, ten thousand, and even twenty thousand people in arenas around the world. People ask me, "Do you get nervous before you speak?"

"No, not at all," I respond.

They're usually baffled by my response. "How can you face so many people and not be nervous?"

I laugh and say, "I know how bad I am, and if grace doesn't show up, we're all in big trouble." Now that I know about God's grace, grace never fails. It is always there!

This is why Paul says, "not many wise according to the flesh, not many mighty, not many noble, are called" (1 Corinthians 1:26). Why? Because the wise, the strong, and the noble will depend on their own ability instead of depending on grace.

Earlier in his life, Paul had been one of the wise and noble ones. "I could have confidence in myself if anyone could," he acknowledged in Philippians 3:4 (NLT). But Paul chose to depend on grace: "I once thought all these things [wisdom, strength, nobility] were so very important, but now I consider them worthless" (Philippians 3:7, NLT). Why were these human attributes worthless? Because Paul wanted to walk in the unmerited resurrection grace over his own natural ability "that I may know Him and the power of His resurrection" (verse 10). This doesn't mean that Paul didn't apply himself. He studied diligently to show himself approved, and he passionately prayed to be filled with the knowledge of God's will in all wisdom and spiritual understanding. Paul applied himself as we all must, but he believed God for the grace to propel his human effort into the realm of divine empowerment.

If you're a student, you should study hard, but all the while you should believe God for the grace to propel you to a level of thought and achievement that your own understanding could not. If you are a doctor, you should stay current with the discoveries of modern medicine, but your trust cannot be in your ability or education. Your trust must be in the supernatural wisdom and creativity of God's grace to help you go beyond the known. If you're a professional athlete, you should work diligently in practice, but your confidence must be in the grace of God to excel beyond the unbelievers in your arena.

Remember how, in the first chapter, we discovered that our loving Creator God wrote each of our biographies before we were born? We saw David's words of praise: "You saw me before I was born. Every day of my life was recorded in your book. Every moment was laid out before a single day had passed" (Psalm 139:16, NLT).

Let me tell you about your biography. It is impossible for you to fulfill your God-scripted biography in your own ability. You just cannot do it. If God had made your biography possible to fulfill on your own, then He would have to share the glory with you. And God doesn't do that! He clearly states, "I will not give my glory to anyone else" (Isaiah 42:8, NLT). So God purposely wrote your biography beyond your natural ability so you would need to depend on His grace to fulfill it. This way, He gets all the glory!

That's what I tell people in regard to the books I've written. Nobody is aware more than I who really authors these books. They're not crafted in my own ability. My name is on these books only because I was the first guy to get to read them. I know I am what I am by His ability, His grace, and that not of myself. It is the free gift of God.

The alarming reality, however, is that only 2 percent of American believers are even aware of grace's empowerment enabling them to achieve their predetermined biography. How can the 98 percent fulfill their calling only in their own ability? The fact is, they can't. Could this be why we are not seeing a huge impact in our communities?

THE ACCESS

A free gift!

This power I write of, the grace of God, you cannot earn, merit, or deserve by your own effort. As Paul confirms, grace is received *only* by faith: "For by grace you have been saved *through faith,* and that not of yourselves; *it is the gift of God, not of works,* lest anyone should boast" (Ephesians 2:8–9). To the believers in Rome he wrote, "We have *access by faith* into this grace in which we stand" (Romans 5:2). What gives us access to the grace of God? It's not working hard, living a good life, praying two hours a day, fasting twice a month—not any of our human efforts. We have access to this grace only by faith!

So why don't we simply believe? Look at it this way. If your fresh-water well runs dry, you have a problem. Without fresh water, you and your family will die in a few days. But just down the road the city has a huge water tower filled with millions of gallons of fresh water, and one of the main pipes from that tower runs along the front of your house. What would you do? You'd go to city hall and get a permit. Then go to the hardware store and buy some PVC piping, return home, and hook up your house's plumbing to the main pipe that runs past your front yard. Now you'll have *access* to millions of gallons of fresh water—more than you and your family need. Simply put, faith is the pipeline of grace. Therefore, we could read Romans 5:2 in this light: "We have *access* by the pipeline of faith into all the water of grace we need." It's that simple: The only way to partake of empowering grace is through faith. This is why the writer of Hebrews states, "For indeed the gospel was preached to us as well as to them; but the word which they heard did not profit them, *not being mixed with faith* in those who heard it" (4:2).

The people he references were the descendants of Abraham—heirs of the promises of God. Figuratively speaking, all of heaven's power and provision ran right by their homes or tents. However, they didn't profit from what God freely provided because they did not hook up their "pipes of faith" to tap into and receive what the Word promised.

In the same light, if only 2 percent of American believers are aware that grace is God's free empowerment—power that gives us the ability to venture beyond our natural ability and enables us to shine in a dark world by doing marvelous works—then how can we as a church believe? How can we partake? Paul put it this way: "How can they believe if they have not heard the message? And how can they hear if the message is not proclaimed?" (Romans 10:14, TEV).

If we Christians remain ignorant of what God's Word declares regarding God's empowering grace, then how can we believe? We cannot believe what we don't know. If we have no pipeline to access this grace, the promise of His Word will not profit us.

> We cannot believe what we don't know.

This must break God's heart. Jesus paid a massive price for us to go beyond what Daniel and John the Baptist were able to do—to be living examples of His abundant life. Yet we've dumbed down the message to include only forgiveness and fire insurance. As crucial and wonderful as these gifts are, we have failed to appropriate and claim the power of God's grace for living life now. Therefore, we are unable to do the works of God in this dark world, unable to live relentlessly for His glory.

The followers of Jesus eventually cried out, "What can we do in order to do what God wants us to do?" (John 6:28, TEV). They were frustrated. They too wanted to help a hurting humanity with God's ability. Jesus charged them to follow His example. Exasperated, they finally cried out, "How do we do what You're doing?" Jesus' simple response? "Have faith." (John 6:29, CEV).

That's it. Faith! Simply believing God's "word of grace" is all that's needed to partake of it. This is how Paul could hearten the believers of Ephesus by saying, "So now, brethren, I commend you to God *and to the word of His grace,* which is able to build you up and give you an *inheritance* among all those who are sanctified" (Acts 20:32).

Paul was leaving those he loved; he knew it would be their final conversation this side of heaven. When you know you're speaking your final words, you tend to be very choosy with the words you leave for your loved ones. Paul commended them not only to God but also to the "word of His grace."

Today I hear so many well-intended Christians say nice things like "You have to trust God" or "All you need is God in your life" or "Just get close to God." While this advice points people in the right direction, it's incomplete. Paul commended his fellow believers not only to God but also to "the word of His grace." God's grace builds us up and gives us our *inheritance.* And what is your inheritance? It's the biography God wrote about you before you were born!

Because of our incomplete teaching on grace, too many Christians (98 percent, to be precise) think that God's incredible empowerment is available only if we pray and fast enough, or work hard enough in Christian service, or live a holy-enough lifestyle. The problem with this incomplete view is that we don't know how much is *enough.* For this reason Paul confronts the Galatians:

> Answer this question: Does the God who lavishly provides you with
> his own presence, his Holy Spirit, working things in your lives you
> could never do for yourselves, does he do these things because of your
> strenuous moral striving *or* because you trust him to do them in you?
> (Galatians 3:5, MSG)

"Strenuous moral striving" gets us nowhere with God because it is all about our own strength and effort. The lesson of this chapter is that the sole determining factor in your access to God's free, empowering grace is that you believe in, trust in, and appropriate His grace by faith.

It's no different from your initial salvation. See how Paul presents it: "Let me put this question to you: How did your new life begin? Was it by working your heads off to please God? Or was it by responding to God's Message to you?" (Galatians 3:2, MSG).

Just as we were first saved by grace by simply believing and responding, so now we are to continue, by grace, to do marvelous works in our field of influence.

CHIHUAHUA OR GRIZZLY BEAR?

Which brings us back to the question we asked in chapter 3. Do we have the power and ability to be *relentless* in our beliefs and pursuits? Are we Chihuahuas or are we grizzly bears?

After pondering the scriptures we have studied, I hope you join me in affirming—with joy and confidence—that you and I are like the grizzly bear. With this confidence in our minds and hearts, let's continue our discovery of what relentless living is all about!

6

SEE OR ENTER

All who receive God's abundant grace and are freely
put right with him will *rule in life* through Christ.

ROMANS 5:17 (TEV)

I t's my hope that if I frequently place Romans 5:17 before your eyes, the verse
will become part of your being, just as I'm sure John 3:16 is. Perhaps you'll
eventually quote these words in your sleep, deeply knowing that it is God's
will that you govern in the realm of life. This firm belief is a prerequisite to a
strong finish, to being identified as an "overcomer" and a relentless believer.

Before proceeding, allow me to reiterate the fundamental truth we've been
unpacking: *All who have freely received God's grace are empowered to be preeminent in this life.* We are to be the head and not the tail, above and not beneath
life's circumstances. We are to be exemplary kingdom influencers who bring
God's way of life to this earth.

WHY DON'T MOST CHRISTIANS RULE IN LIFE?

Why aren't all Christians living in this manner? Why are the majority of believers actually *ruled by life* rather than *ruling in life*?

We've addressed the first and most obvious answer. The national survey
done in 2009 reveals that 98 percent of the believers in America are unaware of
God's grace being His empowerment. I believe that this statistic, unfortunately,
represents the church in general throughout the entire Western world. Due to
their ignorance of God's provision of supernatural power through grace, the vast

majority of believers are unable to live as God intends. They are no different from the African tribe that possesses a powerful Land Rover yet has no knowledge of its ability to transport. They are still limited to traveling by foot and carrying heavy loads great distances on their backs.

The second reason most believers are not ruling in this life will be the focus of the remainder of this book. We'll start by examining Jesus' words to Nicodemus, a Jewish leader who came secretly to inquire of the Master. Jesus' first words to him were, "Most assuredly, I say to you, unless one is born again, he cannot *see* the kingdom of God" (John 3:3).

Jesus speaks of *seeing* the kingdom. But His next statement to Nicodemus reveals something significantly different: "Most assuredly, I say to you, unless one is born of water and the Spirit, he cannot *enter* the kingdom of God" (John 3:5). Why does Jesus shift his emphasis from *seeing* the kingdom (verse 3) to *entering* the kingdom (verse 5)? When we apply only our knowledge of the English language to biblical interpretation, it is often easy to miss the true meaning and significance of the text. Hearkening back to the original languages helps us get a better handle on what God wants us to understand.

When Jesus speaks of the kingdom of God, He is actually referring to the "rule of God." The Greek words most frequently used for *kingdom of God* in the Gospels are *basileia tou Theos. Theos* refers to God, while *basileia* is defined as "royalty, rule, reign." *Basileia* is derived from the Greek word for "base" or "foundation." Some scholars believe the best translation of *basileia tou Theos* is "God's imperial rule" or "God's domain." I love the word *imperial*. One of its definitions is "supremely powerful."

For example, in the Lord's Prayer Jesus instructs us to pray, "Our Father in heaven, hallowed be Your name. Your kingdom come. Your will be done on earth as it is in heaven" (Luke 11:2). He is literally saying, "Our Father in heaven, You are God Almighty. Your supreme, powerful rule come. Your will be done on earth just as it is in heaven." But a problem arises because most people hearing these words think futuristically, when in fact God's kingdom has already come! It has not yet come physically, as Isaiah prophesied, for that is when Jesus will rule forever and ever and Satan's influence will be gone for good. Rather, the kingdom of God has already come spiritually. It is *within us,* God's covenant people, for Jesus says, "The Kingdom of God does not come in such a way as to be seen. No one will say, 'Look, here it is!' or, 'There it is!'; because the Kingdom of God is within you" (Luke 17:20-21, TEV).

Due to Jesus' work at Calvary, the kingdom is now within every Christ follower. We are to spread its domain, its rule, where we are and wherever we go. We are to rule in life by the powerful free gift of God's grace bestowed on us through Jesus Christ.

Let's examine other scriptures where Jesus uses the phrase "kingdom of God" and substitute in its place *"God's supreme powerful rule."* It's amazing how with this change these statements have a more significant meaning for today's believer.

For example, Jesus' teaching in Matthew 12:28 would read, "If I cast out demons by the Spirit of God, surely *God's supreme, powerful rule* has come upon you." The Spirit of God Jesus refers to is the Holy Spirit, the member of the Godhead who enforces the grace (power) of God that we possess. He is called the "Spirit of grace" in the New Testament (see Hebrews 10:29).

Again the words of Jesus: "It is easier for a camel to go through the eye of a needle than for a rich man to enter into *God's supreme, powerful rule*" (Matthew 19:24).

A rich man is one who says, "I have the full adequacy and capability within myself to succeed." Because of his intellect, finances, physical strength, wit, connections, and resources, he believes he's totally self-sufficient. But Jesus sees through the smokescreen. "Blessed are you poor," He says, "for yours is *God's supreme, powerful rule*" (Luke 6:20).

He is not identifying the financially poor; He is blessing those who depend on God's grace. Jesus declared that the Spirit of God was upon Him to preach the gospel to the *poor,* yet many times He would intentionally meet with and minister to some of the financially richest men or women in the communities He visited. When He spoke about a camel going through the eye of a needle, it was right after His encounter with the rich young ruler, who chose to trust in his riches instead of in God.

Consider another statement by Jesus about the kingdom of God: "To you it has been given to know the mystery of *God's supreme, powerful rule;* but to those who are outside, all things come in parables" (Mark 4:11). The authority and power available to us through God's grace is indeed a mystery—a hidden truth that only the Holy Spirit can reveal. "'Eye has not seen, nor ear heard, nor have entered into the heart of man the things which God has prepared for those who love Him.' But God *has revealed them to us through His Spirit*" (1 Corinthians 2:9–10). The fact that you and I can rule in life through the grace of God was hidden until the Holy Spirit revealed it to us through the apostles who wrote the New Testament. All we have to do now is believe.

Here's another assertion from Jesus concerning the kingdom of God: "Assuredly, I say to you that there are some standing here who will not taste death till they see *God's supreme, powerful rule* present with power" (Mark 9:1). This statement from the Messiah himself should secure our belief that the coming of God's kingdom is *in the here and now* as well as in the future. The supreme, powerful rule of God would be within those who followed Jesus once the Spirit of grace came on the Day of Pentecost. In this same light, Jesus said to a scribe who answered Him wisely, "You are not far from *God's supreme, powerful rule*" (Mark 12:34).

As you can see from the few examples I've shared, the kingdom of God takes on a much more powerful and relevant meaning when we read it as it is stated in the Greek. You may find it both enriching and encouraging to continue substituting *God's supreme, powerful rule* whenever you come across the term *the kingdom of God* in the New Testament.

But we must remember a very important aspect of God's supreme, powerful rule. He has delegated His rule to us! "The heaven, even the heavens, are the LORD's; but the earth He has given to the children of men" (Psalm 115:16). Jesus, as the Son of Man, took back what Adam had forfeited. Jesus then declared, "All authority (all power of rule) in heaven and on earth has been given to Me" (Matthew 28:18, AMP). But Christ our Lord and King is no longer here on the earth, so you and I—the body of Christ—are to carry out *God's supreme, powerful rule.* If we don't exercise rule, then it stays within the realm of the forces of this world and life rules us. That's not God's plan! We are empowered by His grace to rule in life through Christ!

SEE VS. ENTER

Now let's examine further Jesus' words to Nicodemus. You'll recall that the Master first said, "Most assuredly, I say to you, unless one is born again, he cannot *see* the kingdom of God" (John 3:3). And just a few moments later, He put it this way: "Most assuredly, I say to you, unless one is born of water and the Spirit, he cannot *enter* the kingdom of God" (John 3:5).

With the insight we've gained from the Greek about the kingdom of God, we're now better positioned to discover why Jesus differentiates between *seeing* the kingdom as opposed to *entering* the kingdom. If we were to view the kingdom of God as a physical place such as heaven, then verse 3 would indicate that being born again is not enough to enter heaven—only enough to *see* it. This, of course, is not true. When you understand that Jesus is talking about God's supreme, powerful rule—or kingdom rulership—then these verses take on a totally different meaning and are much easier to comprehend.

The Greek word for *see* in verse 3 is *eido*. Its primary definition is "to see, perceive, be aware of, or be acquainted with." Jesus is telling us that all who are born again can *see, perceive,* be made *aware of,* and are *acquainted with* God's supreme, powerful rule—the kingdom of God.

In His next statement He no longer uses the word *see (eido)*; He uses the word *enter* in regard to the rule of God. The Greek word for *enter* is *eiserchomai.* Its primary definition is "to arise and come into" or "arise and enter." So in these two statements Jesus moves from *being aware of* to *arising and coming into* God's supreme, powerful rule. See the difference?

To illustrate, when I board an aircraft to fly somewhere I'm quite aware of its ability to defy gravity, lift me high above the earth, and bring me to a set destination. As a passenger, I can see as well as experience the benefits of riding in that plane.

Then one day a friend buys me some flying lessons. After some initial training, I get into a single-engine plane and the instructor tells me what to do. Before long I'm pulling back on the yoke and flying the plane. It's almost a surreal experience. One of my prevailing thoughts on my first flight is the fact I can fly that plane wherever and however I desire. There is no road, no path. Instead, I create the path and the route. I've gone from *being aware of* what a plane can do and experiencing the benefits of riding along as a passenger to now being the pilot and flying the plane wherever I want to. I've *entered into* the freedom of flying.

Jesus' words indicate that there are two types of believers. We could compare the first group to passengers in an airplane who see, perceive, and experience the benefits of flying. Then there are those who arise and enter into the cockpit as pilots who actually do the flying and determine where to go and at what speed and altitude. The passengers, even though they can benefit from the airplane, are at the mercy of those who know how to fly.

To further illustrate the significant difference between seeing and entering the kingdom of God, imagine a small group of people stranded on an island. It's a dangerous island filled with ferocious man-eating wild animals, poisonous snakes, spiders, and scorpions. If that isn't bad enough, there's also a cannibalistic, primitive tribe on this island. Our small group is in great danger. However, there is some good news: located on the island are an airstrip and a fully functional jet. The aircraft is loaded with fuel and sitting on the airstrip. It can easily carry our group of people to safety. But there's a huge problem: no one in the group knows how to fly a plane! All of us are experienced passengers, but none has risen to the status of pilot with the ability to fly a plane. Even though the aircraft gives us the power to fly to safety and freedom, we cannot do it because we don't even know how to start the engines, let alone fly the jet off the island.

This scenario illustrates the difference between the believer who has only *seen or experienced* God's supreme, powerful rule and the believer who has *arisen and entered* God's supreme, powerful rule.

Quite a difference, isn't it? Which type of believer do you want to be?

ENTERING RULERSHIP

The logical question that surfaces now is, How does a child of God move from *seeing* to actually *entering* rulership? In other words, how do we go from being spiritual passengers to spiritual pilots? The apostle Paul addresses this question for us.

Under the direct orders of the Holy Spirit, Paul and Barnabas left their home church and embarked on their first apostolic journey (Acts 13:1–4). After traveling great distances to many cities in Asia, they began their long journey home, revisiting a few of the cities in which they had launched new churches. In those days, of course, travel was more challenging than it is today. I can get on a plane and easily travel to cities anywhere in the world, usually within a twenty-four-hour time span. I'm not prone to think when I leave some location abroad, *Due to the complexity of travel, I wonder if I'll see these people again this side of heaven.* But in Paul's day this was often a nagging thought. When leaving these churches, Paul knew there was a good chance he wouldn't see these dear ones he had birthed into the kingdom again until he reunited with them in heaven. Consequently, we can imagine Paul choosing his words to these new believers carefully. And what he leaves them with directly addresses how we go from *seeing* to *entering* rulership:

> They returned to Lystra, Iconium, and Antioch, strengthening the souls of the disciples, exhorting them to continue in the faith, and saying, "We must through many tribulations *enter* the kingdom of God." (Acts 14:21–22)

Paul didn't leave these three cities with the content of a financial seminar, a church growth conference, a leadership training symposium, or even an uplifting message of hope—though all these topics have their place. No, he left them with words that would empower the young believers to live relentlessly and finish well. His aim was to prepare them to enter rulership.

Paul's words remain true for us today. They should be embedded in our hearts and souls: *We must pass through many tribulations to enter God's supreme, powerful rule.* Stay with me now; this is a message of hope and faith, not gloom. Think of it this way: Tribulation happens! It's inevitable. Jesus clearly communicates that tribulation is a fact of life for His followers. "In the world you will have *tribulation*," He assures us, "but be of good cheer, I have overcome the world" (John 16:33). He has overcome, which means that you and I have been given authority and power over whatever this world can throw against us. We are His body; we are Christ on earth. We have overcome the world in Christ!

The word *tribulation* is defined as "hardship or a state of great trouble." The Greek word is *thlipsis. The Encyclopedia of Bible Words* defines *thlipsis* this way: "The idea of the great emotional and spiritual stress that can be caused by external or internal pressures. Of the fifty-five uses of this root in the New Testament, fifty-three are figurative." The pressure may come from enemies, adverse circumstances, wrong decisions, or passion run awry.

James Strong defines *thlipsis* as "pressure (literally or figuratively): affliction, anguish, burdened, persecution, tribulation, trouble." W. E. Vine defines it
simply as "anything that burdens the soul or spirit."

My own simplistic definition for *tribulation* or *thlipsis* is "the desert."

Today's English Version of the Bible translates Acts 14:22 like this: "We
must pass through *many troubles* to enter the Kingdom of God." To illustrate,
let's imagine that you serve a great king who has conquered an entire country.
He has entered into the capital city and overthrown the beastly lord who ruled
the land with an iron fist. The deposed leader had been cruel to the people,
poisoned their thinking with false propaganda, set them at odds against all that
was good and noble, and incited hatred and disdain for the right ways of the just
and noble king you serve.

The good king commissions his servants to go into the land and enforce his
victory by taking all the enemy's occupied territories and strongholds that remain intact. Throughout the land there are underlords who still hold fortresses
and castles. They continue to propagate the ways of the former evil king. Consequently, there are still many under the sway of the evil lord's system. Even
though the overall war has been won, there is still much work to do to enforce
the victory.

You are en route to conquer a castle in enemy territory. There are many dangers along the way, for you must confront, overthrow, and pass through enemy-
occupied lands. Your foes have set many traps to prevent you from taking this
ground. You'll have to battle through these tribu-
lations one by one. And once you arrive at the
castle you face the most difficult test of all: over-
throwing the enemy stronghold. The good news
is, the more you defeat enemy traps, engagements,
and encampments along the way, the more experienced and battle-savvy you become. If you take
this castle you'll rule this territory. Not only that, but you'll be such a skilled and
trustworthy warrior that you'll be in good stead to maintain your rulership over
the territory you've taken for your king.

> You are en route to
> conquer a castle in
> enemy territory.

The good king in our story represents our Lord Jesus. He has commissioned
us, His loyal soldiers, to go and enforce His victory over the forces of darkness

that are still swaying this world. As we proceed we will encounter battles of hardship but will ultimately liberate those men and women who are still held prisoner by the enemy's tactics, ways, and propaganda.

You and I must pass through many tribulations to enter into rulership. But, as Jesus says, we can be of good cheer because He has overcome the world. Through His grace, we are given power and authority to take on whatever challenges the world hurls our way.

And not only do we have the *empowerment* of God's grace. We who believe in Christ as Savior and Lord also have a very special *position* in God's grace. Read joyfully Paul's words to the Christians in Rome:

> The Spirit Himself bears witness with our spirit that we are children of
> God, and if children, then *heirs*—heirs of God and joint heirs with Christ,
> *if* indeed we suffer with *Him,* that we may also be glorified together. For
> I consider that the sufferings of this present time are not worthy *to be*
> *compared* with the glory which shall be revealed in us. (Romans 8:16–18)

As believers, you and I are God's heirs! We are heirs of God and joint heirs with Jesus Christ. The word *heir* is from the Greek word *kleronomos,* defined as "one who takes possession of or inherits. The emphasis is on the heir's right to possess." My dictionary defines an heir as "a person inheriting and continuing the legacy of a predecessor." There's also a secondary definition: "a person legally entitled to the rank of another." Wow, are you grasping this? God has made us heirs to everything He's accomplished and owns! We own what He owns. We are to rule as He rules.

It all belongs to God, and therefore it all belongs to us. "No one, then, should boast about what human beings can do," Paul writes to fellow believers. "Actually everything belongs to you" (1 Corinthians 3:21, TEV). Everything! You and I are truly heirs of God! The Contemporary English Version phrases it, "Everything is yours, including the world, life, death, the present, and the future. Everything belongs to you." Stop and ponder this for a day or two. In Christ, you and I are far richer than the world's richest man!

But there is one caveat. A very important one. The Romans 8 passage above clearly says *if.* There is a condition on our inheritance; in other words, it's not automatic to every Christian. What is the condition? We must suffer with Him. Read the passage again. In order to enter into the reality of joint rulership with Christ Jesus, we have to encounter, confront, and overcome any opposition that would stand in the way of what belongs to Him, just as He did. Notice the words *suffer with Him.* Overcoming opposition is not a walk in the park or a tiptoe through the tulips. It's warfare, and suffering goes with warfare.

But in our case, it's not a defeated suffering. In Romans 8:18 Paul asserts that facing up to tribulation can be positive and full of hope: "I consider that the sufferings of this present time are not worthy *to be compared* with the glory which shall be revealed in us." Here's the key principle I want you to comprehend and hold firmly:

> No matter the pressure of the *thlipsis* (tribulation) you encounter, the difficulty is nothing compared to the level of rulership you'll walk in after the tribulation has passed.

If we're doing Christianity right, there will be suffering. But with each triumphant battle, a greater glory of strength and wisdom prevails in us. Paul is not just pointing to the glory that will be bestowed on us at the judgment seat in heaven; he is also speaking of the benefit we gain for the present day. When we prevail through tribulation, we move to *(enter)* a greater level of manifest rulership.

SUFFER WITH HIM

As we look at the words *suffer with Him,* we must ask, How did Jesus suffer? This is where many get confused, for there are two types of suffering. One is for righteousness' sake and the other is for the world's sake. Let me explain.

One type of suffering happens because the entire world's system is under the sway of the evil one (see 1 John 5:19). As a result, cruel and evil things happen to people every day. Babies are aborted or abused, girls are forced into sex slavery, diseases take lives far too early, poverty and hunger abound, strife and turmoil rip families apart, addictions drive and destroy—and that's the short list. There is nothing good or profitable in this suffering. It is sad and tragic, but it's consequential to Adam's sin of turning his authority over to a very cruel lord.

The second suffering, for righteousness, is the one on which we will focus, for it is the kind of suffering Jesus and Paul refer to. All suffering for righteousness, when endured with God's strength, is profitable. Its results are always glorious. It strengthens us in our call to rule.

Jesus demonstrates this for us throughout His ministry. Remember, we are destined to suffer with Him if we will rule with Him. So how did He suffer? Jesus had prepared thirty years for ministry and then is baptized in the river Jordan by a well-known prophet named John.

Once Jesus is baptized, the heavens open up and the Holy Spirit descends on Him in bodily form, appearing as a dove. God the Father speaks from heaven for all to hear, "You are My beloved Son; in You I am well pleased" (Luke 3:22). Imagine being among the throng of people witnessing this amazing, heavenly confirmation of Jesus. Many leaders of the nation, both political and ministerial, also witness it.

Now if we were Jesus, most of us would think, *This is the perfect time to launch my ministry! I should give my first message now, with all these people around. After all, I've been preparing for this moment for thirty years. Maybe I should hire a marketing and promotional team that can capture the momentum of this event. Everyone here now knows I'm the man of God for this hour.*

That would be a logical, promotion-wise response, right? But here's what Jesus did instead: "Then Jesus, being *filled* with the Holy Spirit, returned from the Jordan and was led by the Spirit into the wilderness, being tempted for forty days by the devil" (Luke 4:1–2). I've found that many believers think Jesus was tested only at the end of His forty days in the desert. But that's not the case. While the Gospels report three specific tests endured by Jesus, it clearly implies that He was tested (i.e., endured tribulation) the entire forty days.

Notice who led Him into the desert. The devil didn't lead him there. No, His Father, through the Holy Spirit, did. Someone may think, *Why would God lead His Son into the desert where He knows Jesus will face suffering and opposition?* One fact we can be sure of is that God will never lead us into a storm that He doesn't give us the power to overcome. (I'll support and elaborate on this principle in our next chapter.) The immediate takeaway for us here is that God does not author *thlipsis* or tribulation. He knows we live in a broken world and that if we are going to conquer and rule the world, we are going to encounter resistance from its evil forces. Therefore, God trains us in areas He knows we can handle in order to strengthen us for greater conquests.

Jesus went into the wilderness filled with the Holy Spirit immediately after baptism and encountered *thlipsis* over the next forty days. Remember that He had stripped himself of His divine privileges to walk among us as a man filled with grace (see Philippians 2:7 and Luke 2:40). He battled through and overcame all the adversity, never once giving in to the temptations of the devil. Then after the forty days, "Jesus returned in the *power* of the Spirit to Galilee, and news of Him went out through all the surrounding region" (Luke 4:14).

> God trains us in areas He knows we can handle in order to strengthen us for greater conquests.

He went into the wilderness *filled* with the Spirit of God, but after overcoming the adversity of heavy temptation, He returned in the *power* of the Spirit of grace. Recall Paul's words in Romans 8:18: "For I consider that the sufferings of this present time are not worthy *to be compared* with the *glory* which shall be revealed in us." This passage could just as easily read, "For I consider that the sufferings of this present time are not worthy to be compared with the *authority and power* which shall be revealed in us." Jesus entered into a greater level of rulership after He successfully passed through *thlipsis*.

The apostle James underscores it this way: "Blessed is the man who perseveres [relentlessly abides in truth] under trial, because when he has stood the test, he will receive the *crown of life* that God has promised to those who love him" (James 1:12, NIV).

Notice that when you overcome a trial as Jesus did during His forty days in the desert, you receive the "crown of life." I know you can make the case that this crown is awarded in heaven at the judgment seat. And this is true. But I believe James is referring not only to the physical crown awarded in heaven, but to entering *now* into a higher level of rule in this life. A crown speaks of authority. What comes with authority? Power. Jesus went into the wilderness *filled*, but He returned in *power*. Remember, we enter into rulership *if* we suffer with Him. So when we suffer *thlipsis* and pass the test by not giving up—relentlessly obeying God's Word when all hell is breaking loose—there is an immediate benefit: greater authority in the area of life in which we've stood fast.

My Mother-in-Law's Testimony

Lisa's mom is a classic example of this promise. In 1979 Shirley's local doctor in Indiana diagnosed her to have breast cancer. It wasn't caught early, so the cancer also spread into her lymph nodes. Her breast was removed along with 30 percent of her lymph nodes, and the doctor told her she was terminal.

Shirley wanted a second opinion, so she went to MD Anderson hospital in Houston, Texas, considered to be one of the top hospitals in the United States for treating cancer. Her doctor there served as head of the oncology department. His report wasn't optimistic. After giving her the same prognosis she'd received from her first doctor, he said, "You got a stiff indictment, didn't you?" He thought that if she did exactly as he and his staff prescribed, she might live two, possibly three years at the most. Medical science could foresee no cure.

The protocol would be intense radiation, then home to Indiana for two or three weeks of rest, then back to Houston for chemotherapy.

While in Houston, Shirley called a nationally known TV ministry for prayer. It "just so happened" that the man who took her call knew the couple in charge of the outpatient facility at MD Anderson. He proceeded to call and encourage them to look her up and continue to minister to her. The couple connected with Shirley. They took her to their church, to ball games, and out to dinner, the whole time sharing faith-building promises from the Word of God.

Shirley was a new Christian. Prior to discovering the cancer, she had been taught basic principles of the faith by the wife of a couple in ministry. Upon her return to Indiana she had lunch with her mentor, who advised Shirley that God doesn't heal everyone. Her friend gave several examples of other Christians who had not been healed of serious conditions. As Shirley shared the scriptures of hope that the Houston couple had revealed to her, the woman became upset that Shirley was resisting her counsel.

Now Shirley was confused. When she returned to Houston for chemotherapy, the couple continued to meet with her every day, encouraging her from God's Word. Eventually, Shirley came to believe deep within her heart that what the Word of God says about healing is true. There would be no more doubting what God says in His Word. She would be healed!

When Shirley decided to discontinue chemotherapy, her doctor thought she had lost her mind. As she left the hospital, he actually followed her all the way to the elevator, warning her that she was making a life-threatening mistake. But Shirley was resolute. She left and never returned to MD Anderson. She returned home, and there she poured the Word of God into her life each day through books, audio messages, and Bible study.

As of today, thirty-one years later, she is healthy and lives down the street from us. In fact, at age seventy-five she serves in our ministry's church relations department, a team of seven who resource more than twenty thousand churches in the United States with our books and curricula. In her role she has helped countless pastors and church workers find the resources they need.

In all my years of ministry, I've found few people like Shirley who are as easy to pray with for healing. One time not long after Lisa and I married, I came home from work, and Shirley—who was visiting us—had come down with severe flu. When I walked in, Shirley was crawling up the stairs to go to bed. She had no strength to walk. When she saw me she said, "John, I need you to pray for me so I can get rid of this flu."

As I prayed for her, the power of God was so strong, so tangible, that my mother-in-law literally collapsed to the floor. Then she jumped up, started bouncing around our apartment, and said, "I want to make you guys dinner!" She proceeded to cook us a wonderful meal. I laughed within and thought, *Wow, the same thing happened with Peter.* His mother-in-law was sick, Jesus healed her, and she got up and made them all something to eat (see Matthew 8:14–15).

Not only does Shirley receive prayer easily, she's also a power woman when it comes to praying for others to be healed. If she's around anyone who is battling illness or injury, you'd better know that they are going to get a fire-hose dose of God's Word and prayer for healing!

Shirley has remained cancer free and in good health for thirty-one years and counting! By relentlessly fighting her intense *thlipsis* with the Word of God, she has received the crown of life in the arena of healing. She has endured and overcome this adversity and now rules in the area of life in which she persevered.

Overcomers

Others have the same testimony. Consider Oral Roberts, who is in heaven now but whose life and legacy continue. At age seventeen, Oral was about to die from tuberculosis. He relentlessly stood against the disease with the Word of God and prayer, and later was confirmed healed by his doctor. As with Shirley, Oral received the crown of life in the arena of healing, and millions of people were subsequently strengthened and healed through his life and ministry.

I have a friend named Jimmy who has been a pastor for years and influenced many through his ministry. At a young age, he was given up to die by doctors but was taken to an Oral Roberts meeting. After Oral prayed for him, Jimmy miraculously recovered.

What if Oral hadn't persevered as a young man? Where would my pastor friend be today—along with the millions of others who received healing through Oral Roberts's ministry? What about all the people Pastor Jimmy has impacted for eternity—where would they be today? Oral entered rulership. The full result of his relentless belief will be known only at the judgment seat.

Or consider Kenneth E. Hagin. Born in McKinney, Texas, in 1917 with a deformed heart, Kenneth was later diagnosed with a rare, incurable blood disease. He became bedfast at age sixteen and was not expected to live beyond his teens. In April 1933 he died three times and saw hell, and each time Kenneth was miraculously brought back. Kenneth gave his life to Jesus as Lord. He relentlessly believed and fought the disease with the Word of God. A pastor who came to visit and comfort him said, "Hang in there, son, it will all be over in a few days." A year later Kenneth rose from his "death bed" and, shortly after, began to preach.

Kenneth Hagin's ministry became world renowned, with more than sixty-five million books in print and a Bible training center that has graduated more than thirty thousand men and women, many of whom are in full-time ministry. After sixty-five years of ministry, Kenneth is now home with the Lord, but his legacy continues. He received the crown of life in the arena of healing, and, as a result, untold multitudes have been healed and lives changed due to his faithful ministry.

What if Kenneth Hagin had not persevered? How would the millions he ministered to have been affected?

These three people whose stories I've shared—my mother-in-law, Oral Roberts, and Kenneth Hagin—have something in common. They've all been attacked, lied about, and spoken of as evil. The husband of Shirley's hometown friend ceased speaking to her once she decided to believe God for healing. During their lives, both Oral Roberts and Kenneth Hagin were accused of being in error, extreme, heretical, even demon inspired. But what did Jesus say about such things? "Woe to you when all men speak well of you, for so did their fathers to the false prophets" (Luke 6:26).

Interestingly, there are ministers and other believers who have lightened and broadened the message of the kingdom to make everyone feel comfortable. For fear of offending someone or of being labeled "intolerant" or "extremist," they've withdrawn from fighting the good fight of faith. To them, anything that happens is the will of God and should be passively accepted. They've removed "offensive" portions from the Gospels, yet He's referred to as "a rock of offense." The Scriptures also call Jesus a "stumbling stone," but they have reduced Him to a pebble that couldn't cause anyone to stumble.

These pastors, ministers, and believers seem to want to be spoken well of by all; they'd never be accused of being extreme, heretical, or demon inspired. Yet Jesus was considered all of these things. He was relentless in truth. He exposed the deception of those who desired to be well spoken of. He announced, "Count yourself blessed every time someone cuts you down or throws you out, every time someone smears or blackens your name" (Luke 6:22, MSG). Quite the opposite of being well spoken of, wouldn't you agree? Then He gives the reason: "What it means is that the truth is too close for comfort and that that person is uncomfortable."

The reality is this: if you choose to be a relentless believer, one who rules in life, it is highly likely you will be slandered, lied about, misunderstood, and even marginalized by those who profess to follow Jesus but are satisfied with a comfortable life. They will seek to discredit you in order to justify their apathetic ways. They did this with the true prophets of the Old Testament, with John the Baptist, with Jesus, and with the leaders of the New Testament. They do so today. Your greatest resistance will most often be from those who claim to know

God. It will range from lies and slander to exclusion. And it may even go as far as what Jesus foretold: "The time will come when those who kill you will think that by doing this they are serving God" (John 16:2, TEV).

Do you want to rule in life for the glory of God? Do you want to impact lives for His kingdom, forever? Do you want to hear the Master say, "Well done, My good and faithful servant" on that great day? If so, settle it now: You will face *thlipsis*, sometimes quite intensely, and you'll need to endure and overcome.

If you still truly desire to enter rulership and you're willing to endure, then keep reading. The best is yet to come.

7

WHO'S BEHIND THE TROUBLE?

*For to you it has been granted on behalf of Christ, not
only to believe in Him, but also to suffer for His sake.*

PHILIPPIANS 1:29

Philippians 1:29 initially sounds so appealing. "For to you it has been granted...." If we were to hear only those words without knowing the rest of the verse, we'd ask eagerly, "What has been granted to me? What promise awaits me?"

The answer: "to suffer for His sake."

What? Being "granted" the privilege of suffering just doesn't jibe for the human mind. But God is not in the business of deception; it's impossible for Him to even come close to it, for He cannot lie. To the simple mind that verse may seem like trickery, but to one with understanding it is truly an exciting promise. Those who are walking and growing in Christ know this fact, deep down in their hearts: *the greater the battle, the greater the victory.*

Consider a loyal soldier who trains rigorously for a fight. He's well aware of the importance of the battle; it presents the opportunity for conquest. He's a conqueror at heart and longs to serve his king's purposes. When the upcoming battle is announced, he and his comrades rejoice at the opportunity, for in triumph they'll bring glory and honor to their king and benefit their people. To him it is granted, on behalf of his king and kingdom, to suffer the conflict of the battle in order that he may conquer. Do you see the parallel with Philippians 1:29?

You may counter, "But I'm not a soldier. I don't have a conqueror's attitude or outlook." If you are in Christ, you are indeed a soldier, for the seed of Christ has been imparted to your spirit. Jesus is the greatest warrior who ever lived. Hear what the Bible declares of Him: "In righteousness He judges and makes war. His eyes were like a flame of fire.... Out of His mouth goes a sharp sword" (Revelation 19:11–12, 15). You have been re-created in His image and likeness; you have His nature. Since Christ is a warrior, you are also a warrior. Therefore, we are reminded of warfare repeatedly in the New Testament. As Paul writes,

> This is no afternoon athletic contest that we'll walk away from and forget about in a couple of hours. This is for keeps, a life-or-death fight to the finish against the Devil and all his angels. (Ephesians 6:12, MSG)

I love the way The Message captures Paul's charge. We're in a life-or-death combat to the finish, a war that cannot be avoided. He wrote a similar message to the church in Corinth: "We are human, but we don't wage war with human plans and methods. We use God's mighty weapons" (2 Corinthians 10:3–4, NLT). It's clear that we are spiritual soldiers in a war! And you were made for this battle. You're a warrior at heart. Paul exhorts us to "Take your part in suffering, as a loyal soldier of Christ Jesus. A soldier on active duty wants to please his commanding officer" (2 Timothy 2:3–4, TEV). Settle it now in your heart and mind, for it's a fact: in Christ, you are a soldier.

As a soldier, you can take the path of a coward by avoiding or fleeing the battle, or you can take the path of a hero by enthusiastically stepping up and winning the fight. Choose the first and, sadly, you'll be remembered as a deserter. Choose the courageous path and you'll receive a hero's commendation before your king.

Dear friend in Christ, I know it is in your heart to please our king, to glorify Him and live for Him. Only your flesh, if allowed to dominate, would constrain you from the privilege of sharing in Christ's sufferings.

From the book of Romans we have observed that we will reign with Jesus Christ if we suffer with Him. It's obvious that we will need to face and overcome opposition and tribulation. But our perspective should be that of joyful expectation, for we should view suffering as something granted and not dreaded. The greater the battle, the greater the victory—and ultimately, the greater the glory. And here's the really great news: you don't ever have to lose a battle! For we are promised, "Now thanks be to God who *always* leads us in triumph in Christ" (2 Corinthians 2:14).

GOD IS NOT A CHILD ABUSER

In the previous chapter we highlighted the immediate events following the baptism of Jesus. The Holy Spirit led Him into the wilderness where Jesus was tempted forty days and nights. It was God, not the devil, who led Jesus into the wilderness. God knew His Son would be severely tested, but He led Him there for a purpose. The principle we learned is that *God will never lead us into a storm that He doesn't give us the power to overcome.* Brand this truth forever on your heart, for it will strengthen you when you face adversity.

Jesus made clear that He never did or said anything unless it came first from His Father. He was perfectly led by the Spirit of God: "I do nothing on my own authority, but I say only what the Father has instructed me to say" (John 8:28, TEV).

Later in His ministry, following a long day teaching the multitudes, Jesus was exhausted. I have some idea of how He must have felt. On several occasions I've preached four or even five times in a day and have been so exhausted on the ride back to my hotel that night I could not stay awake to chat with my host.

The same would have been true for Jesus. Evening had come and He was ready for a good night's rest, but the Holy Spirit moved Him to tell His disciples to get in the boat and cross the sea. There was a demon-possessed man on the other side to minister to. They all got in the boat, and Jesus fell fast asleep.

A terrible storm arose on the sea. Four of the men on His staff were skilled seamen who had been on the water most of their lives. They knew nautical adversity and how to handle it, but this was no ordinary storm. As wave after wave crashed in over them, these experts finally woke Jesus and cried out, "Don't you care that we are about to die?" They saw absolutely no chance of surviving the intense *thlipsis.*

In the midst of this storm, do you think the Holy Spirit and the Father were panicking? Do you imagine them passionately consulting each other, "We cannot believe this! We had no idea this deadly storm would come up! What are We going to do? Oh, why did We tell Jesus to go to the other side? We've made a colossal mistake!"

Rather funny when you think about it, right? Of course that's not what happened. The Holy Spirit knew the storm would arise, for He knows the end from the beginning. "Only I can tell you what is going to happen even before it happens" (Isaiah 46:10, NLT). He had directed Jesus into the boat with the full knowledge of the deadly storm that awaited. Yet *God never leads us into a storm that He doesn't give us the power to overcome.* Once awake, Jesus went to the front part of the boat and commanded the storm to be still, then turned to His disciples and asked, "Why are you so fearful? How is it that you have no faith?" (Mark 4:40).

> The Holy Spirit... knows the end from the beginning.

Why did Jesus give such strong words of correction after these experts of the sea had fought so hard to survive? Why did He sternly point out that they had "no faith"? Prior to leaving the shore, He had said to them, "Let us cross over to the other side" (verse 35). He didn't say, "Let's go halfway across and sink." They should have known that there was enough grace (power) in Jesus' words to get them to the other side. They should have stood at the bow of that boat and shouted, "Storm, you are not going to kill us, nor will you stop us! We *will* make it to the other side because the Master said 'Go to the other side.' So get out of our way!"

God knew the storm would arise. He led them into it, but He also gave Jesus' disciples the authority and power to rule over the storm. And therein lies the key. What separates those who are defeated by life from those who rule in life is the knowledge that battles and conflicts are inevitable, and that—unlike the natural person—we have power over whatever may come against us. So we can, and must, fight relentlessly until the battle is won. Let the truth of 2 Corinthians 2:14 permeate every fiber of your being: "Now thanks be to God who always leads us in triumph in Christ."

If the situation had been left to the disciples and their limited perspective, all of them would have been dead by drowning. However, Jesus' determined obedience to battle the storm resulted not only in their living another day but also in a demon-possessed man on the other side of the lake being set free.

And the benefit didn't stop there, for this healed man then proclaimed the kingdom of God to the ten cities of the Decapolis. Bottom line, many lives were eventually impacted for the kingdom. The Holy Spirit led Jesus and His team into the storm, they suffered the adversity of it, but it was never God's will for them to be overcome. Rather, God's focus was on the glory on the other side of the storm.

If we could ask the apostles today, "Was it worth suffering the storm to see the man set free?" they would undoubtedly answer, "Absolutely!"

Let's look at another case. The apostle Paul was on a Spirit-led mission to Jerusalem. But here's what awaited him:

> In obedience to the Holy Spirit I am going to Jerusalem, not know-
> ing what will happen to me there. I only know that in every city
> the Holy Spirit has warned me that prison and *troubles* wait for me.
> (Acts 20:22–23, TEV)

The Greek word for *troubles* in the above verse is *thlipsis*. (We've seen that term before, haven't we?) So the Holy Spirit was leading Paul into a place where he would experience intense tribulation. But again, God will always give us the grace to overcome any obstacle we encounter on the course in which He leads us.

What was the outcome of Paul's relentless stance amid adversity? Not only did the Jews and Gentiles of Jerusalem hear the gospel; so did many citizens of the Roman Empire—even soldiers, magistrates, kings of regions, and Caesar himself! All from this one man led into a storm by the Holy Spirit. God didn't author the storm or the suffering, but He knew that Paul would face it due to a fallen world hostile to the ways of God. Nevertheless, the love of Christ compelled Paul to follow the Spirit's leading, and God gave him grace to overcome the adversity. Paul summarized the journey by writing, "Out of them all [tribulations] the Lord delivered me" (2 Timothy 3:11). His words correspond to the psalmist's declaration: "He [God] has delivered me out of all trouble" (Psalm 54:7). Not from some of the trouble or most of the troubles. *All* trouble. That's 100 percent of them!

And the same promise applies to you and me!

Parental Advice

When our firstborn son, Addison, was in first grade he encountered some bullies in his class. Several afternoons he came home in tears over the way these kids treated him on the playground. I bet you can guess what I as his father wanted to do. I wanted to go to that playground, punch the lights out of those kids, then sternly warn, "Don't you ever touch or harass my son again!" But there are three problems with that approach. First, my actions wouldn't have been very godly. Second, such actions would have been counterproductive to developing Addison's character. And third, I had no jurisdiction on that playground. The playground was not my place but my son's place to rule—to take authority.

So once I calmed down, Lisa and I decided that the best thing we could do for Addison would be to teach him how to handle the *thlipsis* he was experiencing. Night after night his mother and I gave him insight and counsel to help him successfully walk through the hardships he'd encounter from the bullies. We sent him to school the next day armed with strategies for handling the difficulties he would face. (Of course if we had felt Addison was in danger, we would have contacted his teacher and principal.)

Consequently, after successfully navigating this and various other tribulations throughout his childhood, Addison became very good at dealing with people. In 2004 he joined our ministry staff in an entry-level position. At that time we had more than forty employees ranging in age from the teens to the sixties. I told the management team that Addison was not to receive any preferential treatment because he was our son. Within six months our leaders said to me, "We want to promote him to become head of the Church Relations Department." Church relations is one of the most crucial functions of the ministry, so I asked why Addison should be promoted to lead that department. "Because your son is a leader," my team responded.

Addison took over the department and it flourished. He won the trust of his people as well as the entire ministry staff as they witnessed his skill and wisdom for solving problems and resolving conflicts. Today, at age twenty-five, he is the Chief Operating Officer of Messenger International and doing a fabulous job. He has won the heart of every employee, no matter their age. They've taken to him, and they trust his leadership.

Now let me ask: to protect Addison in the first grade, should I have pulled him out of the school where he was being sorely mistreated and homeschooled him? Do you consider me mean or abusive for sending him back to school, knowing he would face those bullies each day? Most wouldn't. In the same way, God is not being mean or abusive when He leads us into rough places—places that must be invaded and conquered for the sake of the kingdom. He knows it's for our ultimate good and that it will bring glory to Him and in the end benefit His people if we handle the challenge in the power of His grace.

THE SOURCE OF TRIBULATION

Before proceeding further we should be clear about the source of *thlipsis* and God's will for us in the midst of it. Dealing with this topic is crucial because it can be a stumbling block for many individuals, and especially in three major life areas. Because of its importance I will spend the rest of this chapter addressing it before we continue to explore entering rulership.

The examples we've seen to this point illustrate that God is not the source of *thlipsis*. Instead, *thlipsis,* or severe conflicts, resistance, and tribulation come from the forces of our fallen world. Is this always true? We must pose this question because if you have the slightest notion that God is the author, designer, or instigator of a particular hardship you're facing, then you may not fight to overcome it as you should.

A soldier going to war is well aware of whom he's fighting. And if he's wise, he'll also know his enemy's tactics. There's never a remote question in the warrior's mind as to who his enemy is. However, in my thirty-plus years of ministry, I've encountered far too many believers who aren't certain who's behind the hardships they face. Sadly, they're unaware of their enemy's strategies and activities when we are told to be wise "in order to keep Satan from getting the upper hand over us; for we know what his plans are" (2 Corinthians 2:11, TEV).

How do we know Satan's tactics? Jesus tells us! "The thief's *purpose* is to *steal* and *kill* and *destroy,*" Jesus says, "My *purpose* is to give *life in all its fullness*" (John 10:10, NLT).

Earlier in John 10, Jesus establishes the "thief" to be Satan and his cohorts. Later Jesus refers to him as "the ruler of this world" (John 16:11). Paul calls him "the god of this age" (2 Corinthians 4:4) and "the prince of the power of the air" (Ephesians 2:2). He is the one who sets the course of this world's system. Satan is indeed the source of our conflict. As Paul says,

> For we are not fighting against people made of flesh and blood, but against the *evil rulers* and *authorities of the unseen world,* against those *mighty powers of darkness who rule this world,* and against *wicked spirits* in the heavenly realms. (Ephesians 6:12, NLT)

The Master's words in John 10:10 and Paul's words to the Ephesians (above) clarify beyond a doubt that any hardship that falls under the category of stealing, killing, or destruction is the influence of the various dark forces described in Ephesians 6:12. On the other hand, Jesus' purpose is the Father's will manifested. So God's purpose for you is *life in all its fullness.* Whenever you're faced with pressure, hardship, or suffering of any sort, use the filter of John 10:10 to determine if it is God or the enemy who's behind it. To show how this works, let's consider some common examples.

SHAME, GUILT, CONDEMNATION

If you pass feelings of shame, guilt, and condemnation through the filter of John 10:10, they definitely fall under the category of the thief, not God.

But to be completely sure, let's probe deeper. The psalmist writes, "Bless (affectionately, gratefully praise) the Lord, O my soul, and forget not [one of] all His benefits—Who forgives [every one of] all your iniquities, Who heals [each one of] all your diseases" (Psalm 103:2–3, AMP).

Think of the most trustworthy person you've ever known. Is it your spouse, one of your parents or grandparents, or your doctor? This person has never lied to you nor deceived you. I hope you have someone like that in your past or present life. Imagine this person making these promises we just read to your face. Not only that, but he or she also has the capacity to fulfill them.

Now picture this: God is far more trustworthy than the person you just thought of. He instructs us to *not forget* a single one of all His benefits. *Not one.*

The first benefit is that He has forgiven every one of our sins. Amazing! What kindness, what mercy, what love! If you have not done so already, settle this now: *You are forgiven in Christ Jesus.* There is no sin you've committed that is not eradicated by His shed blood. So if shame, guilt, or condemnation arises in your soul over something you've thought, said, or done somewhere in your past and you've already asked God's forgiveness, *then it is not God who is behind those horrible feelings.* Hear Paul's resounding words on this matter:

> Who dares accuse us whom God has chosen for his own? Will God? No!
> He is the one who has given us right standing with himself. Who then
> will condemn us? Will Christ Jesus? No, for he is the one who died for
> us and was raised to life for us and is sitting at the place of highest honor
> next to God, pleading for us. (Romans 8:33–34, NLT)

It's spelled out so clearly. "Who dares accuse us... Will God? No!... Who then will condemn us? Will Christ Jesus? No." Think of it: God sent Jesus Christ to die for you when you were still His enemy. Jesus agreed to do it, and the Holy Spirit made it happen. Why would God the Father, Son, or Holy Spirit now condemn and put shame or guilt on you when you're no longer an enemy but one of God's children? And why would He put condemnation on you when He already placed it on His sacrificial lamb? Was Jesus' sacrifice not good enough? Was it not eternal?

The writer of Hebrews assures us,

> How much more, then, will the blood of Christ, who through the eternal
> Spirit offered himself unblemished to God, *cleanse our consciences* from
> acts that lead to death, so that we may serve the living God! (Hebrews
> 9:14, NIV)

Christ's sacrifice not only destroyed our sin before God, but it also *cleansed our conscience* from the condemnation, guilt, and shame of sin. So if you are living for Him and seeking to obey His desires, yet are still plagued by these thoughts or feelings, they are originating from the enemy in his attempt to pull you down. You need to confront the source fiercely. How? In the exact way Jesus fought the same enemy who tested Him in the desert: with the Word of God! (I'll get more specific about this in later chapters.)

But if, and I mean *if,* you are living in disobedience to God, then it will be your own heart condemning you. John writes, "If our conscience condemns us, we know that God is greater than our conscience and that he knows everything. And so, my dear friends, if our conscience does not condemn us, we have courage in God's presence" (1 John 3:20–21, TEV). The word *condemn* in this verse does not mean "to sentence to a particular judgment," which often is the meaning. Rather the definition of the Greek word *kataginosko* is "to note against," that is to "find fault with" or "blame."

Our conscience protects and keeps us from slipping out of fellowship with God. If we are in this state and not progressing, then the Holy Spirit will correct us as a loving Father: "My child, pay attention when the Lord corrects you, and do not be discouraged when he rebukes you" (Hebrews 12:5, TEV). He corrects us to restore our fellowship with Him and to make us more like Him—not for the purpose of killing, stealing, or destroying us.

Always remember that condemnation and correction both have an uncomfortable feeling—they're painful! "Now no chastening seems to be joyful for the present, but painful" (Hebrews 12:11). However, there is one huge difference between the two. Condemnation does not give you a way out; it only leaves shame and guilt to permanently plague you. Correction does give you a way out: it's called repentance.

Bottom line, if your conscience knows you're in disobedience, then God knows it too because He is greater than your conscience. Always keep short accounts with Him; immediately repent of your disobedience and confess it to Him. He'll forgive you. It's that simple.

John writes, "I am writing this to you, my children, so that *you will not sin*; but *if* anyone does sin, we have someone who pleads with the Father on our behalf—Jesus Christ" (1 John 2:1, TEV).

Note that John doesn't say "when you sin." No, the goal is that you not sin. A *sin consciousness* will steer you right back into sin, but a *right standing with God consciousness* will keep you strong against sin. This awareness helps you remember that the power of sin has been broken in your life and that grace has been supplied to you to walk completely free from sin, inside and out. "For sin shall not have dominion over you," Paul affirms, "for you are...under grace" (Romans 6:14).

So the goal is not to sin. The grace of God empowers us to attain this goal. But if (and again I emphasize *if*) we do sin, we can immediately address it and believe what God's Word promises: "If we confess our sins to him, he is *faithful* and *just* to forgive us and to cleanse us from *every* wrong" (1 John 1:9, NLT). *Faithful* means He will forgive every time, no matter how many times you've blown it. *Just* means He will do it no matter who you are or what you've done. So when He cleanses you from *every* wrong, which means *any* wrong, then you are clean before Him, and it's as if you've never sinned. The blood of Jesus removes that sin as far as the east is from the west!

One of the greatest hindrances to a believer ruling in life is a sin consciousness. When we continue to battle shame, guilt, or condemnation over a sin we've repented of and confessed before God, it weakens us. I've seen too many people walk away from their faith as a result of plaguing guilt or shame that was from the enemy, not from God. They felt they had sinned one too many times, or that they'd committed an unpardonable sin. Even though God wasn't condemning them, Satan used their unrenewed minds to drive them further into guilt, shame, and hopelessness. So they either walked away or they settled for a fruitless, guilt-ridden version of faith. Instead of ruling life, they were ruled by life.

So settle it now: if you've sinned but have genuinely repented and confessed it to the Lord, you stand before God as if you never committed the sin. By His amazing grace He's made it that simple. You can believe it!

It's important to add this quick note. If you are truly a child of God, you desire above all things to please Him, for His seed is in you. But one who willfully continues in disobedience is not truly born of God. If you are looking for a license to sin, you are on dangerously deceptive ground. To be blunt, you're not truly saved. The Bible makes this clear: "Those who keep on sinning have never known him or understood who he is.... It shows they belong to the Devil" (1 John 3:6–8, NLT).

SICKNESS, DISEASE, PHYSICAL INFIRMITY

What kind of power does grace give us to rule over sickness, disease, or any physical infirmity? Let's review the truth written by the psalmist:

Bless (affectionately, gratefully praise) the Lord, O my soul, and forget
not [one of] all His benefits—
Who forgives [every one of] all your iniquities, Who heals [each one
of] all your diseases. (Psalm 103:2–3, AMP)

Again, think of the person you trust most in your life, then acknowledge that God is even more trustworthy; He never breaks a promise. The first benefit we see in the psalm is that God faithfully forgives every one of our sins. And that's not all, for in the same breath we're commanded to never forget another of His blessings: God, who can never lie, says, "I heal each one of *all* your diseases." He doesn't say most diseases or even 98 percent of your diseases—no, it's 100 percent of our diseases. His healing is part of the redemptive work of Jesus, equal to the forgiveness of our sins. Isaiah foretold what Jesus would endure for the sake of our spiritual and physical freedom:

Surely He has borne our *griefs*
And carried our sorrows;
Yet we esteemed Him stricken,
Smitten by God, and afflicted.
But He *was* wounded for our transgressions,
He was bruised for our iniquities;
The chastisement for our peace *was* upon Him,
And by His stripes we are healed. (Isaiah 53:4–5)

The Hebrew word for *griefs* in Isaiah's passage is *choli*. It's defined by *Strong's Concordance* as "disease, grief, sickness." The renowned biblical scholar and author Henry Thayer defined it as "affliction, disease, grief, illness, sickness." The term is found twenty-four times in the Old Testament, and twenty-one of those appearances refer specifically to sickness or disease. I think it's plain that in the verse above, *choli* could have easily been translated "sickness" or "disease."

The Amplified Bible supports this conclusion: "Surely He has borne our griefs (sicknesses, weaknesses, and distresses).... And with the stripes [that wounded] Him we are healed *and* made whole" (Isaiah 53:4–5). The World English Bible reads, "Surely he has borne our sickness.... And by

> God never breaks a promise.

his wounds we are healed." The New English Translation reads, "He lifted up our illnesses.... Because of his wounds we have been healed."

It's not a coincidence that both the psalmist and Isaiah put forgiveness of all sins and healing of all diseases in the same sentence. Both are part of the redemption package Jesus freely provided for us at Calvary.

In the Gospels you will find that not a single person who came to Jesus for healing was denied. Jesus never once says, "You must put up with this sickness because My Father is teaching you from it." Yet I've heard believers, and even teachers, say this very thing. Let's be logical: Why would Jesus change now? We are told He is the same yesterday, today, and forever (see Hebrews 13:8). He would never turn us away today, just as He never turned away anyone during His earthly life. Furthermore, if you believe God is teaching you something from sickness, why do you go to the doctor for treatment? Why fight against what God is trying to teach you? Do you see how illogical this thinking can be?

Neither does the book of Acts reveal a single person who sought and believed God for healing but was denied. Not one time did the apostles say, "We don't know if it is God's will to heal you, so you will just have to hope He does." Instead, healing was always a sure thing, never denied to any seeker, because according to Isaiah 53 and Psalm 103, healing is as much a part of Jesus' redemption as the forgiveness of sins. If you throw out one, you have to throw out the other!

It's no different today. Sicknesses, diseases, or physical infirmities of any sort all fall under the category of stealing, killing, and destroying. They are hardships we can confidently stand against knowing that we were freed from them through the sacrifice of Jesus at Calvary. They definitely are *not* God's will for our lives. Jesus' redemption package still stands firm and intact! That's why Paul writes, "Now may the God of peace Himself sanctify you completely; and may your whole spirit, soul, and body be preserved blameless at the coming of our Lord Jesus Christ" (1 Thessalonians 5:23). He includes *body* with our soul and spirit, indicating that just as God wants your spirit and soul whole, He equally desires your body to be whole, working in the way He created it to work.

I can hear someone saying, "But I know a person who was believing God to be healed and he died." Let me ask this: Is our faith in God going to be based on another's experience or on what His eternal Word declares? You must settle this firmly within your mind and heart. As Paul writes, "What if some did not believe and were without faith? Does their lack of faith and their faithlessness nullify and make ineffective and void the faithfulness of God and His fidelity [to His Word]? By no means! Let God be found true" (Romans 3:3–4, AMP).

To be straightforward, you don't know for sure what the person who died truly believed in his heart. He may have repeatedly stated his belief in God's healing, but it might have been a front to hide his fear of not being healed. True faith does not doubt God's promise in our heart. A person can say one thing knowing it is correct in his mind, but in his heart he may believe differently.

So how might we process others' experiences that are contrary to what Scripture declares—without becoming judgmental? For example, if a family member or friend departs early in life due to disease? An effective approach I've developed for such scenarios is the following: Scripture teaches we are running a race. In races each participant has a lane to run. If someone's experience doesn't line up with the foundational truths of Scripture, then leave it in his lane but don't bring it into yours. It is between that person and God, who is a merciful and just Judge. This way your faith is not weakened. However, if someone's testimony lines up with the Eternal Word of God, then bring it over to your lane to strengthen your race.

You must embrace at the core of your being what the Word of God states before you can receive its promise. Once you do, you'll be relentless in your belief—just like a man named Bartimaeus.

Jesus was leaving Jericho with His disciples, and a huge crowd surrounded

Him. A blind man named Bartimaeus was sitting beside the road, and when he learned that Jesus was passing by, he cried out for the Master. Numerous bystanders scolded him, urging Bartimaeus not to trouble the Teacher. But he shouted even louder! Here's a guy whose foundation for faith wasn't just in his mind but in his heart. If Bartimaeus did not believe with all his heart that God wanted him healed, he wouldn't have persisted—especially after being scolded by those around him. He would have quieted and resigned himself to this erroneous thought: *Since Jesus isn't going to come over and heal me, it means that God wants me to bear this blindness.* But Bartimaeus didn't buy that lie; he remained determined and vocal. Observe what happened next:

So Jesus stood still. (Mark 10:49)

How amazing! Jesus had set His face like flint to go to Jerusalem to fulfill what He was sent to do; He was focused on His assignment. Multitudes of people surrounded Him and many undoubtedly had physical needs, yet their needs didn't cause Him to stop and put a temporary hold on His mission. However, this one blind man cried out for Jesus and would not be silenced. No adversity, no admonition, could shut him up. It was the sound of his voice, not the silence of the others, that caused Jesus to stand still. Jesus directed, "Tell him to come here." So the disciples called the blind man. "Cheer up," they said. "Come on, he's calling you!" (Mark 10:49, NLT).

It's obvious that the people surrounding Bartimaeus weren't very nurturing. In fact, they were contrary to his cause. Yet it didn't faze him. Bartimaeus would not be stopped in his faith. He threw off his beggar's coat, jumped to his feet, and let the disciples guide him over to Jesus.

Then the Master asked, "What do you want Me to do for you?"

Are you serious? What kind of question is that? A blind man, who has to be escorted, is asked what he needs. It's obvious, so why did Jesus ask this question? Was He ignorant of the beggar's need? Was Jesus insulting him? Of course not! The Master desired to see evidence of Bartimaeus's faith.

If Bartimaeus had said, "I know it's too much to ask for my sight, but could You please heal the headache I've had the past couple of days?" then that is exactly what he would have received. We know this to be true by what Jesus says once the blind man's eyes were opened: "Go your way. Your faith has healed you."

Mark didn't write about the people in the crowd who did not receive healing; he focused on the man who did. Don't allow someone else's story of not getting healed to detract from your firm belief. Hear me carefully once again on this: *Do not become critical or pass judgment on those who didn't receive from God, but do not allow their story to enter into your heart as evidence.* Paul declares, "For what if some did not believe? Will their unbelief make the faithfulness of God without effect? Certainly not!" (Romans 3:3–4). The only evidence we should allow into our hearts should be the testimonies that line up with God's Word.

LACK AND POVERTY

Does grace give us power to rule over lack and poverty?

For some reason, many people believe that godliness is exemplified by not having enough. In extreme cases, some people even take vows of poverty in their service for God. This mind-set fails in the face of Philippians 4:19, where Paul assures his Christian colleagues, "My God will liberally supply (fill to the full) your every need according to His riches in glory in Christ Jesus" (AMP).

If you read that verse in context you will find that Paul is speaking to these believers specifically about finances. Our needs *will* be met—not according to how the economy or stock market are doing but according to God's riches in glory. That's amazing, because He has a lot of riches—an unlimited supply, to be exact! Based on this promise, we can be confident that it is God's will that you never lack any good thing. The psalmist writes, "The young lions lack food and suffer hunger, but they who seek (inquire of and require) the Lord [by right of their need and on the authority of His Word], none of them shall lack any beneficial thing" (Psalm 34:10, AMP). Lack and poverty are *not* life in all its fullness; therefore they cannot be God's will for your life.

The Scriptures declare that a good name is better than great riches or even the precious anointing of God (see Proverbs 22:1; Ecclesiastes 7:1). If we cannot pay our bills, we propagate a bad name. Can you imagine trying to tell your apartment manager about Jesus when you can't pay your rent on time? Why would he or she listen since your life's evidence shouts of failure to keep your word? However, if your apartment manager sees God providing for you and eventually has to say good-bye because God's provision has enabled you to purchase a home rather than rent, how much more does that witness to the unbeliever? God's Word declares, "You will lend to many nations but you yourself won't have to take out a loan" (Deuteronomy 28:12, MSG). What a testimony when we are debt-free—no loan payments to make—and are "lending to the nations" by sharing our abundance with others and giving to the work of the gospel!

From these scriptures, it appears that God's desire is to go further than just *meeting* our needs. It seems that He wants us to *prosper.* Hear His will in the apostle John's prayer: "Beloved, I wish *above all things* that thou mayest prosper and be in health, even as thy soul prospereth" (3 John 2, KJV).

Did you notice the words I highlighted, *above all things*? More than anything else, God desires for you, His child, to prosper and be in good health. Let me say it again: *above all things. More than anything else!* If the apostle's prayer wasn't God's will, it couldn't be written in Scripture. God never exaggerates or overstates. He can't, for it would be a lie and God cannot lie. So you can bank on this, my friend: God's will *above all things* is for you to prosper and be in good health. Amazing!

What is prosperity? It's having more than enough to meet not only *your* needs but also the needs of those in your world of influence. In other words, money should never be the deciding factor in whether you will reach out to the people God calls you to touch in His name. Could this be why God's Word declares, "Always remember that it is the Lord your God who gives you power to become rich, and he does it to fulfill the covenant he made with your ancestors" (Deuteronomy 8:18, NLT)?

God is not opposed to our having money. What He's against is money having us. Money is not the root of all evil; the *love of it* is. It is God's will for you to prosper in every area of life, even financially.

❧

Many young or immature believers struggle with the major areas of life we've just discussed. However, once we're firmly grounded in the fact that God is not the author of shame, guilt, condemnation, sickness, disease, physical infirmity, lack, or poverty, it is easier to discern the other areas of attack that also come from the enemy. Now we are set for the real fight in life—the battle to take ground for the kingdom.

Know this in your heart as you move forward into battle: if opposition falls under the category of stealing, death, or destruction, it has nothing to do with God. It is from the forces of Satan who want to discourage, defeat, and devour you. You and I must battle them *relentlessly* in order to see God's kingdom manifest on earth as it is in heaven.

8

ARM YOURSELF

Therefore, since Christ suffered for us in the flesh, *arm yourselves* also with the same mind, for he who has *suffered* in the flesh has ceased from sin.

1 PETER 4:1

I magine a nation sending its military into war without bullets, guns, cannons, bombs, tanks, planes, or even knives. How would that nation fare in warfare? Would they conquer? Would they contend? Would they even survive? My guess is, a good number would quickly be killed and the rest taken as prisoners of war.

It's a guess because, to my knowledge, such a ludicrous scenario has never occurred. But as ridiculous as it sounds, it's not much different from a believer who is not "armed to suffer." Sadly, most of us are unarmed. When unexpected *thlipsis* strikes, we're caught off guard and enter into a state of shock, bewilderment, or amazement. The result is that we tend to *react* instead of *act*.

In his first letter, Peter, under the inspiration of the Holy Spirit, admonishes us to arm ourselves to suffer in the same manner as Christ did. How did He suffer? Was He plagued with sin? Never, but He did have to resist it. Was He plagued with sickness or disease? No, but He probably had to fight it off. Did He lack enough money to pay bills or to accomplish His mission? No, yet I'm sure He had to trust God for provision. Jesus was tested in all points, yet He never succumbed to one assault hurled by the enemy. We are charged to walk as He walked; therefore, we also are not to yield to any wile of the devil.

As we read more deeply in Peter's letter, we realize that the specific suffering Jesus endured was unfair treatment from people, particularly from the corrupt political and religious leaders of His day. I personally believe this is the highest level of suffering one must endure to enter rulership.

Indeed, unfair treatment was the apostle Paul's greatest struggle. He was stoned, five times whipped, three times beaten with rods, and in nearly constant peril from his own countrymen, foreigners, and false believers. Paul was slandered, lied about, mocked, mistreated, insulted, and falsely accused. He warns us of the same: "Yes, and all who desire to live godly in Christ Jesus will suffer persecution" (2 Timothy 3:12).

If you live as the world lives, you'll not be bothered with persecution; you are virtually a prisoner of war. You're subdued in the enemy's POW camp. You're no longer effectively taking ground for the kingdom, unable to bring God glory. It is the soldiers under fire who are free and fighting to take enemy territory.

> ▬
> If you live as the world lives...you are virtually a prisoner of war.
> ▬

We live in a world that is completely contrary and even hostile to the kingdom of God. The flow of this world's system is directly opposite the flow of God's Spirit. Therefore, if you are truly living for the Lord, you *will* suffer tribulation, affliction, and persecution. It's part of the job description.

Dear friend, whether it's the list of devices described in the previous chapter; or contrary circumstances of nature; or hostility from people, organizations, or entities of this world's system, *you will suffer resistance in your life in Christ.* So, Peter says, you must be prepared. You must, as he puts it, "arm yourselves."

ARMED VS. UNARMED

It may be helpful to first see two examples of unexpected adversity in which one respondent is armed and another is unarmed. Every six to twelve months, a commercial airline pilot is sent for recurrent training. A big part of that training is the high-tech simulator, a training device with a complex computer system, a detailed cockpit replication with all the controls of a specific aircraft, a visual system to replicate the world outside of an aircraft. It's all mounted on motion platforms that move in response to the pilot's control or to outside environmental factors. Simply put, once inside, you can't tell if you're in a real airplane or a simulator.

The instructors who run the simulator throw all kinds of trouble (*thlipsis*) against these pilots, as the simulator is capable of imitating a full range of flight conditions and malfunctions. Pilots encounter simulations of intense turbulence, wind shear, extreme weather conditions, loss of an engine or power, malfunctioning landing gear—and that's the short list. The idea is that if pilots repeatedly, successfully conquer unexpected challenges while training, they will be prepared to solve those crises in actual situations. Many disasters have been averted due to such recurring training in which pilots learn to identify and take charge of emergencies.

I recall an aviation disaster that occurred prior to 9/11/2001. It was a small passenger plane that did not have the standard cockpit doors we see today separating the pilots from the passengers. Shortly after the crash, the black box was recovered and reviewed. Since there hadn't been a cockpit door on the flight, experts could hear the reactions of both the pilots and the passengers. The passengers screamed hysterically as the plane plunged from the sky. The pilots, however, were steady and in control, identifying the malfunctions and working through the situation. They reacted not in fear but according to their simulator training. The pilot in command called out instructions, and the copilot responded to every directive. This continued all the way to the end. Because the pilots had been armed for the unexpected disaster while the passengers had been unarmed, their responses were totally different. The pilots *acted* with purpose while the passengers could only *react* with fear.

I was once a passenger in a private jet when, at 39,000 feet, the door seal broke. The rapid release of pressurized air from the cabin was so loud it sounded like an intense wind tunnel. In just moments the cabin became depressurized. I was caught completely off guard and didn't know what to do. Honestly, my efforts were focused on fighting off the intense fear clutching my chest. I prayed passionately. It just so happened that the pilot in command was a former Navy test pilot with tens of thousands of hours of flight experience and training in numerous types of emergencies. The moment the seal broke, he and his copilot sprang into action. They immediately identified the problem, put on their oxygen masks, and released my mask. Without oxygen they could not have completed the rest of their tasks.

The pilot then started an emergency descent to a lower altitude while giving rapid-fire orders to his copilot. Throughout the crisis, he responded with calm confidence and assurance. His training had embedded within him the exact procedures to follow. I knew we might be in big trouble, but you never would have known it watching the pilot take charge of that situation. I saw no fear in his behavior. His actions were deliberate, automatic, and immediate. He was very much in control.

The pilot brought that jet down to 12,000 feet in less than five minutes—we had dived at a rate of six thousand to eight thousand feet per minute. Not much later, we were safely on the ground. When the alarming situation was over, it was clear to me that my pilot had been "armed" and I wasn't! His training and experience had taught him what to do, which enabled him to rule over a major crisis.

And this is the message of 1 Peter 4:1: We are to be armed for spiritual conflict just as the former Navy test pilot was armed to deal with the unexpected. It's my desire that this book, *Relentless,* become a simulator that prepares you for the hardships you are bound to encounter en route to completing your destiny in Christ and ruling in life.

TRIBULATION WILL HAPPEN

To be armed, the first thing we must know is that tribulation is inevitable. "In the world you *will* have tribulation," Jesus states emphatically in John 16:33. Not "you might," but "you *will*." Paul admonishes, "We must *through many tribulations* enter the kingdom of God" (Acts 14:22). And again he writes, "No one should be shaken by these afflictions; for you yourselves know that we are appointed to this" (1 Thessalonians 3:3).

We are "appointed to hardship" even as a soldier going to war. No great warrior goes into battle to lose. The good soldier sets his or her sights on winning and is determined to fight through the hardship (suffering) in order to win. He or she is armed and prepared for battle. You and I are in a war. Did you think your life would be quieter than before you were saved?

I get upset when I hear newborn Christians being told that they're entering a trouble-free, ideal life—a utopia. I can only imagine that ministers or believers who communicate this nonsense to new Christians either are not truly saved or are more interested in "closing the deal" of salvation than in the welfare of the newborn's soul. I wonder if these "teachers" have pondered Jesus' words in His parable of the sower, where He teaches that once the Word is sown in the heart of a human being, "tribulation or persecution arises for the word's sake" (Mark 4:17). The New Living Translation phrases it this way: "They have problems or are persecuted because they believe the word." To shoot straight, as Christ always did, when you believe God's Word you sign up for problems, hardship, and persecution. You can count on it.

If you're a young believer and don't yet know this from personal experience, then allow me to be the first to tell you: you're in for battles like you've never faced before. However, the great news is, you don't have to lose one of the battles! Not one. You lost in many ways before you were saved, but now, through the indwelling Holy Spirit and God's matchless grace, you have authority and power over any trouble that comes your way.

YOU'RE NOT FACING SOMETHING NEW

The second thing we must know about becoming "armed" for battle is that there's really nothing new under the sun. You will never encounter a difficulty that no one else has experienced, especially Jesus, for He was tested in every way. Paul writes:

> No test or temptation that comes your way is beyond the course of what others have had to face. All you need to remember is that God will never let you down; he'll never let you be pushed past your limit; he'll always be there to help you come through it. (1 Corinthians 10:13, MSG)

Any adversity you face has already been faced, and overcome, by someone else. You can be sure of that! The verse also promises that we will not face any hardship or persecution that is beyond our ability to handle. God will not permit it. You can put away all fear that you might ever face opposition or hardship that you'd be unable to withstand or overcome. Your heavenly Father will not permit it to come your way; He'll block it.

Today's English Version states, "God keeps his promise, and he will not allow you to be tested beyond your power to remain firm." The wonderful, assuring truth is that *the devil does not have free access to you.* His attacks must first be passed through the permission of the Almighty. Your heavenly Father will never author or instigate the tests, but He will sometimes allow them so you can beat up on the enemy and bring glory to Him as you take ground for the kingdom.

> Any adversity you face has already been faced, and overcome, by someone else.

One highly respected early church leader named Tertullian, who lived AD 160–230, commented on this in a profound way:

> By allowing a permission for the operation of [Satan's] designs, God acted consistently with the purpose of His own goodness. He deferred the devil's destruction for the very same reason that He postponed the restitution of man. For He afforded room for a conflict, wherein man might crush his enemy with the same freedom of his will as had made him succumb to Satan.... [And it enables man] to worthily recover his salvation by a victory. In this way, also, the devil receives a more bitter punishment, by being vanquished by him whom he had previously injured. By these means, God is discovered to be so much the more good.[1]

God gives us the privilege of choosing to beat the enemy and in a sense to "get even" for the sinful failures we experienced before we were saved. All the glory goes to God. The enemy can no longer sneer at mankind, God's handiwork. He did after Adam's fall in the Garden, but then Jesus came and whipped him on his own turf. Now God has given us the privilege of completing the devil's whipping.

Paul writes, "I am glad when I suffer for you in my body, for I am completing what remains of Christ's sufferings for his body, the church" (Colossians 1:24, NLT). If these words are read without understanding, one could erroneously

---

1. David W. Bercot, editor, *A Dictionary of Early Christian Beliefs* (Peabody, MA: Hendrickson, 1998).

think Paul is saying that Jesus' suffering was not enough to complete our redemption. For this reason many Christians shy away from this scripture and don't ponder it. (In fact, you'd be amazed at how many trained ministers and believers don't even know this scripture exists.)

But that's not at all what Paul is saying. Rather, he's pointing out our privilege of finishing the work needed to advance the kingdom to the ends of the earth. Jesus gave us the privilege of completing His task of bringing His finished work to the ends of the earth. The enemy resists with a furious vengeance, which brings suffering, but it's a victorious suffering. As Jesus said, "The gates of hell shall not prevail against it." He was talking about His church (see Matthew 16:18, KJV). This is war. We are on the march, we are out to conquer through the empowerment of God's grace, and hell itself cannot stop or defeat us. We have God's Word on it!

Remember: any adversity you may face in your Christian walk is something that another believer, even Christ himself, has already tackled and overcome. Peter encourages us, "Be strong in your faith. Remember that your Christian brothers and sisters all over the world are going through the same kind of suffering you are" (1 Peter 5:9, NLT). The suffering he speaks of goes hand-in-glove with living as God wants us to live, but when we stand strong in the power of His grace, we will be victorious.

You Never Have to Lose

Now we come to the third important point of being "armed": knowing you never have to lose. Don't just glance at these words of Jesus. Drink them in and ponder them deeply:

> Listen! I have given you authority, so that you can…overcome all the
> power of the Enemy, and nothing will hurt you. (Luke 10:19, TEV)

There's so much in this statement! First, recognize His passion as He calls us to *listen*. Observe the exclamation point. If the translators put an exclamation point on a statement of Jesus, that means we should take greater heed. It's a weightier statement.

He then says you've been given *authority,* not over some of the power or even most of the power but over *all* the power of the enemy. That's 100 percent. Not only do you have authority over 100 percent of the enemy's power, but you also have *far greater power* than all evil forces of Satan may throw at you. The King James Version reads, "I give unto you *power...over all the power* of the enemy." This corresponds to Paul's words when he prays that we might know "what is the exceeding greatness of His *power* toward us who believe" and that power is "*far above* all principality and power and might and dominion, and every name that is named" (Ephesians 1:19–21). Not just above but far above!

Not only do we have authority and power far above all the power of the enemy, but also, to back us up, there's one more amazing fact. We're told, "You are of God, little children, and have overcome them [anti-Christ spirits], because He who is in you is greater than he who is in the world" (1 John 4:4). All evil spirits are anti-Christ spirits, and they are the source of all tribulation. We have already overcome them because the One who whipped them is the One who lives in and empowers us.

Luke 10:19 quotes Jesus as promising that "nothing will hurt you" (TEV). There is no evil force—none—that can hurt you. There is no battle you will face that you are destined to lose. If you fight, relentlessly fight, with the weapons God has given you, you'll *always* come out on top. Again you have His Word on it: "Now thanks be to God who *always* leads us in triumph in Christ" (2 Corinthians 2:14).

If we listen to Him, God will lead us to triumph in every situation, in every battle. What Jesus promises, John affirms:

> Every God-begotten person conquers the world's ways. The conquering power that brings the world to its knees is our faith. (1 John 5:4, MSG)

It is our faith that overcomes anything the world can throw at us. Remember, Satan is "the god of this world." We win over anything he tries to throw at us because God has already made the way for our triumph.

According to John, it's our faith that brings the world to its knees. Why faith? Faith is what gives us access to the grace (power) we need to triumph. We've been discussing how we are to rule in life by the grace of God. However, that grace, even though it is freely given to all, can never be accessed unless we believe it (have faith), for faith is the pipeline that brings His grace (power) into any situation we're dealing with and need to overcome. As Paul states, "We have access by faith into this grace in which we stand" (Romans 5:2).

God's grace is free, available to all His children, but if we don't believe (have faith) in the "word of His grace," it's as if we don't possess grace at all. Remember how Paul spoke to the leaders and believers he would not see again: "So now, brethren, I commend you to God and to the *word of His grace,* which is able to build you up and give you an inheritance" (Acts 20:32). He pointed them to what would give them the inheritance of ruling in life for the glory of God: the word of His grace.

GRACE IS SUFFICIENT TO WIN EVERY BATTLE

This brings us to a fourth important truth about arming ourselves: God's grace is more than enough power to rule over any and every adversity you may face.

We can see this in Paul's personal struggle. His insights and revelations were highly damaging to the kingdom of darkness. These truths, downloaded from the Holy Spirit, greatly strengthened the believers of his generation and those generations to follow. Consequently Paul wrote:

> And lest I should be exalted above measure by the abundance of the revelations, a thorn in the flesh was given to me, a messenger of Satan to buffet me, lest I be exalted above measure. (2 Corinthians 12:7)

This specific situation Paul faced has created controversy among Bible teachers. But frankly, it shouldn't. Let's clear up any misconceptions.

First, who gave Paul the "thorn in the flesh"? We know for a fact that it couldn't have been God, for we're told, "Do not be deceived, my beloved brethren. Every good gift and every perfect gift is from above, and comes down from the Father of lights, with whom there is no variation or shadow of turning" (James 1:16–17). We're deceived if we think something other than good or perfect comes from God. A messenger of Satan is in no way good, and certainly not perfect. Someone may counter, "But in a roundabout way it was good because it kept Paul from pride." The apostle James abolishes this erroneous thought: "God is impervious to evil, and puts evil in no one's way" (James 1:13, MSG).

Look at James's statement, "God...puts evil in no one's way." God could never have sent that messenger of Satan or He would have been testing Paul with evil, thus lying through James. And God cannot lie. So without question, we may conclude that the "thorn" was not from God.

Second, what was Paul's thorn in the flesh? Some teachers say it was sickness, trouble with his eyes, or some kind of infirmity in his flesh. They deduce this from what he continues to write,

> Concerning this thing I pleaded with the Lord three times that it might depart from me. And He said to me, "My grace is sufficient for you, for My strength is made perfect in *weakness*." Therefore most gladly I will rather boast in my *infirmities*, that the power of Christ may rest upon me. (2 Corinthians 12:8–9)

I've highlighted two words in the above verse: *weakness* and *infirmities*. Let me focus on the second word first. Confused teachers infer Paul's thorn to be a physical *infirmity* from his statement, "I will boast in my *infirmities*." The Greek word for *infirmities* is *astheneia*. It is used twelve times in the New Testament. Admittedly, in the Gospels this term is predominantly used to identify physical infirmity. However, in most of its occurrences in the epistles, it is used to identify human weakness—our inability to accomplish or overcome something in our own ability. In these situations it does not refer to physical infirmity.

One example is Romans 8:26: "Likewise the Spirit also helps in our *weaknesses*. For we do not know what we should pray for as we ought, but the Spirit Himself makes intercession for us." The Greek word for *weaknesses* is the same Greek word, *astheneia*. I think we can safely say that all Christians don't have physical infirmities (sickness or disease). So what is the weakness every believer possesses in regard to intercessory prayer? The answer: there are occasions when we don't know how to pray due to the limitations of our humanity.

For example, if my mother lives in Florida and I live in Colorado, and an emergency arose in which she desperately needed prayer but she was unable to get in touch with me, I would have the human limitation of not knowing of her urgent need. But the Holy Spirit would help me in this inability (weakness) by directing me to pray for my mother. Again, this Greek word, *astheneia*, has nothing to do with physical infirmity but with natural human inability.

Another example would be Hebrews 4:15, which states, "For we do not have a High Priest who cannot sympathize with our *weaknesses*, but was in all points tempted as we are, yet without sin." The word for *weaknesses* is the same Greek word, *astheneia*. And again, this Greek word is not identifying physical infirmities but our human inabilities compared to God's abilities. Jesus voluntarily took on these human inabilities so He could identify with our struggles and help us effectively by His grace. The account that He "was tempted in all points as we are, yet without sin" obviously doesn't pertain to sickness but to the human inabilities that He voluntarily embraced during His life on earth.

With this in mind, let's return to Paul's statement, which I'll repeat here for ease of reference:

> Concerning this thing I pleaded with the Lord three times that it might depart from me. And He said to me, "My grace is sufficient for you, for My strength is made perfect in *weakness*." Therefore most gladly I will rather boast in my *infirmities*, that the power of Christ may rest upon me.
> (2 Corinthians 12:8–9)

I've again highlighted the words *weakness* and *infirmities*. And here's why: they're both the same Greek word, *astheneia*. So Paul's words could have easily been translated this way:

> "My grace is sufficient for you, for My strength is made perfect in human inability." Therefore most gladly I will rather boast in my human inability, that the power of Christ may rest upon me.

In fact, this passage is translated just this way in other versions. One would be the Contemporary English Version, which reads, "'My kindness is all you need. My power is strongest when you are *weak*.' So if Christ keeps giving me his power, I will gladly brag about how *weak* I am."

We are fooling ourselves if we assume that the only thing the Holy Spirit is referring to is sickness. If that were the case, the passage would read, "'My power is strongest when you are physically sick.' So if Christ keeps giving me his power, I will gladly brag about how sick I am." Wouldn't that be absurd? I think it's amazing how silly these things are when you really think them through.

It's also clear that Paul is not talking about physical infirmity when we read his entire letter in context. Paul identifies the manner in which the "messenger of Satan" was attacking him:

> Five times I was given the thirty-nine lashes by the Jews; three times I was whipped by the Romans; and once I was stoned. I have been in three shipwrecks, and once I spent twenty-four hours in the water. In my many travels I have been in danger from floods and from robbers, in danger from my own people and from Gentiles; there have been dangers in the cities, dangers in the wilds, dangers on the high seas, and dangers from false friends. There has been work and toil; often I have gone without sleep; I have been hungry and thirsty; I have often been without enough food, shelter, or clothing.... If I must boast, I will boast about things that *show how weak I am.* (2 Corinthians 11:24–27, 30, TEV)

Paul lists the hardships caused by the messenger of Satan that repeatedly raged against him. It was impossible for Paul to prevent or stop these unexpected difficulties in his own ability. For this reason he states, "I will boast about the things that show how *weak* I am." It's crystal clear: the weakness or "thorn in the flesh" in this letter has nothing to do with bad eyes, sickness, disease, or any other physical infirmity.

To go even further in showing that Paul's "thorn in the flesh" had nothing to do with sickness, let's look at how it is used elsewhere in Scripture. The phrase appears three other times, and each is in the Old Testament. All three dealt with the Canaanites who persistently attacked the Israelites. God told His people, "If you do not drive out the inhabitants of the land from before you, then it shall be that those whom you let remain shall be irritants in your eyes and *thorns in your sides,* and they shall *harass you*" (Numbers 33:55). In each occurrence, the "thorn in the flesh" metaphor represents people opposing and frustrating a productive life. The phrase is never used in the Old Testament to depict disease or sickness. Paul, a scholar of Scripture, used this phrase in a similar fashion to describe the harassments he faced everywhere he ventured.

THE GREAT PARADIGM SHIFT

I believe that Paul was so frustrated by the interruptions, hardships, and harassments he constantly encountered that he cried out to God—not once but three times—to remove the satanic influencer who was behind them all. I believe God didn't reply to Paul initially because his request was incorrect; Paul was barking up the wrong tree. After Paul's third request, the Lord enlightened him and provided the solution which was in him all along:

> Haven't you figured it out yet? I've given you grace (unmerited empowerment), over all the power of the enemy. So My grace (empowerment) is all you need, for it demonstrates its strength in anything you can't overcome in your human ability. In other words, the greater the resistance, the greater you will see the manifestation of My grace (empowerment) on your life if you simply believe. (2 Corinthians 12:9, author paraphrase)

Once this became clear to Paul, a wonderful thing happened. He embraced a *paradigm shift*—a radical change from one way of thinking to another. His whole attitude changed toward the constant satanic resistance he encountered. He no longer pleaded for it to be removed. Instead, he enthusiastically wrote:

> I *delight in* weaknesses, in insults, in hardships, in persecutions, in difficulties. For when I am weak, then I am strong. (2 Corinthians 12:10, NIV)

His boast now is, "I delight in my human inabilities over any *thlipsis* I may encounter from this moment on!"

Hold on: *delight in*? How could this be? Another translation reads, "I am well pleased and take pleasure in...." Yet another says, "I take pleasure...." Has

Paul lost his mind? Is he exaggerating? lying or overstating? No, anyone who writes Scripture under the inspiration of the Holy Spirit could not do any such thing, for it is impossible for God to lie. So how can someone "take pleasure" or "delight in" hardships, insults, harassment, adversity, and other difficulties? The answer is simple:

Greater resistance requires greater power to overcome;
consequently producing a greater victory.

Many Christians are unhappy when facing extreme hardship. They cringe at having to battle the enemy in difficult circumstances. They would prefer an easy, comfortable, convenient, nonconfrontational life. The truth that Paul discovered is not embedded in their hearts. They simply don't realize that all resistance is merely the opportunity for greater power (grace) to be manifested within them, and to grow to the next level of maturity in Christ. Paul had a similar attitude toward adversity before God challenged his thinking, but one word from God changed his entire paradigm. He wrote 2 Corinthians around the year AD 56. A few years later he wrote his letter to the Romans. Observe an entirely different attitude toward *thlipsis* in his later epistle:

Who shall ever separate us from Christ's love? Shall suffering and affliction and tribulation? Or calamity and distress? Or persecution or hunger or destitution or peril or sword?… Yet amid all these things we are more than conquerors and gain a surpassing victory through Him Who loved us. (Romans 8:35, 37, AMP)

Drink in those words, especially "Yet amid all these things we are more than conquerors and gain a surpassing victory through Him." Before the Great Paradigm Shift, Paul was pleading with God to steer him clear of those rough encounters with hardship. Now his message is resoundingly different: *God's grace is more than enough not only to endure hardships but also to gain a surpassing victory.* Paul's posture now is, "Bring it on! Bring on the opposition so that I may have a great victory for Christ." Paul is "armed to suffer." He's armed to fight to victory and to come out better and stronger than before he entered the battle.

SEE TRIALS AS OPPORTUNITIES

In conclusion, we are "armed" when we are firmly optimistic in heart and mind regarding hardship—optimistic before, during, and after the fight. We can take on a positive attitude because we no longer see tests and trials as obstacles; we see them as opportunities!

The apostle James writes, "Dear brothers and sisters, whenever trouble comes your way, let it be an opportunity" (James 1:2, NLT). We know that the war has already been won in Christ, and we have all the authority and power of heaven backing us up. If we don't give in, if we relentlessly stand and fight, we will always come out on top. It's God's will and destiny for our lives.

As Paul boldly affirms in Romans 8:31, "If God is for us, who can be against us?"

9

STRONG IN GRACE

We are not fighting against human beings but against
the wicked spiritual forces in the heavenly world, the
rulers, authorities, and cosmic powers of this dark age.

EPHESIANS 6:12 (TEV)

Every child of God is at war. If we are not, then we're actually of this world and deceived in our thinking that we belong to God.

I realize that's a strong statement, but allow me to illustrate its reality. Imagine living in Germany during the reign of Adolf Hitler. This tyrant leader ultimately wanted to establish a new order of absolute Nazi German hegemony in continental Europe. He was prejudiced in the purest sense, and those he hated most were of Jewish descent. If you were of German lineage, smart, healthy, and your thinking didn't interfere with the mission of Adolf Hitler, you could live at ease—free from concern of being attacked on any level.

However, if your lineage was Jewish, your life would be completely different. You'd live under constant threat of attack. At any moment you could be slandered, spit upon, vandalized, stolen from; you'd have to be on guard in order to avoid being captured, enslaved, tortured, and murdered. Whether you liked it or not, you were at war. The wiser and more prudent Jewish people armed themselves and did what was necessary to escape Hitler's tyranny. Those who didn't ended up imprisoned in his concentration camps.

Satan and his cohorts are far worse than Hitler and his Nazi regime. If you're of the devil's lineage, you're not a target. You don't have to maintain a posture of being at war. Jesus said to the hypocritical spiritual leaders of His day, "You are of this world" (John 8:23). Then, to ensure they didn't miss His implication, He said directly, "You are of your father the devil" (John 8:44). Even though these leaders believed they were serving God Almighty, in actuality they were serving this world's tyrant leader.

If you're truly God's, then you must be on guard because the world you live in is hostile toward anything that's of God's kingdom. Jesus pointed this out by saying,

> If you belonged to the world, then the world would love you as its own.
> But I chose you from this world, and you do not belong to it; that is why
> *the world hates you.* (John 15:19, TEV)

Notice His words, *the world hates you.* No room for play in this statement. If you're of the world, you'll be embraced by the world; if you're of God, you will be resisted and hated by the world's system.

WEAPONS OF GRACE

So we come to another important aspect of being properly armed, and that is having a working knowledge of the weapons we possess in Christ Jesus. They are both powerful and spiritual weapons, for Paul tells us, "The weapons we fight with are not the weapons of the world. On the contrary, they have *divine power* to demolish strongholds" (2 Corinthians 10:4, NIV).

What's the "divine power" that demolishes strongholds? It's none other than God's amazing grace—His unmerited gift to all believers. Knowing this, let's advance further into Peter's first letter to see this great truth underscored and expanded for us. As we do, keep in mind that we can substitute the words *power* or *empowerment* for the word *grace.* They're interchangeable.

> All of you be submissive to one another, and be clothed with humility, for "God resists the proud, but gives *grace* [power] to the humble." Therefore humble yourselves under the mighty hand of God, that He may exalt you in due time, casting all your care upon Him, for He cares for you. Be sober, be vigilant; because your adversary the devil walks about like a roaring lion, seeking whom he may devour. Resist him,

NEXT PAGE →

steadfast in the faith, knowing that the same sufferings are experienced by your brotherhood in the world. But may the God of all *grace* [empowerment], who called us to His eternal glory by Christ Jesus, after you have suffered a while, perfect, establish, strengthen, and settle you.... I have written to you briefly, exhorting and testifying that *this is the true grace* [power] of God in which you stand. (1 Peter 5:5–12)

Allow me to quickly summarize Peter's rich words, then I will develop his message bit by bit. The main theme of this passage is *the grace of God*. Peter starts by exhorting us to be submissive to one another. Another way of saying this is to "come under the same mission." He then asserts that God gives His grace to the humble, and that we're deemed humble when we expect our cares to be met by His grace (power), not by our own strength.

What kind of cares is Peter talking about? They involve life issues, such as our concerns, responsibilities, needs, or various desires. Our cares can be temporal or, most importantly, eternal: to experience kingdom abundant life and, subsequently, to meet the needs of others in our sphere of influence. In the pursuit of this mission of grace, we will experience resistance from our archenemy, the devil and his cohorts. He can devour us, but that's not God's plan. Therefore, we're to maintain a sober mind, to be well aware of the covenant promises of God, and to be vigilant in prayer. Thus we'll always be well equipped by the grace of God to advance His kingdom purposes and successfully resist our archenemy.

We are not alone in our efforts; our fellow brothers and sisters are on the same mission of grace all over the world and are experiencing similar battles in our overall objective. The good thing about these battles is that they establish maturity and strength. With each victory, we are exalted to a higher place of authority in Christ.

Peter concludes the passage with this invigorating thought: *This is* (the purpose of) *the true grace of God.* Isn't it interesting that the Holy Spirit moved upon Peter almost two thousand years ago to pen the words *the true grace of God*? This was no accident; the Holy Spirit foresaw that in the latter days the concept of God's grace would be reduced (at least in Western Christian thinking) to a mere cover-up for sin and a ticket into heaven. The true grace of God does include both of these, but so much more—it also empowers us to go beyond our natural ability for the mission at hand. A major aspect of this mission is to distinguish ourselves for the sake of glorifying God and advancing His kingdom.

With this knowledge we can easily deduce why more believers are not radiating as bright lights. Distinguishing ourselves comes through tough battles, and most of us naturally shy away from fights. The enemy is not going to just lie down and let us impact the world for Jesus Christ. He's adamantly opposed to our mission, and we must stand up to and resist him to accomplish our God-given goals. The New International Version translation reads, "This is the true grace of God. *Stand fast* in it." After reading that, Paul's words to Timothy become even more potent:

> You therefore, my son, *be strong in the grace* that is in Christ Jesus.…
> You therefore must endure hardship as a good soldier of Jesus Christ.
> (2 Timothy 2:1, 3)

Timothy is not told to be strong physically, socially, emotionally, or intellectually. He is told to be strong in *grace.* It's the weapon we need to finish successfully. After more than twenty-five years of ministry, I've observed that most of us are not using the weapon of grace. After all, 98 percent of U.S. Christians don't fully comprehend this free, powerful gift. We just don't know what we have.

Most of us are not using the weapon of grace.

Just prior to the second chapter of 2 Timothy, Paul corrects the young man of God for succumbing to the resistance and persecution he faced. Apparently, young Timothy's adversaries intimidated him, and he wasn't resisting and fighting as steadfastly as Paul thought he could. Paul reminds Timothy that God hasn't given him a spirit of timidity but of power, love, and a sound mind. As all believers do, Timothy already possessed what it takes to overcome any resistance, so Paul exhorts him to stir up, and be strong in, the grace that is in Christ (see 2 Timothy 1:6–7; 2:1).

Moving into our highest calling is not a walk in the park. We don't tiptoe into greatness or engage "cruise control" for a distinguished life. Paul emphatically states, "I *press toward* the goal for the prize of the upward call of God in Christ Jesus" (Philippians 3:14). If Paul is "pressing," that means there is opposition and resistance.

Recall the vision from our first chapter. Our protagonist, the one rowing the boat, had to press, press, press against the strong current of the river. His strength waned. Why? I can only imagine that observing the party boats float by containing so many at ease, laughing, living what appeared to be successful lives, and experiencing so little opposition—all that grated on him over time. This eventually led to a discovery, one that was an illusion, yet seemed so real. He could live at ease as a "Christian" and, interestingly, experience less resistance. What a deception.

Here's another illustration. A soldier can retreat from battle and consequently experience a much quieter lifestyle than his comrades still on the front line. The war isn't over. It's just that this soldier is no longer in conflict due to his retreat. Similar to our man in the boat, the soldier still looks battle ready: he's wearing a uniform, has all the gear, and is carrying a rifle. But he's experiencing no resistance.

Our objective is not to appear Christlike but to actually be Christlike in advancing the kingdom and destroying the works of the devil (see 1 John 3:8). To do so means we will face opposition and resistance.

We must remember that the grace (power) of God is all we need to overcome any hardship. However, we must cooperate with it by steadfastly believing—and the evidence of our belief is our corresponding action. When Peter walked on the water, he did an impossible and extraordinary feat. Jesus said "Come," and in that one word was all the grace Peter needed to walk on water. But when he stopped believing, the grace (power) waned and he began to sink. There was enough grace in Jesus' word *come* for Peter to walk the full distance to Jesus and even finish crossing the entire Sea of Galilee if he wanted to. But the grace failed because his faith failed. We have unlimited grace in Christ, but we can only access it through faith: "We have access by faith into this grace in which we stand" (Romans 5:2).

The problem is not that grace fails but that our faith wanes. Consequently, the grace (power) is cut off. Then we're left to fight in our own strength. Think of a pipeline that brings water to your home. If the pipe ruptures, the flow of water is cut off. Even though the source has a limitless supply of water, the water can no longer get to your house because the pipe has failed. Faith is the pipe; water is the grace.

To help prevent failure, we must build ourselves up in the faith. How? We get into God's Word; we praise, worship, thank God for who He is and for His provision of grace; we pray in the Spirit. If we don't do these things to build up our faith, we'll eventually stop believing and live in our own strength instead of God's. Then it's only a matter of time before we cease ruling the world and start letting the world rule us.

This is why Peter encourages us to "Continue to grow in the grace...of our Lord and Savior Jesus Christ" (2 Peter 3:18, TEV). We are given the responsibility to grow in God's power. We do so simply by building our faith, and we *can* increase our faith. Paul says, "The righteousness of God is revealed from faith to faith; as it is written, 'The just shall live by faith'" (Romans 1:17). Think of it this way: the more your faith increases, the bigger the "pipe"—and, consequently, the greater the amount of "water" (grace) available to you. Therefore, God can entrust you with more responsibility to go into more needy areas and fight to bring life.

With the writer of Hebrews, I heartily encourage you to

Lift up your tired hands, then, and strengthen your trembling knees!
Keep walking on straight paths.... Guard against turning back from the
grace of God. (Hebrews 12:12–13, 15, TEV)

To turn back from the grace of God is to back down from the enemy's resistance, shift into neutral, become complacent. Why turn back from God's incredible, supernatural power? Why fail to appropriate His amazing grace-empowerment?

We are at war, and the only way to finish strong is to be relentless in our faith. Being relentless is a delight to the Lord and a genuine threat to the kingdom of darkness. This is our calling, our destiny, and our privilege in serving our Lord Jesus Christ.

10

THE ARMOR OF HUMILITY

All of *you* be submissive to one another, and be clothed
with humility, for "God resists the proud, but gives
grace to the humble." Therefore humble yourselves
under the mighty hand of God, that He may exalt you
in due time, casting all your care upon Him, for He
cares for you.

1 PETER 5:5–7

"B e submissive to one another...clothed with humility...humble
yourselves."

Peter's words in the verses above are crucial to living effectively
and finishing well in any aspect of life. The apostle opens with the charge, "Be
submissive to one another." In this context, the word *submissive* means "to unite
under the same mission." How is this possible with our vast diversity of personalities, strengths, and desires? By clothing ourselves with humility. God resists
the proud, and we certainly don't want God resisting us! On the other hand, He
gives grace (power) to the humble.

So, who are the proud, and who are the humble?

THE HUMBLE RECEIVE GOD'S GRACE

Christians who are truly humble believe, trust, and obey God's Word over what
they think, reason, feel, or desire. Consequently, they depend completely on

God's ability rather than their own. They seek His will, not their own or another's. They're on His mission. God's Word tells us, "Behold the *proud*, His soul is not upright in him; but the just shall live by his faith" (Habakkuk 2:4).

Habakkuk 2:4 portrays pride and faith as polar opposites. This verse could have been written, "Behold the one who's *not humble*, his soul is not upright in him; but the just person shall live by his *faith*." Here humility and faith go hand in hand. So do pride and unbelief. To not believe God is to declare that we know better than He does and we trust our own judgment over His. Unbelief is nothing other than camouflaged pride.

Allow me to illustrate. About a year after Israel came out of Egypt, the Lord commanded Moses, "Send men to spy out the land of Canaan, which *I am giving to the children of Israel*" (Numbers 13:2). As usual, God's directive was clear—no gray areas or uncertainty.

So Moses sent out twelve leaders, one from each tribe. However, ten men were very "humble" and two were very "proud." (If you know the story, stay with me here; I'm speaking facetiously to make a point.)

After forty days in the Promised Land, the spies returned. The ten "humble" men spoke first by saying, "We've spied out the land and it is indeed a superb land, flowing with milk and honey. Just look at the fruit we brought back. However, there are mighty armies to contend with—even giants! They're skilled warriors with weapons much greater than ours; we're just a bunch of recently freed slaves. We have to consider our wives and children! How could we possibly subject our loved ones to the cruelty, torture, rape, and even death that await them on the other side of the river? We must be good and responsible fathers and husbands and report to you the reality of this situation. It's impossible to take the land."

Although the people longed for a land to call their own, safety was first. So they commended and applauded the wisdom and humility of these men. I'm sure the majority of fathers and mothers who heard their report were grateful for the meek demeanor of these ten spies. The Israelites comforted themselves by saying to each other, "We're so glad these men went before us. What great leaders—their egos haven't gotten the best of them by putting us in harm's way. What would have become of us if it weren't for their common sense?"

But then the two "proud" leaders, Caleb and Joshua, interrupted and cried out, "Wait a minute! What are we doing here? We need to go and take the land now! We can do it! The Lord God has promised it to us. We have His Word on it! We'll annihilate these people. Let's mobilize at once!"

Everyone was stunned by what they'd just heard. They looked at each other in disbelief. Can you imagine the other ten spies' reaction to Caleb and Joshua's rash and imprudent counsel? I imagine that, after their initial shock, they all responded with something like this: "What are you two talking about? Are you out of your minds? We all saw the same things—we beheld their strength, weapons, and fortified cities. They're huge, skilled warriors, and we're just a bunch of slaves. We're no match for them! You're not thinking of our wives and children, the welfare of our nation. You're arrogant, foolhardy, and idealistic! Shut up, you egomaniacs!"

I envision the crowds sighing in relief. "Whew, thank God the wiser ones aren't backing down. We are so fortunate that the majority of the spies are humble and prudent. Can you just imagine what would have become of us if all of them were proud and arrogant like Caleb and Joshua?"

But, as He always does, God had the final word. "How long will these people treat me with contempt?" He thundered to Moses. "How long will they refuse to *believe*?" (Numbers 14:11, NIV). God was not happy with the crowd mentality. What they thought was humility wasn't humility at all. In actuality, their unbelief was pride. They were basing all of their calculations on their own wisdom, ability, and strength.

Much later in the Old Testament God declares, "Cursed are those who put their trust in mere humans...but blessed are those who trust in the LORD and have made the LORD their hope and confidence" (Jeremiah 17:5, 7, NLT). Ten of the spies had seen how big the giants were and based their timid prospects on their own strength. But Caleb and Joshua saw how big God was compared to the enemy and based their estimates entirely on God's grace. These two, Caleb and Joshua, ended up blessed; the other spies and everyone else who disbelieved were cursed.

So which of the spies were truly humble and which were truly proud? In God's eyes, the ten were proud and only two were humble.

It takes genuine humility to have faith, because when you are humble you rely on and trust in God's ability (grace) to pull you through—not on your own ability. If the ten spies had humbly relied on God's promises, they would have moved out and conquered the land. They would have submitted to the Word of the Lord rather than their limited strength and human reasoning, and thus they would have been submitted to one another—*under the same mission.*

It takes genuine humility to have faith.

Once they were in battle, an onlooker may have assumed the descendants of Abraham were operating in their own strength, but in reality it would have been God's grace—His supernatural power—working through them. When we're empowered by God's grace, there are times when what we accomplish appears to be by our own ability. On other occasions it is clearly evident that it's God's ability. But no matter how it appears to the outsider, we can know and trust completely in His power and move forward based on our confidence in His Word.

That, my dear reader, is relentless faith. But it all starts with a spirit of humility before God and each other.

To be clothed in humility is to wear His armor rather than our own. First Peter 5:5–6 commands, "Be clothed with humility.... Therefore humble yourselves under the mighty *hand* of God." In the Scriptures, the *hand* of God always speaks of His ability, power, might, or strength; it's His armor.

How does this translate practically? We're to humble ourselves under God's might and strength. We refuse to allow human ideas and experiences (ours or others) to rise above the Word of God. Instead, we *believe,* regardless of our natural reason or logic, and allow His Word to dictate our actions.

Four hundred years of subjugation in Egypt had taught the children of Israel that they could not defend themselves against an army of greater strength that possessed more powerful weapons. Egypt had dominated them. They could do nothing to free themselves; it had taken God himself. He gloriously had delivered them by His *mighty hand.* As Moses recalled, "For with a *strong hand* the LORD has brought you out of Egypt" (Exodus 13:9). Yet we also know that "They soon forgot His works" (Psalm 106:13). They clung to their longtime experience of slavery instead of to the hand of God that delivered them. The same strong hand that defeated Egypt would also defeat the Canaanite armies, who in fact were far inferior to the Egyptian armies.

But before you and I come down too hard on the weak-faithed Israelites, we need to look in the mirror. How often do we do the same? Before we joined God's family, we were under Satan's tyrannical rule. We possessed his nature and had no hope of escaping. But God mightily "rescued us from the power of darkness and brought us safe into the kingdom of his dear Son" (Colossians 1:13, TEV). If He accomplished this impossible feat, how much more can He handle far less complex and difficult situations in our lives? Situations like healing sickness and disease, providing for any need, granting wisdom, and empowering us to be distinguished and overcome "impossible" odds. Let's not repeat Israel's folly and "soon forget His works." Let's you and I stay clothed in the armor of humility as Caleb and Joshua did.

HUMILITY MISUNDERSTOOD

Sad to say, humility is often mistaken as being weak, wimpy, or spineless. In actuality, it's quite the opposite. And, often in the Bible, those who are truly humble are mistaken for being prideful or arrogant. Take David, for example. At his father's request he visits his older brothers who are at war against the Philistine army. When he arrives at the battle scene, he notices all the soldiers, including his brothers, in a strange new military position: hiding behind rocks and shaking with fear. They are intimidated by the size, strength, and reputation of the Philistine giant, Goliath. David learns that this has been going on for forty days, and he questions in no sheepish tone, "Who is this uncircumcised Philistine, that he should defy the armies of the living God?" (1 Samuel 17:26).

David's attitude infuriates his oldest brother, Eliab. Can you imagine Eliab's thoughts? *My little brother is not only a brat, he's full of himself.* He snaps back at David, "I know *your pride* and the insolence of your heart" (verse 28). Wow, what a direct rebuke! Today's English Version translates Eliab's words as "You smart aleck, you!" and the New International Version reads, "I know how *conceited* you are." David's brother clearly views young David as impudent, arrogant, and proud.

But wait, which sibling was really the proud one? Only a chapter earlier, the prophet Samuel had come to Jesse's house to anoint the next king. Eliab the firstborn didn't make the cut. Both Jesse and Samuel had assumed that

Eliab would be the chosen one because he was the oldest and most likely the tallest and strongest of Jesse's sons. But God firmly stated, "I have rejected him" (1 Samuel 16:7, NIV).

Why did God reject Eliab? Could it be that the very pride Eliab accused David of resided in his own heart? God later commended David's humility by declaring how David has been a man after His own heart (see Acts 13:22). Humility characterized David's life, and we all know that this great leader was far from being weak, wimpy, or spineless. He's the one who wrote, "The LORD is on my side; I will not fear. What can man do to me?" (Psalm 118:6).

Back on the battlefield, David shakes off Eliab's verbal assault and challenges the giant with confidence, letting Goliath know in no uncertain terms that he is about to lose his huge head. Then David runs toward the enemy camp, kills Goliath with a single stone from his slingshot, and does exactly as promised: He takes Goliath's head.

David's oldest brother and siblings had based their calculations for battle on their own strength, just as the ten spies had done. David, on the other hand, envisioned the battle through God's strength or *mighty hand*. He clothed himself with humility. King Saul had offered David his armor, but the lad refused; he trusted in the armor of God. But once again, just as with Caleb and Joshua, David was viewed as arrogant and proud by those who trusted in their own strength.

I believe that the enemy has worked hard to pervert our definition and understanding of humility. Many well-meaning Christians have joined the unbelieving world in viewing humility as being soft-spoken, weak in demeanor, and nonconfrontational. But this is light years from the true meaning of the word. Consider two more biblical examples, Moses and Jesus.

In the book of Numbers we read, "Now the man Moses was very humble, more than all men who were on the face of the earth" (Numbers 12:3).

Wow, that's quite a statement! Wouldn't you and I love to have this said about us? Of course, we'd never dare say it about ourselves because only an arrogant, conceited, egotistical person would tell everyone how humble he was, right? But guess who wrote the book of Numbers—Moses! This amazing man of God described himself as the most humble man on the face of the earth.

How could this be? Can you imagine a minister standing before a Christian conference and saying, "Everyone, I'm very humble, so let me tell you all about it." He would be laughed off the stage.

Now hear what Jesus says: "Come to me, all you who are weary and burdened...and learn from me, for I am...humble in heart" (Matthew 11:28–29, NIV).

Jesus is saying, in essence, "Hey, come to Me. I'm humble and I want to teach you about it." Like Moses' statement, Jesus' self-proclaimed humility wouldn't go over very well in today's world. But the problem is not what Moses and Jesus said; the problem is that *we have drifted in our comprehension and understanding of humility.* We've missed its true meaning because we now think it means to live as unworthy worms and to speak only of our incapability and wretchedness. Meanwhile, humility as God designed it is a very positive, powerful character quality. True humility is absolute obedience and dependence on God. It puts Him first, others second, and ourselves third in all things. Humility has nothing to do with being soft-spoken and self-demeaning and has everything to do with living boldly, relentlessly, in the power of God's free gift of grace.

HUMILITY KEEPS US RELENTLESS

Remember how those who endure relentlessly and finish well receive the reward? Paul cautions against letting *false humility*—which can have an appearance of wisdom—cheat you of this reward: "Let no one cheat you of your reward," he warns, "taking delight in false humility" (Colossians 2:18). The ten spies and the timid nation of Israel illustrate how false humility can actually cost us our God-intended reward.

The ten spies counseled against entering the Promised Land. Their reasoning seemed sound, logical, and prudent, but they drew from the tree of the knowledge of good and evil rather than the promise and wisdom of God. They cheated not only themselves but also their families and millions of others: they never entered the Promised Land. That's a lot of people who missed their destiny due to false humility. Caleb and Joshua, the two spies who reported back in a spirit of humility, were the only adults of that generation whom God allowed to enter the new land. With Joshua as leader, the new generation of Israelites entered boldly, humble in the power of God's mighty hand. And they conquered.

A man once asked me, "John, would you rather preach to millions of people with varying backgrounds or to only a dozen leaders?"

"The millions," I responded.

He said, "You choose unwisely, for the ten leaders who spied out the land were responsible for causing millions of people to miss their destiny."

We're all called to be leaders and influencers. So how are you leading? Are you armed with humility in coming under the mighty hand of God, or do you have an appearance of humility but still operate in your own strength?

Paul further writes that "we are more than conquerors" (Romans 8:37), but that our own ideas, plans, or directives that are outside the Word of God may "seem wise because they require strong devotion, humility, and severe bodily discipline. But they have no effect when it comes to conquering" (Colossians 2:23, NLT).

Everyone in Caleb and Joshua's generation had been positioned to conquer. Eliab and his brothers should have conquered the Philistines long before young David arrived on the scene. But false humility stole their strength, promise, fruit, ability to rule in life, and ultimately their eternal reward. For this reason Paul strongly exhorts us,

> Be of the same mind toward one another. Do not set your mind on high things, but associate with the *humble*. Do not be wise in your own opinion. (Romans 12:16)

The humble mind is not wise in its own opinion. I recall the time a prominent international magazine was writing an article on a controversial subject. The editor contacted our office requesting my comments and views, and my assistant relayed the request. I told her, "Let me think it over."

The next day I felt troubled in my spirit, but I couldn't put my finger on the reason. I kept asking myself, *What's wrong?* But I couldn't articulate what was bothering me. I finally brought it to the Lord in prayer, and a day or two later it suddenly hit me. I was talking to Lisa and said, "I know why I've been troubled about the magazine's request. It's simple: Who am I to give my opinion? Do ambassadors give their own opinions?"

The Bible says, "We are *ambassadors* for Christ, as though God were pleading through us" (2 Corinthians 5:20). If the President of the United States sends an ambassador to deliver his message to another nation and the ambassador gives *his own* message or comment in the President's stead, he's in a heap of trouble. When I speak on the behalf of God the Father and Christ Jesus my Lord, I must speak His Word. Who am I to give my own opinion? It's the folly of the ten spies. This magazine came to me, a minister of the gospel, for my opinion, which would insult the stewardship of the grace of God committed to my trust.

This incident caused me to flash back to what God had spoken to me in prayer years earlier. The first four years of our ministry were tough going—a desert, so to speak. Lisa and I drove our small Honda Civic up and down the eastern half of the United States, with babies in car seats and our luggage crammed into every available space. We prayed hard for doors to open to us. Most of our meetings were in churches of a hundred or so members that did not seem to be growing and were of minimal impact in their communities.

After four years of this labored ministry, God spoke to me in prayer one morning: *John, I've sent you to churches and conferences that carry smaller influence for these past four years, and you have faithfully obeyed Me. I will continue to care for these you've ministered to, but now I'm going to make a significant change. I will now bring increase beyond what you've dreamed. Your reach will multiply many times as you'll be invited to churches and conferences carrying significant influence in cities and nations. You will be blessed financially, socially, and spiritually in an exponential way. You steward what is Mine, and it's time for the message you carry to go to the masses.*

(Allow me to interject this important point in regard to numbers. There are large churches that lack influence in their communities and, conversely, there are small churches that are very influential. The important aspect of an effective church is not numeric but the quality of their outreach and influence.)

I was stunned and excited in what I so clearly heard God say to my heart. I later told Lisa and she was delighted, too. But only a few moments later, the Lord continued to whisper to me: *This will also be a test. When you went to the smaller venues lacking influence, you had to believe Me for every penny and trust Me for every word. You consistently sought My counsel because you knew that if you missed My will in your labor, you would significantly suffer.*

Will you now spend money loosely because I've financially blessed you? Or will you still seek My counsel as you've done through the dry times? Will you now go wherever you desire instead of seeking My direction? Will you now give your personal opinions from the pulpit instead of believing Me for every word as My oracle? Son, My children are tested in two major areas: in the desert and in the abundant place. Most who have failed have not failed in the desert but in the abundant place.

I was trembling. After coming out of prayer, I immediately shared with Lisa what God had spoken to me. She responded, "John, when I heard the first part of the Word God gave you, I wanted to dance all over the kitchen. Now that I've heard the complete message, I'm trembling with fear!"

"That's good," I replied, "because that's the right response: *the fear of the Lord.*"

Many don't understand that the fear of the Lord does not mean to be scared of God. Rather, it means being scared—even terrified—to be away from Him! The fear of the Lord is the root of a healthy, wise, powerful, secure life. When it comes to riches, for example, they're good if handled properly and kept in perspective. However, deceit can easily attach itself to our wealth. Jesus warns of "the deceitfulness of riches" in Matthew 13:22, but such deceit will not trick or harm us if we stay in God's counsel, Word, and wisdom—the fear of the Lord.

> The fear of the Lord is the root of a healthy, wise, powerful, secure life.

To give my personal opinion as Christ's ambassador would be a lack of godly fear, nothing other than pride. This is why Paul says, "Associate with the humble. Do not be wise in your own opinion" (Romans 12:16). Caleb and Joshua didn't adhere to the opinions of their contemporaries; God had already clearly made His will known. They feared God and consequently finished well. As the book of Proverbs states, "He [God] mocks proud mockers but gives grace to the humble" (3:34, NIV).

No one in his right mind would ever want God mocking him. Yet this is exactly what transpires with the self-sufficient. The Lord of glory doesn't tolerate pride. He hates it. Lucifer was close to Him, the closest of all angels, but he lacked the fear of the Lord and therefore he definitely did *not* finish well. We are told,

"The fear of the LORD is clean, enduring forever" (Psalm 19:9). The fear of the Lord is the staying power that gives us the ability to finish well. Adam and Eve walked in the presence of His glory, but they didn't fear God enough to fear being away from Him. As a result, they didn't endure forever in Eden.

Godly fear, faith, and humility is the true threefold cord that can't easily be broken (see Ecclesiastes 4:12). If you fear the Lord, you'll believe Him in the face of impossible circumstances. If you fear Him, you will be humble—not wise in your own opinions. Even so, pride, rebellion, and unbelief are a threefold cord of darkness that is difficult to break. Show me a man who discounts or ignores what God says in His Word as he clings to his own opinion, and I will show you someone who will not endure. His only hope is true repentance and humility.

BACKSIDE ARMOR

Pride is very deceitful. I believe it is the enemy's most effective weapon to prevent us from finishing well. The proud can't see the enemy's advances because they're hit from the backside. Blindsided. How often you and I have heard from those who have lost everything, "I didn't see it coming!"

There's a reason for this. If we look at the armor of God in the Bible, it's all there to protect us when we're *facing forward.* The belt of truth, the breastplate of righteousness, the shoes of the gospel of peace, faith as a shield, salvation as our helmet, and the Word of God as our sword… When you think about it, they all cover frontal attacks. So what covers our backside? The prophet Isaiah supplies the answer: "The glory of the LORD shall be your rear guard" (58:8).

The New Living Translation says God's glory "will protect you from behind." His glory protects our back. But we still must keep in mind God's emphatic assertion that He will not share His glory with another (see Isaiah 42:8). When we exalt our opinion over His, we act in pride and lose our rear guard of His glory—and our backside becomes uncovered!

When I consider how misinformed we've become in regard to true humility and pride, I shiver. God says, "My people are destroyed for lack of knowledge" (Hosea 4:6). How many of us have been, or will be, destroyed because of ignorance? If the ten spies and all of Israel mistook Caleb and Joshua's humility for pride, and if Eliab mistook the humility of David for pride, then how about today?

It could be compared to going on a long journey and not knowing that along the way certain locations are teeming with deadly, aggressive animals. If you were to get out of your vehicle and wander into the wrong place, you could end up a shredded fatality.

Once Lisa and I were treated to a safari in Africa. It was a nice place, a five-star accommodation where each couple had their own private bungalow. Every night an armed ranger escorted us on the pathway from the open-air dining facility to our bungalow. It was a fair distance. The first night the ranger sternly warned Lisa and me, "Under no circumstance come out at night, because you can easily be attacked. There are wild, hungry animals out hunting at night, and there are no fences to keep them out."

What if we hadn't known this and I decided to go to the food area for a midnight snack? I would have probably become the midnight snack. I would have been destroyed for a lack of knowledge. Based on what we've explored in this chapter, Hosea's words might be phrased this way: "My people are destroyed for a lack of knowing the difference between true humility and pride."

I'm so glad you are taking the time to learn what it means to arm yourself with humility. But don't stop here. Search the Scriptures and ask the Holy Spirit to enlighten you. Don't get blindsided and taken down in life because of a lack of knowledge. You are destined to finish well. Hear God's promise:

The humble also shall increase their joy in the LORD. (Isaiah 29:19)

What a great promise! We all love joy. But why is it also a crucial promise? Because "the joy of the LORD is your strength" (Nehemiah 8:10). Strength to finish well. We cannot relentlessly run the race and finish the course without it. God promises that you and I will increase in joy, or strength, if we remain clothed with humility. He also promises,

For thus says the High and Lofty One
Who inhabits eternity, whose name *is* Holy:
"I dwell in the high and holy place,

With him *who* has a contrite and humble spirit,

To revive the spirit of the humble,

And to revive the heart of the contrite ones." (Isaiah 57:15)

When God dwells within us, we can without a doubt run our race with endurance. A visitation from God is not what we're after. Rather, we should desire for Him to dwell within us. This fosters the sustained strength for endurance.

So, dear one, "Be clothed with humility, for 'God resists the proud, but gives *grace* to the humble.' Therefore humble yourselves under the mighty hand of God, that He may exalt you in due time."

11

THROW OFF THE WEIGHT

All of you be submissive to one another, and be
clothed with humility, for "God resists the proud, but
gives *grace* to the humble." Therefore humble yourselves under the mighty hand of God, that He may
exalt you in due time, casting all your care upon Him,
for He cares for you.

1 PETER 5:5–7

A prime aspect of clothing ourselves in humility is to place ourselves
under God's mission, as did Caleb and Joshua. When we do, any
adversity standing between our present position and the completion
of our divine mission becomes conquerable. In humility we base our calculations on God's strength or His mighty hand. In humility we believe His report
even over what the best human logic or reason dictates. In humility we walk by
faith, not ruled by our senses or natural knowledge.

To realistically live in this manner we must cast all our cares on Him. Not
some cares; *all* cares. This is what Caleb and Joshua did in regard to their wives
and children. As fathers and husbands, they too cared deeply for their families.
But for them, the Word of the Lord took precedence over human logic and fear.
They understood that by putting God's will first, their families would be protected and provided for. Caleb and Joshua were truly humble before the Lord
and, as a result, their family concerns were in the most capable hands in the
universe.

CASTING ALL OUR CARE ON HIM

Casting all our care on God gives us the ability to remain relentless in our mission. In order to press on, we cannot carry cumbersome weights. The Bible instructs, "Let us *strip off every weight* that slows us down... And let us run with endurance the race that God has set before us" (Hebrews 12:1, NLT).

Weights slow us down and can keep us from finishing well. Can you imagine running a marathon with a forty-five pound plate hanging from each hip? It would be extremely difficult to run at all, let alone finish the race!

One very heavy weight that hinders our progress is our care and concerns. It's the very thing that weighed down the ten spies who didn't finish well. Their heavy care regarding the possible danger to their wives and children kept them from moving forward in God's promise to do His will.

It's important to clarify that our families are *not* the weight; it's the *concern* for our families that becomes the weight. If we question God's ability or desire to provide and protect, we insult His integrity and strength. It's interesting to remember that Caleb and Joshua eventually proved the error of their contemporaries when, forty years later, they indeed went to battle with the same Canaanites, and their families were not harmed in any way. In fact, doing battle actually blessed their wives and children by giving them a fruitful land for their inheritance.

Think through the different outcomes carefully. The ten spies, who sought to protect their families instead of trust in God's direction, caused their families to inherit the desert. It was definitely an undesirable end, filled with forty years of hardship and lack of abundance. But the two leaders who believed and obeyed God's Word, and entrusted the care of their families to His integrity, caused their families to inherit the Promised Land, the land "flowing with milk and honey." It was their destiny.

> **Each of us has to choose between security and destiny.**

At various times in our lives, each of us has to choose between security and destiny. Will we choose the path leading to *significance,* or will we attempt to *secure* our comfort and well-being? If you choose self-preservation, its end will not be your divine destiny. You may succeed in maintaining your sense of security, but you'll eventually discover, at the judgment seat of Christ, the abundant fullness of life that you forsook for the sake of maintaining your temporary comfort zone.

It's a fact, verified again and again throughout God's Word: if you are going to fulfill your God-planned journey, you'll need to leave the weight of your cares and concerns with Him. His path is one of adventure and faith, and the reward is always far greater than your sense of security and comfort. Strip off the weight that slows you down by casting your care on Him.

OUR PERSONAL CHALLENGES

Allow me to share with you some of the weights I've had to cast off in my personal race. As I was growing up, I recognized the importance of a father and husband providing for his family. My dad modeled this beautifully, teaching us that a penny saved was a penny earned. The role of the husband and father in providing a secure, stable household was drilled into me as a boy. I wanted to become a pilot, but my father discouraged it because in those days being a pilot wasn't considered a secure job. Dad directed me toward a more stable career. I studied engineering and, in 1981, took a position with Rockwell International.

I made a handsome salary as a junior engineer. It was a good feeling to provide adequately for my wife. I was following what had been modeled before me as a young man. However, I struggled with an inner conflict: I felt a burning call to enter ministry. It had been on me for a few years, but I saw no way to provide for my wife and eventually our children on a minister's income. So Lisa and I came up with a plan.

I had learned from another employee that the company paid an extremely large salary if an employee took a position overseas, especially in the Middle East. So I went to the personnel director and inquired about being transferred to Saudi Arabia. Lisa and I figured we could endure living there for a few years, save the extra money, come back to America, pay cash for a modest house, then go into the ministry.

One problem: our plans were all based on our own ability.

One night a young minister, who had known Lisa and me for a couple of years, sat me down and rebuked me for two hours. In essence he said, "John, the call of God is on your life, and you are doing nothing about it. If you stay on the same path you are on now, you'll end up being an old engineer who missed his destiny."

I was shaken by his words, but I knew he was right. I came home that night and said to Lisa, "I'm going to make myself available to the church to work in any position. The first door that opens, I'm going to walk through it. Are you with me?"

"I'm with you," she said,

I prayed passionately over the next few months for God to open a door for me to serve in the ministry. In the meantime, I did all I could to serve in our church on a volunteer basis. I became an usher, joined the church's local prison ministry, and even taught my pastor's children how to play tennis. (I had been a tennis instructor for three years at a swim and racquet club while in college.)

A few months later, in 1983, a door opened for a full-time position in ministry. I left Rockwell and started working for my local church. I took a huge pay cut to accept the new position, and my dad thought I had lost my mind (as did my boss at Rockwell). Other friends questioned my decision, and I, too, fought thoughts about how I would provide. On paper it just didn't work; our monthly income was lower than the total of our expenses.

But I knew that it was God's plan for me to take this position. So Lisa and I left the *care* of provision with God. We never missed a meal, always had enough to meet our needs. Time and time again, without our uttering a word to anyone, we saw God provide miraculously. Lisa and I would privately voice our necessities to God, resist discouragement from the enemy with God's Word, and witness one miraculous provision after another.

I recall once having to make the choice of whether we would give our tithe or buy groceries. It wasn't much of a struggle because we had already decided to put God first in everything. So we placed 10 percent of our salary in the offering, which meant we had nothing left for groceries because the other 90 percent had to go toward paying bills and other unforeseen expenditures—one being our car.

At the time, we had only one car and the alternator had failed. Extremely busy with my church work, I didn't have time to fix it. Besides, I drove the church's van, so I had the transportation I needed to and from work. So our car sat. Then, a few days after the alternator failed, a rear tire went flat. To make matters worse, our spare was unusable. We lived in Dallas, Texas, and the heat that summer was extreme. One evening I came home from work only to find that one of our car's windows had shattered into hundreds of little pieces. Turns out that the inside of the car had become so hot that the air expanded to the point of exploding one of the windows.

The frustration mounted. I was in a pickle. Even if I fixed the alternator, I still couldn't drive the car because I had no tire. We covered the window with a garbage bag and tape, but I knew that if a strong rain came, our patchwork window covering would give way and water would get into the car. Over time, moisture could rot the interior of the car. I couldn't ignore it another day. I called several garages, but all the estimates were beyond what we could pay. We just didn't have the money to fix our car. With my previous engineering salary it would have been an easy matter. I had to battle thoughts of self-pity and visions of our car rotting away in the parking lot.

Finally, I was fed up. I found a secluded place for a meeting with God and screamed out, "Lord, You said I am to cast all my care upon You. So at this moment I take the care of this automobile and I put it in Your hands completely and totally. It's no longer my care, it is now Yours. If the car rots, it's not my fault because the concern is no longer mine! I'm staying focused on what You've told me to do. Now I thank You for providing the solution."

I was loud and strong in my words and really meant what I said. And for the first time since the alternator died, I began to feel peace in my soul. It was just as God's Word promises:

> Don't worry about anything; instead, pray about everything. Tell God what you need, and thank him for all he has done. If you do this, you will experience God's peace, which is far more wonderful than the human mind can understand. His peace will guard your hearts and minds as you live in Christ Jesus. (Philippians 4:6–7, NLT)

Then I started in on the enemy. I spoke violently and passionately, "Satan, you listen to me. My God, my Father, supplies all my needs according to His riches in glory. I have no lack, for I seek first His kingdom and all I have need of is added to me. So I resist you in the name of Jesus and command you to take your filthy hands off our finances and our car."

It felt as if something snapped. Almost immediately I found myself laughing. I thought, *Have I lost my mind?* Yet the joy was coming from a well deep within me. I knew it was the joy of the Lord, which would be the strength I needed. With that strength I knew I could keep running my race relentlessly. My care was now in God's mighty hand and the enemy was bound up. I was in a state of anticipation of God's provision.

The very next day, a friend of Lisa's came over and saw our damaged car in the parking lot of our apartment. It was indeed an eyesore. She said, "Lisa, I have a friend who is a mechanic. Why don't you let me get hold of him to see what he can do for you and John." Her friend ended up fixing everything at a fraction of what the other garages wanted to charge us. We saw God provide in an amazing way, and it strengthened us.

But because of giving our tithe, we still didn't have any money for groceries, and I wouldn't be paid for another twelve days. One night we sat in the car and cried together. Our tears were not of unbelief but of frustration. We didn't understand why we had to fight for everything while others lived at ease. As with the apostle Paul, we lacked understanding of what was being accomplished in the midst of our trial. We saw the trials as bothersome, irritating, and a waste of our time. We didn't realize we were being strengthened in God's grace so we could later face bigger challenges in order to bring God greater glory. After a few tears, Lisa and I affirmed our belief in God's Word and kept on with our divine mission.

Two days later, a visiting couple from San Antonio, whom we'd met only that week, approached me. They said, "John, we don't know why, but God keeps speaking to us to give you this." They handed me an envelope containing a check for $200. Lisa and I were amazed. Nobody except God knew our situation, and He provided for us once again.

A NEW LEVEL OF RELEASING CARES

After a few more years of growing and developing in our faith and maturity, I accepted a position as youth pastor for a very large church in Florida. We again faced the same financial challenge of another pay cut for this position. This time we had an eighteen-month-old son, so getting by was even more challenging. Again we gave our care to God, resisted the enemy, and saw miraculous provision. I stayed focused on the mission, and the provision came again and again, often in spectacular ways.

In September 1988, God showed me that the time had come to move into the next phase of ministry—traveling and speaking full-time. I had submitted to my pastor's leadership, so I decided to not say a word and wait for God to show him what was next for me. No one else knew what I was shown in prayer except for Lisa and a friend who lived in another state.

In February 1989, my pastor came into our staff meeting and told of a vivid vision he had had the night before. He shared how he saw Lisa and me leaving from the church to travel and minister on a full-time basis. As I listened to him, I started to weep. The Holy Spirit had confirmed His will, just as He did with Barnabas and Paul in Acts 13:1–5.

Six months later, in August 1989, within a three-week period I received invitations for seven future speaking events. I told my pastor and he smiled, laughed, and said, "This is what the Lord showed us. Looks like you're on your way." Then he said, "John, travel as much as you can this fall and the church will continue to pay your salary through the end of the year. On the first of January you'll be on your own financially."

Over the next few months I traveled to those seven places and had good meetings, but no other invitations came. I was looking at soon being launched but with no place to go. My pastor noticed and, two months before I was to go off salary, he gave me a remarkable letter of recommendation and the addresses of six hundred churches in America in which he had spoken. (He was a very well-known minister, both nationally and internationally.)

Immediately I began to address his stationery with the addresses he gave me. My plan was to put his letter and a letter from me in the packet to all six hundred churches. I had completed about forty of the envelopes when I heard the Holy Spirit say to me, *Son, what are you doing?*

"I'm letting these pastors know I'm available to come to their churches," I responded.

You'll get out of My will.

"But God," I blurted out, "nobody out there knows who I am."

I do. Trust Me.

At that point I had a decision to make. I could choose *humility* by submitting to God's directive spoken in my heart, or I could secure provision through my own marketing efforts. In other words, would I give my care and concerns to Him, or would I keep my care and concerns in my own hands? I made the decision immediately. Before my intellect or emotions could talk me out of it, I tore up the forty addressed envelopes. *Either I'm hearing from God or I'm crazy,* I thought.

Time passed. It was now mid-December and I had booked only two meetings. One would be the first week of January in a tiny town in South Carolina, at a small church that met in a funeral home. The other was booked for the end of February in a small church in the hills of Tennessee.

At this point our pastor was very concerned for us. He was about to start his daily television program that would eventually air all over the world. Lisa had television production experience, so our pastor offered her a job producing the new program for $45 per hour. I was so relieved and excited! So was Lisa. This would bring in much-needed money while my traveling ministry gained momentum.

But a few days later while I was in prayer, the Holy Spirit once again spoke to my heart. *Son, if Lisa accepts the job of television producer, then whatever she makes financially I will deduct from the offerings taken for your ministry on the road. I don't want her working for your pastor. I want her by your side.*

I was in shock. I shared this message with Lisa and, to my surprise, she agreed. She had received the same message during her prayer time! We graciously turned down our pastor's offer, but he was still concerned for us.

We were now at the end of December. My income from the church was about to stop, and I still had only the two meetings booked. Once again our pastor approached me. "John, on Sunday morning during our televised service I'm going to get you up on the platform and announce to all the pastors who watch us nationwide that you are being launched into a traveling ministry and are available to come to their churches. Furthermore, our church is going to give you monthly support."

Again, I was quite happy. This man of God was perhaps one of the most well-known pastors in America with millions watching his program. I was sure this was God's way of getting me out onto the field to do what He'd called me to do.

But a few days later while I was praying, the Holy Spirit spoke again: *Son, your pastor will not announce you on the church's televised program, and the church will not give you monthly support.*

Now I was getting frustrated. "Why not?" I protested. "Our pastor said he would!"

Immediately I heard in my heart, *Because I won't let him do it, and he is a man who listens to Me.*

"Why won't You let him do what he promised me?"

Then the Lord said something to me I will never forget: *Because if he does, when you run into difficult times, you'll run to him instead of to Me.*

Sure enough, our pastor never stood me up in front of the television audience. In fact, he never mentioned my new ministry at all, and he didn't give me monthly support. And I'm so glad he didn't do either. It forced me to entrust my cares to God, to pray and fight rather than give hints to men who had the money or influence we needed.

So January came and, sure enough, the church stopped our salary. Lisa and I had $300 to our name. We now had two small children—Addison, who was three and a half, and Austin, who was nine months old. Our monthly payments were $1,000 for our house mortgage and $200 for our car. I didn't know where my next penny was coming from. I prayed like my life depended on it, which, of course, forced me to draw near to the Holy Spirit.

We saw doors open in the most unique ways. My first speaking engagement, for the church that met in a funeral home, was a terrific set of meetings. They were extended to another week. Word got out and another pastor attended from Columbia, South Carolina. At the final meeting, he asked me if I would come to his church. Lisa and I went, and his church led to another. And so it continued.

A couple of months went by and again my schedule was wide open. We were under a lot of pressure financially, but we hadn't been late on one bill. Early one morning I went outside to pray. "God, my Father, I'm doing what You told me to do," I shouted out. "If You don't provide meetings and finances for my family, then I'm going to get a job sacking groceries, and I will tell people You couldn't provide for us. Father, I refuse to sell myself. If You've called me, You'll open the doors. I give this care totally to You."

I then turned to the north and commanded doors to open. Then I faced the south, the east, and finally the west, each time commanding doors to open. Then I commanded the enemy to back off, telling the devil that he could not hinder the steps that God had ordered for us to take.

Shortly after that prayer session, a church in Michigan brought me in for four days of meetings. A genuine movement of God broke out. The four-day meeting turned into weeks of meetings. People drove to the services from as far as ninety miles away, packing the church to capacity every night. I called Lisa, who was with our sons at the public pool near my parents' house in Florida. I told her about the meetings, that there was no end in sight, and that I was sending airline tickets for her and the boys to join me in Michigan.

A pastor on vacation was sitting near Lisa and overheard her side of the phone conversation. He approached her and said, "Please forgive me, but I was listening to your phone call with your husband. I pastor a fifteen-hundred-member church in upper New York. I'm so hungry for a movement of God among our people. I felt the Lord told me to invite your husband."

So after the meetings in Michigan, we went to New York. These also turned out to be powerful services. We returned to that church frequently. This type of thing continued week after week. In fact, in the first four years of traveling ministry we never wrote one letter or made one phone call to a church. Every meeting just opened up as I've described or in other strange ways.

CONTINUED PROVISION

I'll say again, I was raised with a mind-set that it is extremely important for a man to provide for his family. First Timothy 5:8 confirms this conviction by stating that if I don't, then I'm worse than an unbeliever. To provide for my family was a valid and godly concern. However, if I had made this care my top priority, I would never have stepped out in obedience to God. That concern or care would have been the weight that would have greatly hindered my race.

After being on the road a few years, I had the opportunity to observe other ministers who had chosen differently—who had not given the care of their provision completely over to God. As with the ten spies, they seemed to calculate their provision by their own ability. I would observe them selling themselves, dropping hints, playing political games. I grieved for them, knowing that the call on their lives was genuine but that they had sold themselves, and God, short. Even today, many of these ministers still haven't entered kingdom rulership. It saddened my heart when I heard one pastor say, "Don't you know, faith without hints is dead."

Our first year traveling, Lisa and I saw God provide in amazing ways. One month we needed almost $700 to pay our mortgage, which was due the next day. I went to the mailbox and there was a letter from a hippy couple who lived in Alabama. They had eight children and slept on the floor with a box spring and a mattress. The letter read, *John and Lisa, we don't know why, but God put it so strong today on our heart to send you this check for $300.*

That night I spoke to a church of just forty people. The pastor gave me the offering in a paper sack. I came home and went to bed, then realized I had forgotten to count the offering. Because Lisa and I had given our care to God, I honestly was not worried about the house payment that was due the next day. I got up and counted the offering. It was $397.26. This combined with the gift from the hippies was enough for our house payment. Once again, God had provided.

Over time, I came to understand the process that God used to train us. Lisa and I first had to learn how to cast our care upon God in smaller matters, like a car alternator. It was important that we learn how to believe and fight when our salary was low. Why? Because when we entered full-time traveling ministry, we went from low salary to no salary. We had grown in faith and were ready for a more difficult mission. The challenges faced during our first year traveling helped us grow even more and prepared us for the next level of faith we would need.

As I write this book, our budget at Messenger International is more than $100,000 per week. If I had not learned how to give my cares to God and believe Him step by step, I would be overwhelmed now. But the good news is, *I've never lost a minute of sleep over our provision.* The peace of God, which *does* pass understanding, has remarkably guarded and kept our hearts and minds in Christ Jesus, just as God promised.

FROM FAITH TO FAITH

The process God uses to build our faith reminds me of bodybuilding. When I was thirty-five I was so busy traveling and speaking that I viewed going to the gym as a waste of time. Consequently, I almost fainted on a platform one Sunday in Atlanta, Georgia.

Our next-door neighbor was a professional wrestler for what was then the World Wrestling Federation. He, his wife, and his children had become good friends of ours. He had previously offered to take me to the gym, but I had rejected the offer. After my incident in Atlanta, my attitude had completely changed. I asked him if he'd help me get in better shape.

My friend was massive, weighing 260 pounds with only 4 percent body fat. His biceps and triceps were bigger than my thighs. We started going to the gym regularly. Early on, I met some of his huge bodybuilding friends and observed their training techniques. I discovered that lifting low weights with high repetitions ("reps") didn't build big muscles. Rather, these guys would weight the bar heavily enough for a maximum of three or four reps. I watched them push the weight up three times, but the fourth rep was when all the action happened. The man on the bench really didn't have the strength to get the fourth rep up, but his face contorted, his veins bulged out, his body trembled, and his friends all screamed "Push!" or "Explode up!" And he would push with all his might to get that fourth rep up. *That* is when the muscles in the body respond and grow.

My first time in the gym I could bench-press only 95 pounds, and it stayed that way throughout my first month. Then I graduated incrementally to 135 pounds; after six months to 185 pounds, and eventually to 205 pounds. However, I got stuck at 205 for a few years.

Then a former bodybuilder came to work for our ministry. As we talked he refreshed my memory of what was required to build strength and muscle. I had forgotten that to build muscle you must "max out" at low reps. So we started the building process again and continued until he accompanied me on a ministry trip to Fresno, California. During a break in the conference, several of us went to the gym, where they decided to gang up on me. "John," my colleague said, "you're going to lift 225 today."

I said, "No way."

"Yes, you are! Just get on the bench and we'll spot you."

Sure enough, I did 225 pounds. I was so excited. I kept training and got up to 245 pounds. But again I got stuck. My goal, which I actually thought was unattainable, was to one day push up 315 pounds.

I went to a church in Detroit, Michigan, where the pastor told me one of his members was a nationally known trainer for bodybuilders. The pastor himself had recently bench-pressed 545 pounds. The day after our Sunday services, the pastor got me together with the trainer and I benched 265 pounds. I was so excited! He put me on an intense program, which my staff member and I diligently adhered to over the next several months.

The next time I returned to the Detroit church, I preached about the Holy Spirit in both the Sunday morning and Sunday evening services. On Monday morning we went to the gym, and the same trainer said to me, "John, last night I had a dream that you pushed up 300 pounds on the bench."

"No way," I chuckled.

He looked at me and said, "Hey, man, you spoke all day yesterday on how the Holy Spirit communicates to us. He communicated to me last night. So be quiet and get on the bench. You're going to push 300 pounds today."

I wisely shut my mouth and reclined on the bench. After warmups, my friend put 300 pounds on the bar. He spoke intently: "Just explode up when the bar comes down. Don't even think about it. Just explode!"

He and the others around us shouted, "Push! Push! Push!" as the bar came to its lowest point and I pushed with all my might. It went up! All the way up! They took the bar, and I leaped from the bench, yelling for joy. I was amazed.

My trainer friend let me celebrate for five minutes, then looked me square in the face. He had that same intense look. "Now you're going to go for 315 pounds."

"No way—did you dream about that last night too?" I said.

He just smiled and politely said, "Shut up and get back down there."

Sure enough, at the age of forty-four, I bench-pressed 315 pounds. I was jumping up and down with excitement. I'll never forget calling Lisa from the Detroit airport to tell her the news.

Later, God showed me that those coaches—my staff member, the pastors in California, and the national trainer in Detroit—were all like the Holy Spirit. Recall Paul's words:

> God keeps his promise, and he will not allow you to be tested beyond
> your power to remain firm; at the time you are put to the test, he will
> give you the strength to endure it, and so provide you with a way out.
> (1 Corinthians 10:13, TEV)

Those trainers knew what I could and couldn't handle. They knew not to put 405 pounds on the bar when I could only push up 315. They were skilled and could recognize potential. I was so impressed with their ability to see beyond what I could see. Every time I couldn't imagine myself pushing up as much as they did. They saw strength and potential I didn't know was there.

The Holy Spirit is the same. He knows what you can and cannot handle. If my professional-wrestler friend had put 315 pounds on the bar the first time we went to the gym, what would have happened? The bar would have come down almost at the speed of gravity, crushed my rib cage, and possibly killed me. I had to start at 95 pounds and work my way up.

The Holy Spirit knows what you can and cannot handle.

Likewise, the Holy Spirit knew what was in store for Lisa and me. "I alone know the plans I have for you," God says (Jeremiah 29:11, TEV). He had to build our faith, and in the building process, we had to learn to cast our cares on Him. It never was comfortable, but it was always beneficial.

Many times I fought the emotions of wanting to quit or give up, but I just couldn't do it because Jesus never quit on me. We stayed steadfast in our divine mission and kept overcoming the resistance along the way.

In looking back now, the low salary, alternator problems, cash-flow challenges, and other trials we walked through were building blocks to strengthen us for what was to come. If we'd had to start out believing God for $100,000 per week, it would have been like putting 315 on the bar during my first visit to the gym. No, the Holy Spirit had to gradually, steadily build us to the place where we could trust God for the bigger things.

Don't Circumvent Your Training

The resistance we faced in the early days of our training process dealt with our personal needs: fixing the car, paying for groceries, paying bills, making the house payment. But the resistance we face now rarely involves our personal needs but instead is for the welfare of the multitudes God has entrusted to our ministry. If we had circumvented God's training process in the beginning, we wouldn't have the strength for those He sends us to now. He would have had to get someone else to do it.

How many ministers were not able to reach the people God called them to reach because they didn't complete the training process? If they didn't use their faith to push up the 145-pound challenges back then, they can't handle the 405-pound challenges now. Sadly, God had to get someone else to complete their assignments.

How many businessmen and women are stuck far below where God has called them because they didn't enter into rulership through the trials they faced? Instead of believing God, they went to institutions of men and used manipulative or domineering techniques to overcome their trials. As a result, they've fallen far short of their God-given potential.

I'm almost certain that Israel's ten spies didn't go through the training process as Caleb and Joshua did. They more than likely found ways to get around trials and hardships apart from believing God. They didn't build up their faith. So when their life-defining moment came, they didn't have the faith-strength to believe.

Our Father knows the best training course for each of us. And although He doesn't author the hardships, He permits them in order to strengthen us for the destiny He has for us.

Don't circumvent your training process. *The trials you face today are preparing you for the great feats you'll accomplish tomorrow.* Always remember, my friend, that *God will not bring you into a challenging place without first making available the training you need to come through it successfully.*

Learn to cast your cares on Him in true humility so that you can go from glory to glory, faith to faith, and strength to strength.

12

Be Sober and Vigilant

Be clothed with humility, for "God resists the proud, but gives *grace* to the humble." Therefore humble yourselves under the mighty hand of God, that He may exalt you in due time, casting all your care upon Him, for He cares for you. Be sober, be vigilant; because your adversary the devil walks about like a roaring lion, seeking whom he may devour. Resist him, steadfast in the faith.

1 PETER 5:5–9

Before we continue mining Peter's rich exhortation, let's briefly summarize: The apostle is discussing the true grace of God. Grace is not only for our salvation, the forgiveness of sins, but it also empowers us to shine in a dark and lost world. But distinguishing ourselves doesn't come without resistance; there will be a fight. Therefore, we must also be armed with the weapons of grace.

Arming ourselves begins with humility because grace is given to the humble. Paul exhorts us to "be clothed" with humility, and a crucial aspect of true humility is giving our cares to Him instead of trying to handle life's challenges solely in our own ability. We cannot run the race, fight effectively, and endure to the finish if we're weighted down with personal concerns. Worry, anxiety, and fear are enemies of our destiny. Releasing their load to God enables us to run faster and wield our swords with greater strength.

Bottom line: true humility liberates us to freely make positive progress against the current of this world's system. The alternative is to drag an anchor through the muck and mire of worry—an impossible task coupled with the resistance of the river's current.

Then Peter exhorts us to be sober and vigilant.

BE SOBER

The word *sober* can be defined as "serious, sensible, and solemn." The Greek word is *nepho,* defined as the antithesis of being drunk with wine. It means "to be of a sound mind."

I took up drinking alcohol during my junior year of high school, and it continued on weekends through my senior year. However, during my freshman year of university, the drinking accelerated because I was no longer under my parents' direct supervision. Joining a fraternity didn't help either, as we viewed college life as one big party with some studying in between. It wasn't long before I became a regular and excessive drinker. I'm so glad Jesus rescued me my sophomore year—God only knows what disastrous end I was spared from.

Several times I had gotten drunk only to learn from friends the following day the stupid and ridiculous things I had said and done. Simply put, a drunken person loses his edge; he's far from alert. Our fraternity was loaded with jokesters, and it didn't take us long to discover how easy it was to mistreat a drunken frat brother. We were able to do things we'd never get away with if he were sober.

One prank was stealing. The guy wouldn't even know that a valued possession was taken. The next morning would be pandemonium as the victim frantically searched his room and the entire fraternity house. He was clueless as to how and when the heist happened. In a panic, he'd run through the house moaning, groaning, and even sometimes yelling as he searched for his missing lab project, wallet, girlfriend's picture, or some other article of value. Everyone would snicker and laugh as they watched the show. When we felt that our brother had suffered long enough, we'd return the missing item, laughing uproariously.

Of course we were only joking, but what if someone had been serious about stealing his valuables? If not sober, he was easy prey and could have lost something very valuable for good.

Intoxication also creates a huge disadvantage in fighting. I recall a party where I watched two of my friends get into a fistfight—one friend was drunk, the other sober. On any other day my drunken friend could have easily whipped the sober one, but because he was drunk he got beaten badly. It took someone stepping in to prevent severe physical harm.

Recall from our introduction the true story behind the movie *The Ghost and the Darkness*. I shared of the two brave men—Patterson, the railway engineer, and Remington, the famous American hunter—who took down the two lions that were responsible for taking more than 130 men's lives. What I didn't tell in the introduction is the fact that in the end Remington lost his life to one of the lions. After days of hunting, the two men had successfully shot and killed the first lion. That evening, in celebration, Remington drank himself to intoxication and as a result lost his life to the second lion. Patterson shortly afterward brought the second lion, which had killed his friend, to its death.

Remington was world renowned for his hunting skills, but they were of no value and his life was lost to his enemy because of his intoxication. He had a weapon that was far superior to the lion's ability, but he was not sober and therefore not alert to fend off the animal's deadly attack.

Spiritual Inebriation

The same thing happens spiritually. The enemy can easily steal from or destroy those who aren't sober-minded. We should be able to beat him soundly with our weapons of grace, but if we're in a drunken state we'll lose our edge and he can defeat us.

> The enemy can easily steal from or destroy those who aren't sober-minded.

Peter warns that Satan is walking about seeking whom he may devour (see 1 Peter 5:8). He can devour the proud and those weighted down with cares, but the easiest prey is a believer who's drunk.

Is Peter referring to alcoholism? Probably so, but even more, he's referring to the believer who's drunk on the wine of the world.

Toward the end of the book of Revelation, John describes the judgment of the great harlot, Babylon. An angel is saying to him,

Come here, I will show you the judgment of the great harlot who sits on
many waters, with whom the kings of the earth committed acts of
immorality, and those who dwell on the earth were *made drunk with the
wine of her immorality.* (Revelation 17:1–2, NASB)

There are different views as to what this harlot represents. Some say it is the
Catholic Church. Others believe it refers to the ancient city of Babylon, and still
others believe it is the city of Rome or the Roman Empire.

Personally, I believe "the great harlot" is the world's financial system. One
reason for my belief is the mysterious name written on her forehead, "Babylon
the Great, Mother of All…Obscenities in the World" (Revelation 17:5, NLT).
Other translations use the word *Abominations,* but I don't believe ancient Babylon, Rome, the Roman Empire, or the Catholic Church is the Mother of *All*
Obscenities and Abominations on the earth. But the Scriptures do tell us that
"the love of money is the root of all evil" (1 Timothy 6:10, KJV) and we could
easily replace the word *evil* for *obscenities and abominations* and stay true to the
verse's meaning. This is not worth a lengthy debate, but it's something to
consider.

My point is, the ways of this world's system are alluring to the senses and
thus can be intoxicating. Notice John's words in the Revelation passage above:
"Those who dwell on the earth were made drunk with the wine of her immorality." In becoming caught up with the intoxicating wine of the world's cares,
riches, and pleasures, one can easily be drawn away from intimacy with the
Holy Spirit. It's a very deceptive state, for a believer may have an *appearance* of
godliness while being drunk on the desires of this world. With one's spiritual
edge lost, he or she becomes an easy target for the enemy's theft, deceit, destruction, or even death.

This inebriated state is a good description of what happened to Solomon. He
started out seeking to know godly wisdom. It was granted, and, as always, wisdom
enabled Solomon to achieve great success and wealth (see Proverbs 8:11–21).
However, over time, King Solomon became intoxicated with the benefits of wisdom and lost sight of God who had granted them. He drank in the pleasures,
lusts, and riches of this world. Now drunken, he inevitably did what he would
never have even considered in his sober mind: he started worshiping other gods.

It has bothered me greatly that Solomon could ever succumb to such a travesty, especially after he had seen God twice. But if you look at what he did in light of what I described above, it becomes easier to comprehend. When my fraternity brothers or I were stone drunk, we did things we never would have done in our right mind. Solomon was no different.

How do we guard from such folly and stay sober-minded? The answer is to continually feed on and drink in the Lord, who truly satisfies. "Do not get drunk with wine, which will only ruin you," Paul writes. "Instead, be filled with the Spirit" (Ephesians 5:18, TEV). I don't believe he's speaking only of physical wine but of anything that can intoxicate us and weaken our focus on God's ways. It could be excessive attention to business, the opposite sex, a sport or hobby, social networking—the list is endless.

In themselves, the activities may be harmless, for we know that God "generously gives us everything for our enjoyment" (1 Timothy 6:17, TEV). It's perfectly fine and healthy to enjoy recreation, clean entertainment, athletic competition, food, nature's beauty, and even the fruits of technology. But if we participate in excess and draw our satisfaction from them instead of from God Himself, they become intoxicating addictions.

Jesus is to be our first love and passion; we are to be intoxicated only with His Spirit.

GIVE YOURSELF PERIODIC CHECKUPS

To stay sober—to prevent the things of this world from inebriating and weakening us—every child of God should do periodic checkups. We must honestly ask ourselves, "What do I hunger and thirst for?" Don't be superficial with this; be brutally honest. What do you find yourself dwelling on in your free time? What do you constantly gravitate to in your thoughts or actions? If it's football games, then you are drinking in too much of the NFL or NCAA; it's gone beyond enjoyment and is now excessive. Is the opposite sex your favorite drink? Is making money consuming your thoughts? Then you're discovering what intoxicates you. For this reason we are told to read, give attention to, and meditate on the Word of God. What you drink in most is what you will thirst for. What you eat most is what you will hunger for.

I remember observing my high school tennis coach becoming addicted to Coca-Cola. It started with one a day, went to two, then three. This pattern continued until he craved Coke so much that he consumed a case every day. I remember opening his refrigerator and seeing two or three cases of Coke, and beside the refrigerator were several more cases waiting to replace those consumed.

I've seen others become overweight and struggle with health issues because they drank excessive amounts of soda. As a young believer I knew my body was God's temple, that I was responsible for stewarding it correctly. I no longer wanted to ingest the horrible ingredients found in sodas, so I determined to stop consuming them. It wasn't easy! I found myself craving these soft drinks. I had to deny myself for a season.

Jesus tells us, "If anyone desires to come after Me, let him deny himself" (Matthew 16:24). To break free from intoxication, we have to deny ourselves what we crave. I learned to replace sodas with something better—a glass of water with lemon. I didn't crave water or thirst for it—I *wanted* soda—but I forced myself to drink a half gallon of water a day. In a few months, I didn't crave sodas any longer. Today I don't have any desire for them. Today I crave water!

It's no different with the Word of God. Jesus' words are spirit and life and truth. In order to reignite our passion for God's Word, we must sometimes deny ourselves because our appetites and thirst have become misdirected. For example, if I find the media is consuming too much of my thoughts and time, then I go on a media fast. I cut it off for a season and replace it with quality time with God and His Word. Some of the most meaningful, effective fasts I've been on were not food fasts but media fasts.

When we fill ourselves with His Word and obey it, when we invest quality time in prayer and obey His direction, we are filled with His Spirit. The intoxications or addictions of Babylon lose their grip on us. Other people might think we are strange, but we've just changed our drinking habits. We now crave the wine that will truly satisfy, empower, and remain.

Now we'll think more clearly, make right decisions, and easily spot the enemy when he comes seeking to devour. Satan cannot defeat a sober-minded believer, for we know and claim the covenant promises of God. We're alert and serious. We are armed and ready for the battle.

BE VIGILANT

"Be sober, be vigilant," Peter instructs in 1 Peter 5:5–9. You cannot be vigilant without first being sober, but soberness does not necessarily assume vigilance. Being vigilant is a conscious act of the will of a sober-minded believer.

For our discussion we'll define *vigilant* as "keeping careful watch for possible danger or difficulties," and as another source defines it, "ever awake and alert; sleeplessly watchful." The definitions should describe the state of every follower of Christ. Vigilance is another crucial, nonoptional factor in being armed.

A few chapters earlier we glimpsed life in Nazi Germany during the time of Hitler. Just as the wise Jew lived on alert during those horrific years, so a believer should be vigilant every moment of every day. Danger is all around us since the devil walks about seeking whom he may devour. But there's a huge difference between the Nazi state and our present world: the Jewish people had no authority over Hitler, but we do have authority over our enemy. Our enemy rules the world, but he doesn't rule us. But he can put up a good fight and, if we allow, he can devour. For this reason the apostle Paul admonishes you and me to "Continue earnestly in prayer, being *vigilant* in it" (Colossians 4:2).

Our primary way to keep an alert watch is through prayer. It opens our eyes to the spiritual realm, enabling us to see beyond the natural and detect dangers and attacks before they manifest in our natural world. This truth is perfectly illustrated by the evening before Jesus' crucifixion.

During the Last Supper, Jesus knew in His spirit the intense trial He would shortly face. Nothing seemed out of the ordinary, all appeared well and peaceful, but He was well aware of what was

> **Our primary way to keep an alert watch is through prayer.**

brewing. After supper He took His disciples to one of His favorite locations to pray, the garden of Gethsemane. There He shared with Peter, James, and John, "My soul is exceeding *sorrowful*, even to death. Stay here and *watch* with Me" (Matthew 26:38). Notice that the Master specifically says, "Watch with Me." One of the definitions of *vigilance* is "keeping careful watch for danger." Jesus was already vigilant and alert, but He was also well aware that His disciples were insensitive to the warning signs of the mounting danger, and thus ignorant of it.

Jesus said His soul was "exceeding sorrowful," and therein lies the primary secret to staying vigilant: prayer. Maintaining a consistent prayer life enables your soul to become more in tune with what is going on in the realm of the spiritual world. We are then more apt to recognize the warnings, interpret them, and act accordingly. This is crucial in staying ahead of the enemy.

THE WARNING SIGNS

In the early years of our marriage, Lisa and I had some difficult times. We both were new Christians and had come from families that had endured recurring hardships for generations. On Lisa's side was a family history of intense strife, divorce, and multiple marriages. Satan didn't want to relinquish this stronghold he had held in the family line for years, so Lisa and I experienced multiple attacks on our marriage.

I spent at least an hour and sometimes up to two hours in prayer each day, and consequently became very sensitive to the realm of the spirit. Periodically, an overwhelming *sorrow* would hit the core of my being—an alarm in my heart telling me something was very wrong. It's not easy to describe, but it was like a gnawing, penetrating, driving irritation deep within. It definitely can be described as a sort of "sorrow" within.

When this first started I couldn't figure why it was occurring. Usually everything seemed fine and there were no outward signs of danger; Lisa and I were getting along just great. Unfortunately, the first several times the sorrow came over me, I ignored it. But every time, within just a few hours, it seemed all hell broke loose against our marriage. We would argue, fight, and utter words that would take days, weeks, and even months to heal from.

As time passed I began to recognize this pattern, so I made it a practice that any time this sense of sorrow came over my soul—no matter how good things looked outwardly—I would slip away and pray earnestly for our marriage. Sure enough, the devil would still attack, but because I was earnestly resisting him in prayer beforehand, his attacks would subside quickly with little or no aftermath.

Today the enemy doesn't hit us nearly as easily or frequently. We believe he grew weary of being assaulted by the "sword of the spirit" every time he was planning an attack. Don't get me wrong: Lisa and I still have to be vigilant. We cannot become complacent or let our guard down. We still have to consciously and prayerfully resist the enemy, but not nearly as frequently as when we were first married.

The positive lesson we've learned from these struggles is to recognize the warning signals of an imminent enemy attack. We're now aware of the importance of staying vigilant in *all* areas of life, of detecting the sorrow that arises within our hearts just prior to attacks on our finances, our health, our relationships, and our ministry. I've learned to ask the Holy Spirit to assist me, as I often don't know how to pray specifically when it comes to advance warnings. He helps me, and He will do the same for you. He's *for* you! He'll help you, even to the point of praying through you if you yield to Him. God's Word promises,

> And the Holy Spirit helps us in our distress. For we don't even know
> what we should pray for, nor how we should pray. But the Holy Spirit
> prays for us with *groanings* that cannot be expressed in words. And the
> Father who knows all hearts knows what the Spirit is saying, for the
> Spirit pleads for us believers in harmony with God's own will. (Romans
> 8:26–27, NLT)

These groanings are the sorrows we experience deep in our soul, as Jesus experienced in the garden the night before His crucifixion. Once we recognize sorrow, we must respond. We can choose the opposite of being vigilant—slothfulness—and quench the sorrow by repeatedly ignoring or suppressing it. Or we can be vigilant and yield to the Spirit of God.

The Holy Spirit's goal is to move us beyond the groanings and to ultimately give specific utterance to deal with the situation at hand. Paul writes, "I will pray with my spirit [by the Holy Spirit that is within me], but I will also pray [intelligently] with my mind and understanding" (1 Corinthians 14:15, AMP).

WATCH AND PRAY

In the garden of Gethsemane, after Jesus informed His disciples of the deep sorrow or groanings of His soul, He charged them, "Stay here and *watch* with Me"

(Matthew 26:38). Then He separated himself from the three by walking a little farther into the garden where He prayed for an hour.

When He came back, He found them *sleeping.* Sleeping! Why were they sleeping? Was it too late at night? Were they exhausted from a full day's work? Did they eat too much at the Last Supper? Luke's gospel tells exactly why they were sleeping: "When He rose up from prayer, and had come to His disciples, He found them *sleeping from sorrow*" (22:45).

They, too, were about to come under attack, so they experienced a *sorrow* similar to that of Jesus. At the Last Supper, Peter had boldly declared that he would die before ever denying the Lord. Peter believed in his own ability to remain relentlessly firm to the end. The other disciples declared the same, that they would stand loyal to their Master. Yet Jesus knew that not only was He about to be severely tested in His allegiance to the Father but also that His disciples would be severely tested in their allegiance to Him.

Listen to how Jesus addressed His sleeping disciples.

Then He came to the disciples and found them sleeping, and said to Peter, "What! Could you not watch with Me one hour? Watch and pray, lest you enter into temptation. The spirit indeed *is* willing, but the flesh *is* weak." (Matthew 26:40–41)

Here again is the key to whether we will remain relentless in our obedience to God or merely possess the desire but fall short. It comes down to strengthening ourselves through watching (vigilance) and praying. Jude writes, "But you, beloved, building yourselves up on your most holy faith, praying in the Holy Spirit" (verse 20). Prayer quiets our flesh and builds up our inner person.

Our flesh is weak; it will always seek the path of least resistance which most often is the wrong path. Our flesh doesn't want to fight against the strong current of the world's forces. Prayer, on the other hand, builds our inner strength to override the desire of the flesh. It keeps us from fainting. Jesus declares, "Men ought always to pray, and not to faint" (Luke 18:1, KJV). In other words, we'll faint if we don't pray, especially in those times when sorrows (groanings) come over us.

Fainting is what happened with the disciples that night in the garden. These men slept when they should have been praying. They were not alert to the danger that lurked. They were not vigilant, they were slothful.

Today you and I have other means of quenching or suppressing the warnings of the Spirit: We can turn on the TV, surf the Web, text friends or check Facebook with our ever-present cell phones, play computer games, engage in busywork, or go to the refrigerator and feed our flesh. We become less and less sensitized to the guidance and warnings of the Holy Spirit. Consequently, we lose our ability to stand strong through hardships. We lose the relentless strength that's freely available to us through God's grace.

So Jesus confronted His closest staff members and directed them to "Watch and pray, lest you enter into temptation" (Matthew 26:41). He went a short distance away and prayed for a second hour, then returned only to find them sleeping again. This time He didn't wake and warn them; they had made their choice.

Many times God will warn us once, perhaps twice, but if we ignore His first warnings He will remain silent thereafter unless we repent. When trouble overtakes us we'll ask in frustration, "Where were You, God?" He had warned us, but we just wouldn't listen.

Jesus returned to the same location a short distance from the sleeping disciples and prayed for a third hour. When He finished, they were still asleep. And that's when Judas, the betrayer, and the guards of the Sanhedrin came to the garden and arrested Jesus.

THE DIFFERENCE BETWEEN SUCCESS AND FAILURE

Jesus succeeded in His incredible mission of grace by remaining sober, vigilant in prayer, and relentlessly firm to the end. On the other hand, the disciples had expressed their desire to remain firm; they thought they could do it, but they didn't possess the strength. Just as Jesus predicted, each of them was attacked and failed: "Then all the disciples forsook Him and fled" (Matthew 26:56). Peter did exactly what he said he would *not* do: he denied Jesus. One positive thing can be said of Peter. At least he followed Jesus to the trial. The others, with the exception of John, immediately fled the garden to their own safety.

How often do we hear fellow believers' good intentions but see their lack of follow-through? Why is this? Because, like the disciples in the garden, they're not vigilant in prayer! Their spirit is willing, but their flesh is weak. Not being properly armed keeps them from reaching their desired end.

Who better to write the exhortation to "arm yourselves" than the apostle Peter? On that crucial evening he was bold in word, yet he failed in action. Jesus had specifically forewarned him, "Simon, Simon, Satan has asked to have all of you, to sift you like wheat" (Luke 22:31, NLT). But Peter and the others lacked the relentless strength needed to stand strong throughout the night. Therefore, later in his life, he warns you and me to arm ourselves in order to finish strong, whether for an evening, for a season, or for our entire lives.

Arming ourselves for battle includes staying sober and vigilant. We must not allow the allures of this world to deaden our resolve or our commitment to Christlikeness in all things. And we must be on alert, vigilant at all times, for if we don't *relentlessly* watch out for the devil who seeks to devour us, he will wreak havoc.

13

RESIST THE DEVIL

Be sober, be vigilant; because your adversary the devil
walks about like a roaring lion, seeking whom he may
devour. Resist him, steadfast in the faith.

1 PETER 5:8–9

N ow we come to the section of Peter's exhortation that deals directly
with the fight. He declares that the devil (including any of his cohorts) is like a lion, seeking whom he may devour.

For clarification, *lion* is not the devil's identity; in Scripture he's called a serpent,
dragon, thief, and a few other names, but not a lion. Jesus is the true Lion, the "Lion
of the tribe of Judah" (Revelation 5:5). However, Peter's point is the devil is *like* a
ravenous lion on the prowl for those he can devour. And he will indeed devour,
without mercy, if given the opportunity. Make no mistake about it. He is a defeated
foe, but he's a ruthless opponent and should never be taken lightly. He has no affec-
tion or compassion for us, and he has one mission: to kill, steal, and destroy.

If you were on the plains of Tanzania in the territory of a man-eating lion,
you wouldn't want to walk through the region unarmed. If you did, chances are
good you wouldn't come out alive. If you're wise you would carry a powerful
rifle and know how to use it. If armed, sober, and alert, you'd be prepared to
fight and win. You'd remain unharmed. This is Peter's emphasis.

RESIST THE DEVIL

In verse 9 Peter strongly exhorts us to *resist* the devil. The word *resist* is the
Greek word *authistemi*. Thayer's defines it this way: "to set oneself against, to

withstand, oppose." Strong's adds, "to stand against." My dictionary defines *resist* as "to prevent by action or argument." There's no question, the word embodies aggressive conflict.

But as we prepare for armed conflict, listen to Jesus' words of assurance: "Behold! I have given you authority and power…over all the power that the enemy [possesses]; and nothing shall in any way harm you" (Luke 10:19, AMP). Isn't that heartening? God's promise ensures that if you walk in His powerful grace, no one or nothing can harm you—not even the devil himself! That's significant.

However, you have to *use* the power you've been given. If you don't, the promise will not be in effect and you can be harmed. For this reason Peter charges us to *resist* the devil. He doesn't say, "Pray and ask God to remove him." We are to directly, boldly, and purposefully resist him.

Nowhere in the New Testament will you find a scripture instructing us to ask God to remove the devil from our lives. The fact is, God cannot do it! I realize you may think I've lost all reason by using the word *cannot* in relation to God. But it's true. God gave man authority on the earth, and He will not override His own word. This is why He didn't interfere with the serpent and Adam's encounter in the garden. It's why Jesus had to come as the Son of Man to defeat the devil. And it is why the body of Christ must directly resist Satan and his cohorts.

> By decree, God gave all authority to Jesus, and Jesus in turn gave it to us.

By decree, God gave all authority to Jesus, and Jesus in turn gave it to us. As His body, we must do the fighting, but according to the Scriptures it's a "good fight" (see 1 Timothy 6:12).

OUR BEST EXAMPLE

If we are going to learn how to resist the devil, then who better to learn from than Jesus? We can learn much from His time in the desert.

> Then Jesus, being filled with the Holy Spirit, returned from the Jordan
> and was led by the Spirit into the wilderness, being tempted for forty
> days by the devil. (Luke 4:1–2)

The enemy's temptations took place over a forty-day span. That means Jesus had to resist quite a bit. The first recorded confrontation was near the end of the forty days; it was the attempt to get Jesus to use His divine power to prove He was the Son of God. Jesus was hungry, so the enemy suggested He turn a stone into bread. Jesus boldly retorted, "It is written, 'Man shall not live by bread alone, but by every word that proceeds from the mouth of God'" (Matthew 4:4).

There are at least three lessons for us in this situation. First, Jesus recognized and dealt with the temptation swiftly. He didn't think on it or entertain the idea, which would have given Satan's suggestion opportunity to be conceived in His heart. We should follow His example.

Second (and very importantly), Jesus spoke directly to the devil. He did not pray to His Father to remove the tempter or the temptation. Nor did He communicate to the enemy indirectly by saying something like, "It's not God's will for Satan to overcome Me, so I will not succumb to this trial." No, He dealt directly and sternly with Satan. You and I should do the same. We're exhorted, "Don't give the Devil a chance" (Ephesians 4:27, TEV).

Finally, Jesus spoke the written Word of God. Note His words, "It is written." Why is this so important? Because the Word of God is our sword. Paul says, "And take the...sword of the Spirit, which is the word of God" (Ephesians 6:17). God's Word is not a physical weapon, but it's an extraordinary spiritual weapon. Jesus literally stabbed the enemy with His spiritual sword, and there's no doubt it hurt. However, the enemy is extremely tenacious and he didn't give up. He took the painful thrust and kept attacking.

In the next recorded attempt, Satan offered Jesus a shortcut to regain the kingdoms of the world, which Adam's sin had turned over to the devil. All Jesus had to do was fall down and worship him. But Jesus replied, "Get behind Me, Satan! For it is written, 'You shall worship the LORD your God and Him only you shall serve'" (Luke 4:8).

Jesus told the enemy to get behind Him. This would be similar to you or me saying boldly, "Back off!" Jesus then used the Word of God to jab the enemy once more.

The temptations continued until the enemy had taken all the piercings he could handle in one encounter. Luke records, "The Devil retreated temporarily, lying in wait for another opportunity" (4:13, MSG).

A PASTOR HINDERED

Some years ago a pastor I'll call Ken came to my office. Ken was young, strong, and handsome and blessed with a great wife and children. Prior to becoming a believer, he'd been involved in illicit drugs. Ken was so grateful for deliverance and salvation, he would often weep during worship. It touched my heart deeply to see the intense love this man had for Jesus. Ken was tender, a good husband, and a tremendous father. He was definitely aware of how much he was forgiven, and therefore he loved much.

But he had been in a severe battle for months and had kept it to himself. Finally he couldn't stand the pressure any longer and decided to confide in me. As he entered my office he had a pitiful look on his face.

"What's wrong?" I asked.

Ken began to tell me some of his family history. It so happened there was a lot of heart disease and consequential early death among males in his family. "John, I fight intense fear of dying of a heart attack," he said. "I've scheduled doctor checkups, and so far I appear to be okay. However, I just can't shake the fear of suddenly dying. I live with it, but sometimes it completely overwhelms me. I'll start sweating profusely—my clothes become soaked from my sweat. It happens during the night, or when I'm alone, or even when I'm with people or in church services. I seem to have no control over the fear—it comes on suddenly, without warning, and overwhelms me.

"I've prayed passionately. I've asked God to remove the fear and help me not to succumb to the overwhelming feelings."

That's when I jumped in.

"Ken, that is why you aren't seeing any results. You are praying to God, but you're not speaking directly to the enemy as Jesus did in the wilderness. God's Word specifically instructs us to 'Resist the devil and he will flee from you' (James 4:7). You have to do it! Jesus defeated Satan, but then He left for heaven and He's seated at the right hand of God. Before going, He gave us His authority and power to execute His will over His defeated foe. Jesus makes it so clear when He says, 'The spirits are subject to you' (Luke 10:20). They *must* obey you. We are instructed to use the Word of God, speak to the enemy, and command him to obey God's covenant promise."

My friend was listening intently, so I continued. "Ken, there are times the enemy harasses me and it starts to get out of control, so I'll go outdoors to a secluded place where I know no one can hear me. Then I start yelling out loud, because *fervent* means giving it all I've got—spirit, soul, and body. The 'body' part here often naturally means raising my voice, so I say, 'Okay, Devil, if it's a fight you want, it's a fight you're going to get! But I'm telling you in advance that you're just going to get whipped again because I have a sword and you don't. So I'm going to take the sword of the Spirit, and I'm going to cut you up into pieces, and by that time if you haven't had enough and fled, then I'm going to cut the pieces into smaller pieces until you run in stark terror. Now, the Word of God states....'"

Ken listened as I shared some passages from God's Word about healing, freedom from fear, provision, and deliverance. I showed him how to take the written promises and turn them into a battle sword. I told Ken that he had to speak directly and fervently to the spirit of fear. We talked for a while longer, I prayed for him, and he left.

Six months later Ken returned with a solemn look. I could see the heaviness still on him. I asked how he was doing, but I already knew what he was going to say.

"John, it's worse now than ever before," he said. "I'm fighting the fear more frequently than I was six months ago. It seems to happen almost every day: I sweat profusely, my clothes are soaked from the inside out, my confidence is shaken. And I'm having trouble ministering to other people because of my own battle."

Ken leaned forward and admitted with dismay, "John, I have fasted, prayed, and even cried out to God profusely and passionately to help me. I'm just not getting any relief or answers. I'm about to lose my mind."

I was incredulous. "Ken, have you done what I told you to do several months ago? Have you gone out to a remote place and fought the devil directly? Have you spoken God's Word to him?"

"Well...not really."

Now I was angry. "Ken, nothing will happen, there will be no change, unless you directly confront the enemy with the sword of the Spirit, the Word of God."

He bowed his head, and I could see he was starting to withdraw. I don't think Ken had ever agreed with my counsel, but he had come back because he knew others had come and received help. He was a man of faith and really believed God was powerful enough to answer his cry, but he wasn't seeing results and was desperate.

I sat searching for an illustration when suddenly the Holy Spirit gave me a relevant example. "Ken, the President of the United States is the official Commander in Chief of all U.S. armed forces. Simply put, he's the head, leader, and boss of all military personnel.

"Imagine one of our soldiers on the battlefield in Iraq. The enemy is shooting at him from all sides, but our soldier isn't shooting back. Frantic and fearful, he gets on the radio and is able to call the White House. Once the President answers, the soldier pleads, 'Mr. President, I'm under heavy fire. The enemy is shooting at me and he's trying to destroy me. Mr. President, please come and kill the enemy who is trying to put me to death. I'm desperate and scared! I beg of you, come to my assistance!'"

I asked Ken, "Admittedly, this soldier's life is in great danger, but even so, how would the President reply to his frantic request?"

I proceeded to answer my own question. "The President would yell at the soldier, 'What are you doing calling *me*? I gave you the best military training on this planet. I gave you the finest weapons available. I gave you the authority of the United States of America to destroy the enemy. Soldier, get off the phone and shoot back! Engage the enemy!' Then the President would hang up and expect the soldier to do his job."

I could see a light coming on in Ken's eyes.

"Ken," I continued, "you've been given a sword, and the enemy you're fighting has none. In fact, he's been completely disarmed because our Lord 'disarmed principalities and powers, He made a public spectacle of them' (Colossians 2:15). You have a legitimate weapon; the enemy has only intimidation. Not only that, but you've also been given all the power and authority vested in the name of Jesus. We are told that every knee must bow to His name and every tongue must confess His Lordship (Philippians 2:10–11).

"You've been given the armor of God: the breastplate of righteousness, the shield of faith, the helmet of salvation, and so forth. Your shield of faith will quench not *some* but *every* fiery dart the evil one throws at you. God has told you in His Word, 'No weapon formed against you shall prosper, and every tongue which rises against you in judgment *you* shall condemn. This is the heritage of the servants of the LORD' (Isaiah 54:17). Ken, God specifically says that *you* are the one who has to fight off the assaults. He doesn't do it; *you* must address the devil and speak to him. You keep calling out to God, but God is saying back to you—just like the President—'Shoot him!' Or 'Stab him with the sword!'"

Ken was now looking straight at me. He saw the wisdom of the example the Holy Spirit had relayed through me. He left my office with hope and faith. Three weeks later he returned to my office grinning from ear to ear. He had a skip in his step, a twinkle in his eyes, and a spark in his voice. "John, you have to hear what happened!"

I leaned forward anticipating a great report.

"I was on my way to church Sunday morning when it started again," Ken said. "The awful fear arose in me that at any moment I would drop dead of a heart attack. I started sweating and my clothes were getting wet. But instead of crying out to God as I always had done in the past, I got fed up. I got steaming angry at the devil. The anger boiled in me and, without any warning to my wife who was sitting next to me, I slammed my fist on the dashboard of the car. She about jumped through the roof! I hollered out, 'Devil, I've had it! I'm through with you and this fear!' Then I started quoting loudly, passionately, what the Word of God states concerning my life.

"John, when I pounded my fist on the dashboard and shouted, 'Devil, I've had it!' I suddenly had a vision within my heart. I saw Jesus on His throne in heaven, and the moment I confronted Satan, I saw Jesus jump up with excitement, His arms extended upward, and He cried out, 'Yes!'"

Ken started laughing as he said, "John, it was as if Jesus was saying, 'I've been waiting all along for you to do this. I'm so glad you've finally acted.'"

Ken never succumbed to the fear again. He never again fought depression over his fear. Today, more than twenty years later, this dear man of God is still alive and healthy and has a large church in the southern United States. He's doing very well—physically *and* spiritually.

Resist Relentlessly

Now look a little more closely at Peter's words:

> Be sober, be vigilant; because your adversary the devil walks about like a roaring lion, seeking whom he may devour. Resist him, *steadfast* in the faith. (1 Peter 5:8–9)

If you recall from chapter 1, the word *steadfast* is a synonym for *relentless*. The Bible doesn't teach that if we resist the enemy once, he's forbidden to come back and try again. No, quite the opposite: he can try again and again. Through the years I've learned that this is where many Christians get discouraged and experience defeat. They think, *I guess it doesn't work* or *I must not have what it takes.* These are huge lies. We cannot afford to entertain them—ever.

Another story illustrates this point. Lisa had colic when she was a baby. This condition occurs in infants, usually babies under one year of age. All babies cry, but a baby with colic will cry for hours at a time, and there is nothing you can do to alleviate the pain. The incessant crying occurs almost daily, and the condition can last for months. Doctors aren't sure what causes colic, but many believe it's a result of an immature digestive system.

Our firstborn son, Addison, fought colic too. I remember him crying intensely for seemingly no reason. The first few times it seemed to be endless. We patted his back, rocked him, and sang to him, yet he just continued screaming. We felt helpless because he couldn't be comforted. After a while I'd take him in my arms and command the pain to leave his body. I would speak directly to his digestive system. Then I'd pray aloud and strongly in the Spirit, and Addison would fall asleep.

One night Lisa was in the master bathroom and I was already in bed. Suddenly we heard a bloodcurdling scream from the nursery. "John, it's the colic again!" Lisa called out.

I got up from bed and glanced at the bedside clock. 12:11 a.m. I hurried into the nursery, lifted Addison from his crib, and commanded the pain to leave my child's body in Jesus' name. Then I prayed in the Spirit until Addison fell asleep. This took about fifteen minutes.

The next night we were both in bed when again we heard the horrible scream. I have to admit that my first thoughts were, *It doesn't work! You keep praying for him and he's not getting any better. You are ineffective and have no faith.* I had to consciously cast the thought from my mind and replace it with what God's Word says about answered prayer. I said to Lisa, "I'll take care of this."

I got up and glanced at the clock. Again it was 12:11 a.m. *That's a coincidence,* I thought. I hurried into little Addison's nursery, hugged him close, commanded the pain to go away in Jesus' name, and prayed in the Spirit until he fell asleep. Again, it took ten to fifteen minutes.

The next night, Lisa was removing her makeup in the master bathroom and I was in bed. For the third straight night we heard the bloodcurdling scream. This time my thoughts were a little stronger: *John, you've been praying for Addison for almost two weeks. You prayed last night and the night before. Just face it; you're not doing your child any good! Your prayers aren't working!* Again I fought off the thoughts by replacing them with God's Word and got out of bed again.

My eyes went to the clock, and I did a double take. For the third straight evening, the scream had come at 12:11 a.m. Now I was furious! I stormed into the nursery, saw my suffering child, reached into his crib and placed my hand on his chest. I looked down at my little boy and sensed that it wasn't just me looking down at my son; it was as if the Holy Spirit was looking at him through my eyes.

With anger and great authority I shouted, "You foul spirit of colic and infirmity, I've had it with you tormenting my son! I break this curse that's gone back throughout Lisa's family, and I command you in the name of Jesus to take your filthy hands off Addison! You must leave at once, and don't come back!" You would think that this would have terrified the baby, but just the opposite occurred. Little Addison immediately stopped crying, looked at me tenderly, then closed his eyes and fell asleep. That was the last time he ever cried from colic. From that night on, he was a normal, happy baby. The enemy had had enough; he was tired of getting jabbed with the sword. He fled Addison to return no more.

Our second son, Austin, came into our family less than three years later. A few months following his birth, he started showing the same symptoms. I knew what was up and was ready for another fight. I spoke with authority a time or two, and the horrible crying stopped. The colic ceased in a couple of days and never bothered Austin again. When our third son, Alec, was born a few years later, he had no problems with colic. The cycle had been broken. I imagine the enemy thinking, *If I try again, I'm just going to get slammed and jabbed with the sword—Word of God.*

Dear friend, be relentless in resisting the devil. Rebuke him directly and sternly in the authority vested in you by the Lord Jesus Christ. *Our determination to be free from bondage must be greater than our adversary's determination to enslave us.*

I will never forget hearing the testimony of a great missionary to the Indians of Mexico. He works predominantly in the small villages in the mountains, and nearly everyone in one village was a believer as a result of his team's ministry. One evening he was awakened by the villagers. They were frantic. The baby of a couple who attended the mission church had just died. Family members urgently asked the missionary to come and pray. He immediately got up, went to their home, and commanded the spirit of death to leave the baby. Within minutes the infant started coughing, sneezing, and breathing. The baby was back from the dead! Everyone celebrated, and the missionary returned to his residence and fell back asleep.

A little while later the same people again knocked at his door. The baby had died a second time. The missionary got up, rebuked the spirit of death, and the baby came back to life. The missionary reported that he had to resist death several times that night before it left the child for good.

The baby lived, and at the time of the missionary's report, he was one of the healthy children of the village.

HOLD FAST

Too often I've witnessed believers suffer tragic losses. Well-meaning people have genuinely received blessings, healings, and miracles from God, but within days, weeks, months, or sometimes years they lose what they received. That's why the

Bible instructs us to "Hold on to what is good" (1 Thessalonians 5:21, NLT). Every believer should ponder, memorize, and stand firm in this exhortation, which I learned early in my Christian walk.

For most of my teenage life I suffered from irritating lower back pain. After I'd been a believer for about a year, I attended a meeting with a friend. The lady conducting the service announced, "There is someone in this meeting tonight who suffers from back pain, particularly in the low area of your back."

I immediately knew she was referring to me, but I was a little leery of what was transpiring. I'd been in Catholic masses most of my life and wasn't comfortable with a minister calling out someone's issue. I stayed in my seat. When the lady moved on, I was relieved.

Ten minutes later she said, "I'm sorry, the Lord just won't leave me alone about this issue. Someone in this meeting needs their back healed."

Again I thought, *I'm not going up there in front of all these people. I'm not moving.* However, this time the Holy Spirit was tugging at me, so I pushed aside my apprehensions and decided to respond. The lady and her husband prayed for my back, and it was immediately healed. I was amazed! My back hadn't been pain free in years. I was truly in awe of what God had done in my body that night.

For the next couple of weeks I enjoyed a pain-free back. It was amazing. I loved leaning over to brush my teeth or to shave and not having to clutch my back in agony as I straightened back up. I was so happy and grateful for what God had done.

About a month later I was lying in bed, about to fall asleep, when something came into my room. I couldn't see it, but I definitely could sense it. My room was moonlit from the window, but oddly enough it seemed to get darker. As the presence entered, so did fear. Suddenly I felt the same pain in my lower back that I'd struggled with for years. The thought went through my head, *You've lost your healing! Your pain-free days are over. You'll have a bad back the rest of your life.*

As a young believer I had immersed myself in the Word of God and was knowledgeable enough to know that this was an attack. The enemy was trying to get me to buy the lie so the pain could stay. I immediately jumped from my bed and started pacing the floor, yelling out, "Satan, I got healed in that service two weeks ago. I'm holding on to it! The Bible says that by the stripes of Jesus

Christ I am healed. You are not putting this pain back on me. I will remain pain free. So I command you to leave my body, my room, and my apartment now in the name of Jesus!"

The room actually lightened up. The fear and the presence that accompanied the attack were immediately gone, and the pain was gone too. I have never had to fight against that back pain since.

Jesus says, "Keep safe what you have, so that no one will rob you of your victory prize" (Revelation 3:11, TEV). We must be relentless in holding fast what we've received from God.

One of the saddest stories I've witnessed is a man who received a miraculous healing one night in a church service where I was speaking. The crowd was large, so consequently at the end I prayed a mass prayer. I noticed a man bowed over, weeping amongst the sea of people before me. I went over to him to see what had happened. It turned out that he had endured several surgeries on his back and was on lifelong disability.

> We must be relentless in holding fast what we've received from God.

He had lived in chronic pain but was now completely healed. He wept and wept and wept with joy, like I've never seen a grown man weep, for the amazing freedom he received.

Weeks later we ran into each other in a restaurant. He was all smiles, full of vitality, and shared how he'd come off disability and was enjoying his newfound freedom. I was so happy for him.

A little more than a year later I saw him again. He didn't come up to me with a smile as he had before. In fact, he didn't come to me at all. I recognized him and asked how he was. He told me that his back problems had returned. He questioned whether the healing he received in the service that night was authentic. He tried to assure me that his relapse wasn't a completely bad thing because God was teaching him life lessons through the pain. I tried to share with him Jesus' words to "hold fast," but he wasn't interested in what I had to say. He had convinced himself otherwise.

To this day he's a good man, a great dad and husband, but, unfortunately, he is carrying a load that Jesus paid a heavy price to free him from.

IT'S IMPOSSIBLE NOT TO RECEIVE

What I have to say now is really important. If you believe and are steadfast in your resistance of evil, you'll *always* win. Lay hold of, declare, and act upon the promise boldly: "Resist the devil and he will flee from you" (James 4:7).

The Greek word for "flee" is *pheugo.* It means "to vanish, escape, flee away, and seek safety by flight." I've even heard it taught that *pheugo* means "to run in stark terror." That's so good! God's Word doesn't say the devil *might* flee from you. No, if you resist him, he *will* flee. He *hates* bold, biblically based resistance!

You must know that the enemy is afraid of you! When he looks at you, he doesn't see who your friends see; he sees Christ. You are the body of Christ; you are God's anointed one. You're made in the image of the One who destroyed Satan and took away all his armor and weapons. You are a huge threat. So many of us have allowed our imaginations to puff up the power of Satan, but he's beneath you—beneath the feet of the body of Christ. Even if you were the smallest toe in the body of Christ, all the power of the enemy is far beneath your position in Christ. In fact, Scripture declares,

"How you are fallen from heaven, O shining star, son of the morning!
You have been thrown down to the earth, you who destroyed the nations
of the world. For you said to yourself, 'I will ascend to heaven and set my
throne above God's stars. I will preside on the mountain of the gods far
away in the north. I will climb to the highest heavens and be like the
Most High.' But instead, you will be brought down to the place of the
dead, down to its lowest depths. Everyone there will stare at you and ask,
'Can this be the one who shook the earth and the kingdoms of the
world?'" (Isaiah 14:12–16, NLT)

Historically, Isaiah writes of the king of Babylon. However, prophetic Scripture often has two different applications and fulfillments—one natural, one spiritual. As Isaiah writes of the one whose forces destroyed individuals, families, and nations, it's without question that on the spiritual level he's addressing Satan.

According to Isaiah, his end is the lowest depths of the lake of fire where he and his companions will be "tormented day and night forever and ever" (Revelation 20:10, NLT).

It's impossible to not receive blessing and deliverance from God if you believe and stand against the opposing forces of darkness. It may be in the area of finances, wisdom, health, business, ministry, or, most importantly, your ability to aid others. If you fight with the sword of the Spirit, you'll come out on top every time, just as Jesus did.

A WORD OF CAUTION

Before closing this chapter I want to address two extremes I've witnessed in the body of Christ. The first extreme is to look for the devil behind every bush. Christians in this group have become so demon conscious that they've taken their gaze from the Master. This is very unhealthy.

The second extreme is to love God but completely ignore the enemy, like Pastor Ken who visited my office. The predominant mind-set of Christians in this group is: *If I pay no attention to evil, it will eventually go away.* That thought is futile and far from the truth. We are commanded to actively resist the enemy and to continue doing so until the will of God prevails. We must keep in mind that what we do not confront in Jesus' name will not change. Don't shy away from confrontation! It's your duty as a citizen of the kingdom, it's your obedience to God, and it's within the magnificent power God has bestowed upon you by His grace.

The Bible teaches us how to live in a spiritually healthy manner. We are instructed, "Let us run with endurance the race that is set before us, *looking unto Jesus,* the author and finisher of our faith" (Hebrews 12:1–2). A wholesome lifestyle is founded upon fixing our gaze on Jesus and keeping it on Him. If the devil or any of his cohorts get in the way, blast away at him! Resist and he will flee! But then refocus your attention right back on Jesus. He's the one who gave us our faith, and He's the one who will perfect us in it.

14

THE HIGHEST FORM OF RESISTANCE

*Resist him, steadfast in the faith, knowing that the
same sufferings are experienced by your brotherhood
in the world.*

1 PETER 5:9

Suppose a wicked military force has invaded your country and held it captive for years. To bring true liberation, you must not only confront the enemy in direct battle, but you must also eliminate the strongholds they've established. These can be hidden land mines, booby traps, bunkers, and bases—to name a few.

However, one of the most difficult strongholds to contend with is the twisted, evil mind-set the enemy has instilled in the citizens of your captive nation. This kind of opposition cannot be resisted by direct combat, for it is psychological, not physical. But if you do not win this most insidious aspect of the war, any gains made in direct combat may eventually be lost.

In this chapter we're going to arm ourselves for this type of resistance. As with direct combat, it too must be steadfast—relentless. If not, all other forms of battle become inconsequential. The apostle James emphasizes this aspect of warfare when he writes, "Submit to God. Resist the devil and he will flee from you" (James 4:7).

In this verse James reveals that the foremost method of combating the devil is to submit to God. This means living in consistent trust and obedience to Him. By doing so we can usher His ways, His mind-set, and His principles into the twisted and perverted areas of the world around us. *Absolute obedience* is the principal method of fighting off the strongholds or attacks of the enemy and for us to rise to a new level of authority and rulership. Listen to Paul's words:

> For though we walk in the flesh, we do not war according to the flesh. For the weapons of our warfare are not carnal but mighty in God for pulling down strongholds, casting down *arguments* and every *high thing* that exalts itself against the knowledge of God, bringing *every thought* into captivity to the obedience of Christ, and being ready to *punish all disobedience when your obedience is fulfilled.* (2 Corinthians 10:3–6)

The devil's strongholds are thought processes, mind-sets, reasonings, intellectual views, imaginations, or any other psychological patterns that are contrary to the knowledge or will of God. These would include but are not limited to jealousy, greed, selfishness, manipulation, lust, hatred, strife, seduction, and envy. These heart and mind positions are adversarial to God's truth, and they create real spiritual conflicts. However, as Paul wrote, our obedience empowers us to stomp out these forms of disobedience.

GROWING UP IN CHRIST

As stated in an earlier chapter, our level of authority and power increases as we successfully handle adversity. In other words, we evolve and grow into our rulership. Returning to Peter's exhortation to "arm ourselves" gives us more insight:

> Since Christ suffered for us in the flesh, arm yourselves also with the same mind, for he who has suffered in the flesh has *ceased from sin,* that he no longer should live the rest of his time in the flesh for the lusts [desires] of men, but for the will of God. (1 Peter 4:1–2)

Those who have suffered adversity have *ceased from sin.* What does Peter mean by this? He's speaking of attaining spiritual maturity, of becoming a full-grown man or woman in Christ. A "spiritual adult" in the kingdom no longer lives for the desires of men but is fully committed to and obeys the will of God.

He or she no longer gives in to the pressures of the world's system but can now tear down its strongholds. Paul describes this power in 2 Corinthians 10:6 as "being ready to punish all disobedience when your obedience is fulfilled."

We must remember that, no matter what our physical age, we were birthed as babies into God's family. And He expects us to grow up. He commands us, "As newborn *babes,* desire the pure milk of the word, that you may grow thereby" (1 Peter 2:2). Just as we have different stages of physical growth (babyhood, childhood, and adulthood), so we have stages of spiritual maturity. Paul states, "And I, brethren, could not speak to you as to spiritual people but as to carnal, as to *babes in Christ*" (1 Corinthians 3:1). These Corinthian Christians may have been adults in age but they were babies as far as spiritual maturity. That's a sad place for any believer to stay.

In a different letter, Paul illustrates the next stage of spiritual growth, childhood: "that we should no longer be *children,* tossed to and fro and carried about with every wind of doctrine" (Ephesians 4:14). And again Paul writes, "Brethren, do not be children in understanding; however, in malice be babes, but in understanding be *mature*" (1 Corinthians 14:20). We're to be as guileless as babies only when it comes to malice; in understanding and steadfastness we're to be mature adult believers.

A baby will respond according to whatever training he or she receives, whether it's good training or bad. Children are also vulnerable, easily influenced. However, an adult most often knows where he or she stands and cannot be so easily swayed by the wrong forces. We are admonished to grow in Christ so we will be able to stand strong in truth and effectively push back or punish all disobedience. According to Paul, it takes understanding to be mature in Christ. But there is more involved, and Peter addresses it.

How do we grow spiritually? It will be helpful to first consider physical and mental growth. What is physical growth a function of, and what is it limited to? *Time.* Have you ever seen a six-month-old who is six feet tall? No, it usually takes fifteen to eighteen years to attain adult height. Physical growth is a function of *time.*

Mental growth, in comparison to physical growth, is not limited to time. I've met fourteen-year-olds who've graduated from high school and are referred to as "child prodigies." I've encountered fifty-year-olds who've not graduated high school. So mental or intellectual growth is not a function of time but a function of *learning*. You must go from first to second grade, then continue to third, fourth, fifth, and so on. But you can do this as fast or slowly as you desire.

So is spiritual growth and maturity a function of, and limited to, time? Well, I've observed people who have been born again for only one year who have already grown to maturity. Then I've beheld others who've been saved for twenty years but still wear "spiritual diapers" and cause a lot of trouble for their Christian leaders, as well as their fellow believers. So spiritual maturity is not a function of time.

Is spiritual growth and maturity a function of, and limited to, learning? The Pharisees could quote the first five books of the Bible from memory, but they couldn't recognize the Son of God when He was healing the sick and casting out devils right in front of their faces. Their lives embodied hypocrisy, and they were spiritually blind to the arrival and ministry of the Messiah.

So what is spiritual growth a function of? What's it limited to? The answer is *suffering*. Look again at Peter's words: "He who has suffered in the flesh has ceased from sin" (1 Peter 4:1). Someone who has ceased from sin has reached complete spiritual maturity.

An argument that may come up is, "I've observed people who've suffered, and they're now bitter." And that happens. So there must be another element that's key to spiritual maturity. The writer of Hebrews enlightens us: "Though He was a Son, yet He learned obedience by the things which He suffered" (Hebrews 5:8).

> Spiritual growth doesn't come when the sun shines brightly on our lives.

This verse tells us that Jesus didn't automatically bring obedience with Him when He came to earth; He had to learn it, which He did perfectly: He never sinned or made a mistake. For our discussion, the key point is that *Jesus learned obedience by suffering.* Coupling this scripture with Peter's words reveals that spiritual growth doesn't come when the sun shines brightly on our lives, when everyone speaks well of us and treats us nicely, and everything goes smoothly. No, we grow spiritually when we continue to obey God in the midst of a trial. We grow stronger as we submit to God's wisdom whenever people slander us, gossip about us, mistreat us, or try to hurt us...or when we've just lost our job, received a bad report from a lawyer or doctor, or don't know where needed funds are going to come from.

We choose amid the hardship to believe God, even if it appears to be to our disadvantage. We choose to resist the evil that attacks us, first and foremost by obeying God's Word. This is when true spiritual growth occurs. This is exemplified beautifully in the life of Joseph, son of Jacob.

Joseph's Dream

God made a covenant with Abraham. The promise passed down to Isaac, his son, and to Jacob, his grandson. Jacob had twelve sons; the eleventh was Joseph. Joseph's older brothers despised him, and Scripture gives clues as to why. Young Joseph was a tattletale (Genesis 37:2) and a bit of a braggart (verse 5). And their father, Jacob, favored Joseph above the others and further spoiled him by giving him an elaborate coat of many colors. None of these factors promoted goodwill with Joseph's older brothers.

With their relationships already strained, the tipping point came when God gave Joseph two dreams. In the first dream Joseph saw bound sheaves in a field. His own sheaf stood upright while his brothers' sheaves bowed low to his. In the second dream Joseph saw the sun and moon and eleven stars bowing to him. Joseph naively and enthusiastically shared both dreams with his brothers along with his interpretation that he would one day rule over them. Not surprisingly the brothers didn't share Joseph's enthusiasm but hated him even more.

Later, the ten older brothers went a long distance from home in search of fresh fields to graze their father's flocks. Time passed, and Jacob sent Joseph to see how they were getting along. As his older brothers saw Joseph coming, they conspired, "Here comes our little brother, The Dreamer, Mr. Leader, Our Illustrious Ruler. Let's kill him! Then we'll see what becomes of his dreams" (my paraphrase).

So they tossed him into a pit with the intent of leaving him there to die. However, a few hours later a caravan of Ishmaelites passed by on their way to Egypt. Judah, the fourth born, got a bright idea. "Hey guys, hold on a moment.

If we let him rot in the pit, it'll be no profit to us. Let's sell him as a slave and make some money. He will be as good as dead and will never again bother us, and we'll all share in the spoils. On top of that, we won't be responsible for killing him" (my paraphrase).

The brothers who were present liked the idea, so they sold Joseph for twenty pieces of silver. Their envy, hatred, and wicked thinking fueled actions that were intended to rob Joseph of his inheritance and family. Keep in mind, these were his siblings who did this!

It's hard for us today to comprehend the injustice done to Joseph. Selling him into slavery was almost as cruel as taking his life. In those days it was very important to have sons, for sons carried on a father's name and inheritance. Joseph's brothers deprived him of this honor. They erased his name, completely stripping him of his identity. Back then, when a man was sold as a slave to another country, he would remain a slave until death. His wife and children would all be slaves. For Joseph, all he knew and all that was dear to him were gone. It was extremely difficult to be marked as a slave for life but indescribably more difficult to be born an heir of a wealthy man only to have it all stripped away— and by your own flesh and blood! It was almost as if Joseph was now a living "dead man." I imagine Joseph had to fight thoughts of wishing he were dead rather than be sold into slavery. What Joseph's brothers did was indescribably cruel and wicked.

When the caravan arrived in Egypt, Joseph was sold to a man named Potiphar, an officer of Pharaoh. He was now Potiphar's property. You and I can read this story in the Bible thousands of years after it happened, so we know the outcome. But remember, Joseph didn't have the book of Genesis to read. He didn't know what the future held except for slavery in a foreign land. It appeared to him that he'd never again see his father, friends, or homeland. It also seemed that he'd lost all chance of seeing the fulfillment of his dreams. How could they ever come true? He was a slave in Egypt; he couldn't leave, for he was bound to another man for the rest of his life.

But we walk by faith and not by sight.

Joseph served Potiphar for ten years. There was never a word from home, and each passing year only solidified the heartbreaking reality that his brothers had reported him dead to all those he loved. He was certain by now that his father, Jacob, had mourned his loss and moved on without him. There was no hope of a father's rescue or reunion.

As time passed, Joseph found favor with Potiphar. He was placed in charge of Potiphar's household and all that he owned. But at the same time, something terrible was brewing under the surface. Potiphar's wife had cast longing eyes on Joseph, and she wasn't shy about it. In fact, she was rather persistent, for she approached him every day. She was a wealthy woman accustomed to getting her way. She was not only determined but also dressed and scented with the best—and almost certainly she had a strong, seducing spirit.

Joseph, however, wisely resisted her every attempt: "You're his wife, after all! How could I violate his trust and sin against God?" (Genesis 39:9, MSG). Even though his young life had seemingly been ruined by betrayal and disappointment, Joseph was a man of truth, submitted to His God, and that was his bottom line.

One day Joseph and Potiphar's wife were in the house alone. Still intent on seducing him, she grabbed his garment and urged him, "Please, my husband is away, let's go to bed with one another. No one will know it. We can fill the day with fun and pleasurable lovemaking" (my paraphrase).

Again, Joseph resisted sexual immorality and fled the house. He darted away so quickly that he left his garment in her clutched hands. The scorned woman's embarrassment quickly turned to anger, and she screamed, "Rape!"

Without delay, Potiphar had Joseph thrown into Pharaoh's dungeon. Once again, just as when he was sold by his brothers, in a single day every good thing in Joseph's life had been lost.

WARFARE IN THE DUNGEON

Our prisons in America are nothing compared to Pharaoh's dungeon. I've ministered in several prisons, and, as unpleasant as they are, they would still be viewed as nice hotels compared to a Middle Eastern dungeon. I've also visited a couple of these ancient prisons in that part of the world. They're cold, damp, dreary, and void of sunlight and warmth. Unlike America's prisons, they have no workout areas, televisions, cafeterias, toilets, sinks, or mattresses to sleep on. They're just sunken rooms or empty cisterns cut from the rock. Most cells are only four to five feet tall and are crude and dehumanizing.

In those days, prisoners were given only enough water and food to remain alive, because dying would be too easy for them (see 1 Kings 22:27). According to Psalm 105:18, Joseph's feet were hurt with fetters and he was placed in irons. Potiphar had put him in this dungeon to die. If he'd been Egyptian, he might have had some chance of release, but as a foreign slave accused of raping the wife of one of the king's top officers, Joseph had no hope. Joseph had descended as low as a person could without being dead.

Can you imagine the thoughts he had to ward off in that damp, dark dungeon? With all kinds of time on his hands, I'm sure the enemy attacked his mind and imagination without mercy. Can you hear Joseph's thoughts? *I served Potiphar and his household faithfully, with honesty and integrity for more than ten years. I've been more loyal to him than his own wife. I stayed faithful to God and my master by daily fleeing sexual immorality. What is my reward for my obedience? A dungeon! Why didn't I just behave as any normal red-blooded male and enjoy the pleasure of that woman? If I had just had sex with her when we were alone, nobody would have known and I would not be in this dungeon.*

If Joseph had bought into these lies, it would have opened the door for his thinking to plunge to even lower levels: *So is this how a loving, faithful God cares for those who obey Him? Why, He's not faithful at all—in fact, He abuses His servants. He's allowed the wicked to prosper and triumph while I am tormented for my obedience. What good is it to obey God? He gives me a dream of leadership, I simply share it with my brothers, and what does that get me? The pit and slavery! Then I obey God and flee sexual immorality, and what is my reward? This dungeon! It seems the more I obey, the worse my life gets. Serving God is just a mean joke!*

Joseph had very limited freedom in prison, but he still had the right to choose his responses to all that had happened to him. Would he become bitter and resentful? Jaded and cynical? Would he despise the Word of God, entertain thoughts of revenge, and embrace the hatred that was knocking at the door of his heart?

Or would he *steadfastly resist* the rush of negative thoughts and emotions that undoubtedly flooded his soul?

I doubt that it ever crossed Joseph's mind until much later that this horrific series of events was God's way of preparing him to rule. Joseph was learning obedience through suffering. His obedience muscles were being stretched to the max. It was as if 315 pounds were put on the bar and he was on the bench with everything inside screaming out, *Give up!* Would he heed heaven's cries of *Push! Push! Push!* or would he listen to his human logic, choose the easiest path of bitter revenge, and cave in to the pressure of the weight?

WAS GOD CAUGHT OFF GUARD?

For Joseph, the bottom line was his brothers. If it weren't for them, he'd never be in this awful place. During the two years he lived in the dungeon, I'm sure it crossed his mind many times how different things would have been if his brothers hadn't betrayed him.

How often do we fight off the same thoughts? You know, all those *If* thoughts:

- *If it weren't for my boss, I would have been promoted instead of fired.*
- *If it weren't for my ex-husband, we wouldn't be in the financial mess we're in.*
- *If it weren't for the man who slandered me at work, I wouldn't have lost my job and faced this threat of eviction from my apartment manager.*
- *If my parents had not divorced, my life would be normal.*

It's easy to blame everyone else for adversity and to imagine how much better off you'd be if it had not been for all those who seemed to oppose you. But the ironic truth is that such thoughts only weaken our resistance to what will ultimately harm us. *The real threat is not our adverse circumstances but the wrong beliefs and thoughts that try to slip in during our hardship.* We must be relentless in our belief in God's sovereign plan and firm to resist any logic contrary to His Word.

Ultimately, this truth must be solidly established in our heart: *No man, woman, or devil can ever get us out of the will of God! No one but God holds our destiny.* Joseph's brothers tried hard to destroy the vision God gave him. They thought they had ended it. They even said to each other, "Come therefore, let us now kill him and cast him into some pit.... We shall see what will become of his dreams!" (Genesis 37:20). They purposely set out to destroy him. It wasn't an accident; it was deliberate! They wanted no chance of Joseph ever fulfilling any dream.

Do you think it caught God off guard when they sold him into slavery? Can you imagine God the Father looking at the Son and Holy Spirit and in a perplexed and frantic tone saying, "What are We going to do now? Look at what Joseph's brothers have done! They've ruined Our plan for his life. We'd better think of something quick! Do We have a back-up plan?"

If we consider the typical responses of many Christians to crisis situations, it would seem that this is exactly what transpires in heaven. Can you see the Father saying to Jesus, "Jesus, Pastor Bob was just kicked out of his denomination because he prayed for someone to be healed! Sure didn't see that one coming! Do you have another church for him to lead?" Or how about this: "Jesus, Sarah and her children don't have any income because her husband divorced her and is not paying alimony or child support. To make matters worse, the economy is bad, and she has very little education, skill sets, or formal training! What are We going to do?"

It sounds absurd, yet the way we so often react to trials suggests that this is the way we view God.

JOSEPH'S GREATEST TEST

How about getting even? If Joseph had been like many of us, do you know what he would have been doing? Plotting revenge. He would have consoled himself with ideas contrary to the Word of God (see Romans 12:19). *If I get out of this prison, I'll make them pay for what they did. I'll hire the finest lawyer, bring the brothers to court, and sue their pants off! Or better yet, why waste the money and time? I'll just kill them. I'll make it look like it was an accident, just like they did with me.*

But if Joseph had actually thought this way, God would have been forced to leave him in the dungeon to rot. Why? Because if he had carried out a plan such as this, he would have killed the heads of ten of the twelve tribes of Israel! This would have included Judah, who carried the lineage of King David and, most importantly, Jesus Christ. That's right, the ones who treated Joseph so wickedly were the patriarchs of Israel!

Joseph had to relentlessly resist reasonings, arguments, thoughts, and imaginations that exalted themselves over the ways of God. He had to remain firm in his belief in God's promise, for his most crucial test of trust and obedience was still to come.

Two new prisoners arrived in the dungeon. They were Pharaoh's butler and baker. In time, each of them had troublesome dreams and told Joseph about them. What was Joseph's test? *Could he proclaim the faithfulness of God to these two men when he had not seen one shred of evidence of God's faithfulness in his own life in more than ten years?* Think of it: Joseph had had a dream of leadership in which his brothers would serve him. Yet not one single facet of that promise had come to pass. If Joseph had been like many today, he would have said to the two men, "So you guys had dreams last night. Yeah, right, I had a dream once. Leave me alone."

If this had been his response, he would have died in the dungeon a very bitter man, muttering "God is not faithful. He doesn't keep His promises." He would have destroyed the pathway to his destiny, for two years later it was the butler's report to Pharaoh of Joseph's ability to interpret dreams that ultimately brought Joseph out of prison to interpret Pharaoh's own dream. That single incident vaulted Joseph from the depths of the dungeon to second in command over all of Egypt—and eventually, nine years later, to seeing his brothers literally bow down to him exactly as promised in his long-ago dream.

Joseph didn't see that God-given promise fulfilled for twenty-one years. Yet it was indeed fulfilled because God is faithful to keep His promises. How many of us give up if we don't see our prayers answered in three years? Or three months? Or three weeks? If God's methods and timing are different from ours, we tend to give Him a bad rap. But it's not God who aborts the dream; it's us! We have need of endurance, of relentless faith and obedience, and the power we need is available in God's economy of grace. It's His free gift available to all; we just need to trust His Word and stand fast in our faith in Him. We'll reap if we don't faint.

As I've stated, no man or demon can stop the plan of God for your life, and if you become established in this truth, you will be an unstoppable force in His kingdom. However, there is one exception to this truth that you need to know about: *only one person can destroy your destiny, and that's yourself!*

Consider the nation of Israel. God sent Moses to lead them out of Egyptian bondage into the Promised Land. His will was for them to enter into

Canaan a year after leaving Egypt. However, due to unbelief, wrong thoughts, complaining, and

No man or demon can stop the plan of God for your life.

blaming Moses, they never entered their destiny. Instead, that entire generation except for two, Caleb and Joshua, died in the wilderness. They constantly groused that God was not faithful, but in reality they were not faithful to God. Because they weren't relentless in their faith and obedience, they self-sabotaged their destiny.

THE CHARACTER TO RULE

Joseph started out as a tattletale and braggart and was a tad haughty. But he didn't remain this way. He obeyed through adversity, and consequently he developed the character he would need in order to eventually rule effectively. He became the second most powerful man on earth. If he had harbored bitterness, offense, unforgiveness, and hatred toward his brothers he could have easily executed revenge. His brothers came to Egypt for food during the worldwide famine. He could have thrown them in prison for life, or tortured and even killed them. However, Joseph did just the opposite. He gave them grain at no charge and the best land in Egypt for their families. They ate the finest food the country offered. Bottom line, he gave his undeserving brothers the best of all Egypt. Mature character had established, strengthened, and settled in Joseph's heart—Christlike character—for he blessed his brothers who cursed him and did good to those who hated him (see Matthew 5:44–45).

Look closely now at the conclusion of Peter's exhortation:

Resist him, steadfast in the faith, knowing that the same sufferings are experienced by your brotherhood in the world. But may the God of all grace, who called us to His eternal glory by Christ Jesus, after you have suffered a while, *perfect, establish, strengthen,* and *settle* you. (1 Peter 5:9–10)

May the God of all grace…perfect, establish, strengthen, and settle you. Those are four very powerful, promising words for you and me. Allow me to cite James Strong's definitions for each:

1. *Perfect*—"to restore or complete through repair, adjusting, or mending."
2. *Establish*—"to set fast, to turn resolutely in a certain direction, to fix, establish, steadfastly set."
3. *Strengthen*—"to confirm or strengthen in spiritual knowledge and power."
4. *Settle*—"to lay a basis for, i.e., to literally erect."

Each of these words describes what God did within Joseph while preparing him to rule. He was fixed or mended, no longer a tattletale or braggart or haughty. He became powerful, elevated by God's incredible grace into his place of destiny. He became spiritually strong in that he blessed and didn't curse his brothers. His relentless obedience through what appeared to be hopeless situations forged undeniable wisdom, courage, and character.

In the last chapter we examined the importance of engaging in direct combat with our enemy by laying hold of and speaking the Word of God. However, speaking the Word is actually not our greatest weapon. Our most powerful weapon for direct combat is to stand firm in our obedience to God's Word. It's thinking, speaking, and living His truth. God cries out through the prophet Jeremiah, "Where are those who are valiant for truth on the earth?" (see Jeremiah 9:3). He's looking for the Josephs of our generation. If we're relentless in our obedience and speak the Word of God boldly, we'll reap a bountiful harvest of fulfilled promises, matured character, greater authority, and destroyed strongholds. Those within our world of influence will benefit remarkably from our steadfast faith and obedience.

What a great life God has called you to! His plans for you were set before you were formed in your mother's womb. Like Joseph, He's calling you to greatness. Peter summarizes it all at the conclusion of his exhortation:

I have written to you briefly, exhorting and testifying that this is the true grace of God in which you stand. (1 Peter 5:12)

The power to relentlessly obey is found in the grace of God. I hope you will never again reduce God's amazing grace to only a covering for sin and a ticket to heaven. It is so much more! By His grace we are to distinguish ourselves for the absolute glory of our Lord Jesus Christ.

15

RELENTLESS PRAYER

> Most assuredly, I say to you, whatever you ask the
> Father in My name He will give you.
>
> JOHN 16:23

Our discussion of *Relentless* wouldn't be complete without addressing our personal interaction with God himself. How are we to approach and petition Him? Should we come with a timid disposition, cowering in posture? Should we only ask for "big items" with a "hope so" attitude so we're not disappointed if we don't see answers? Should we expect a small, medium, or large percentage of our prayers to be answered?

I know these questions might sound absurd to you, but after traveling for more than twenty years and praying with many leaders and believers, these questions really are not so far-fetched. I've witnessed countless mundane prayers with no strength of conviction or passion in them. I've attended prayer meetings in which people looked around, read their Bibles, or listened to the worship music while we were supposed to be interceding. I often wonder whether these Christians assume that by their attendance God will answer, or if they long ago gave up on praying with resolute, relentless faith and trusting God in all things?

Too many times my heart has ached as I listened to leaders pray shallow and unspecific prayers. The thought has crossed my mind, *If he went into a civil leader's office in the same manner as he's petitioning God, the official would probably respond, "What are you here for? You're wasting my time!"* It's as if these Christian leaders choose their words to sound spiritually acceptable, not wanting to get people's hopes up and set them up for disappointment. It's so very sad because it demonstrates how unrealistic the spirit realm is to so many Christians today.

BE BOLD AND FERVENT

We are cordially invited by the God of the universe to come "boldly to the throne of grace" (Hebrews 4:16). To be *bold* is to be confident, courageous, forward, strong, and firm. Antonyms to *bold* include *timid, hesitant,* and *bashful.* Think of it: God invites and instructs you to come to Him with confidence, strength, and firmness in order to receive your needs from Him. This is His desire!

The apostle James tells us, "The effective, fervent prayer of a righteous man [or woman] avails much" (James 5:16). *Fervent* means to "have or show great intensity of spirit, feeling, enthusiasm." The dictionary reveals that synonyms include *passionate* and *heartfelt.* James is saying that an effective prayer is a fervent prayer. On the other hand, an ineffective prayer is one that is subdued, impassionate, and not heartfelt.

When you hear *fervent,* do you also hear *relentless?* You should. James underlines his point by recounting the great prophet Elijah:

Elijah was a man with a nature like ours, and he prayed *earnestly* that it would not rain; and it did not rain on the land for three years and six months. And he prayed again, and the heaven gave rain, and the earth produced its fruit. (James 5:17–18)

Elijah prayed earnestly—*relentlessly*—and experienced miraculous results. The word *earnest* is a synonym for *fervent.* It is defined as "serious in intention, purpose, or effort; to be sincerely zealous." Are you grabbing hold of God's Word on how to pray effectively? It's clear: God is looking for heartfelt, relentless passion when we approach Him with our needs and requests.

Sometime following Elijah's prayer for rain to cease, he began praying for rain to return. The biblical account tells us, "Elijah went up to the top of Carmel; then he bowed down on the ground, and put his face between his knees" (1 Kings 18:42).

The New Living Translation reads, "fell to the ground and prayed." I can picture him crying out to God with great passion. He's in a kneeling or seated position, rocking back and forth with his head between his knees, and he's shouting, "God of Abraham, Isaac, and Jacob, You spoke to me that Your desire is for the rain to return. So I call upon You to bring in clouds and rain so that fruit may return to this land! I request that You not delay, but bring the rain so that Your people may once again re- joice in Your goodness!" He petitions boldly, re- lentlessly, with heartfelt passion. Then Elijah in- structs his servant, "Go up now, look toward the sea" (1 Kings 18:43).

> God is looking for heartfelt, relentless passion when we approach Him with our needs and requests.

Years earlier, when Israel received regular rains, they would come from the Mediterranean Sea to the west. Elijah orders his servant to go look in that direction for the clouds. He puts action to what he believes. When we truly believe, this is exactly what we'll do. Elijah's servant comes back and reports, "There is nothing."

Many of us would have stopped right there, wouldn't we? We'd say, "Well, maybe I heard wrong. I guess God wants to continue punishing Israel for its wicked behavior. As long as Ahab's king we probably won't see any rain." We wouldn't have stood firm in faith; rather, we would have stopped petitioning God and, consequently, missed His will. But not Elijah.

Elijah knows the will of God and will not be denied. He cries out once again, this time boldly and fervently thanking God, by faith, for hearing his prayer. He sends the servant up to the summit of Carmel a second time.

Prayer and faith without corresponding action is nothing other than reli- gious exercise and a waste of time. To be fervent in prayer means your heart, mind, soul, and body are determined to receive, and you act accordingly. Be- cause you are confident that you are acting in God's will, you refuse to take no for an answer. You know that circumstances and conditions can and must change.

But Elijah's servant comes back with the same answer. "There's nothing."

The majority of us, if we hadn't given up the first time, would give up at this second report. We'd find a good theological reason as to why God wasn't grant- ing this particular request at this particular point in time. But not Elijah! He again storms the throne room of heaven, and for the third time sends his em- ployee up the mountain. Again, the same answer. He does it a fourth time, a fifth time, a sixth time, and a seventh time! (What a superb employee; he was asked seven times in one day to climb to the summit of Mount Carmel, and he did it. Not only was Elijah fervent, but his servant was as well!) After the servant's seventh round trip, he reported, "There is a cloud, as small as a man's hand, rising out of the sea!"

A cloud the size of a man's hand certainly cannot produce the kind of rain Elijah prayed for. But it's all Elijah needs to stop petitioning and to go into action. He knows his prayer has been heard.

> So he said, "Go up, say to Ahab, 'Prepare your chariot, and go down
> before the rain stops you.'" Now it happened in the meantime that the
> sky became black with clouds and wind, and there was a heavy rain.
> (1 Kings 18:44–45)

Seven times he had prayed, and seven times he sent his servant. Elijah was relentless in his request, determined to receive an answer. This is the example James refers to when he's talking about effective, fervent prayer. It's fervent in belief, speech, perseverance, and action.

SMALL CLOUD RISING

Elijah's rising small cloud foreshadows the assurance we can have when we pray with relentless faith. The Holy Spirit bears witness with our spirit (see Romans 8:16). This is our small cloud. Sometimes it's a word, other times a release of joy, and still other times it's an awareness in our heart that what we've been asking God for is done. Once we see our small cloud rising, we can act accordingly, as Elijah did.

I remember when Lisa was due to give birth to our fourth son. She was five days overdue, but she had a history of carrying our babies past the due date. However, this time Lisa had an awareness that something wasn't right. The baby began thrashing in her womb. She called the doctor to report her concern, and he instructed, "Come to the hospital tomorrow morning and we'll induce labor."

The next morning the doctor broke her water and informed us that she would almost certainly go into labor without delay. He sent us on a walk in an attempt to kick-start the contractions. Lisa and I walked all morning with no progress. Around noon she grew tired, so we returned to the hospital room for rest. Lisa said, "John, please go out and pray. If I don't go into labor soon, they'll have to take more severe measures to get the baby to come, and I do not want that to happen."

One of the measures would be to give her a drug called Pitocin and an epidural. She had gone through this procedure with our first baby, and it had resulted in long-term complications in her back. There was another deterring factor: it was an expensive procedure. Because our ministry was still in its infant stages, we did not have medical insurance. We were a low-income family and didn't have the money for other than basic expenses.

At noon I left the hospital and found a nearby secluded place where I could raise my voice to heaven. I prayed fervently. Forty-five minutes later I returned to Lisa's room, only to find no progress. I spent another hour with Lisa and then went out to pray a second time. My appeals to God grew stronger. I returned midafternoon to once again find no progress.

We spent another hour together. Lisa's concern was mounting for many reasons, but mainly for the safety of our baby. She pleaded, "John, please go and continue to pray. I'm very concerned."

I went back a third time to my secluded spot of prayer. This time I was even more passionate and intense. My prayers were firm and loud; I was determined to be heard. I had seen the fearful look on Lisa's face, and I wanted to be able to comfort her. I prayed in English and reminded God of His covenant promises. Then I prayed fervently in the Spirit.

After several minutes I heard clearly in my heart, *Your baby will be born today, and both mother and baby will be home by this time tomorrow in good health.* The Holy Spirit bore witness with my spirit that my prayer was heard by giving me a word. He had given me "a small cloud the size of a man's hand." I now was ready to act.

I got back to Lisa's room at 5 p.m. and told her, "Arden will be born today and both you and he will be home tomorrow in good health." She was comforted. But after a while with no change, the promise really didn't look possible. There were still no labor contractions. How could a baby be born so quickly? But I had seen the small cloud!

The evening went on, and the nurses and doctor were now discussing next steps. Lisa asked more than once, "John, shouldn't you go out and pray again?"

"No need. The baby will be born before midnight," I said.

With each hour that came and went, my thoughts intensified about giving up and letting go of the word that I'd heard so clearly in my heart. However, I was certain that God had heard me, and I refused to relent.

Finally, a little past 11 p.m., Lisa's contractions kicked in. Arden was born at 11:51 p.m. When he came out, the umbilical cord was wrapped tightly around his neck. I remember the horrifying sight of his head being a different color than his body. He was in the process of being strangled. The doctor quickly cut the cord, and they rushed Arden away for close observation.

The next day we checked out of the hospital at 3:30 in the afternoon. Lisa and Arden were home by 4:30 p.m. What God had whispered to me came to pass exactly as He had said it would.

ASK, AND KEEP ON ASKING

Most of us are familiar with Jesus' words, "Ask, and it will be given to you; seek, and you will find; knock, and it will be opened to you" (Luke 11:9). These are taken from the New King James Version of the Bible. However, a look at the Amplified Bible's translation reveals something more:

> So I say to you, ask and keep on asking and it shall be given you; seek and keep on seeking and you shall find; knock and keep on knocking and the door shall be opened to you. For everyone who asks and keeps on asking receives; and he who seeks and keeps on seeking finds; and to him who knocks and keeps on knocking, the door shall be opened. (Luke 11:9–10)

You can see that Jesus encourages us to relentlessly ask, seek, and knock. Why? Is God hard of hearing? Definitely not! It's a matter of our truly believing. I've witnessed people who are *determined* to receive and others who *aspire* to receive. There is a huge difference. If someone's *determined*, he is tenacious, ardent, and bold. Coming away empty-handed is not an option. On the flip side, if he only *aspires* to receive, he's prone to give up more easily. If we truly believe, we'll continue to ask and become more intense the longer it takes.

Consider this lesson from the Master Himself:

One day Jesus told his disciples a story to illustrate their need for constant prayer and to show them that *they must never give up.* "There was a judge in a certain city," he said, "who was a godless man with great contempt for everyone. A widow of that city came to him repeatedly, appealing for justice against someone who had harmed her. The judge ignored her for a while, but eventually she wore him out. 'I fear neither God nor man,' he said to himself, 'but this woman is driving me crazy. I'm going to see that she gets justice, because she is wearing me out with her constant requests!'" Then the Lord said, "Learn a lesson from this evil judge. Even he rendered a just decision in the end, so don't you think God will surely give justice to his chosen people who plead with him day and night? Will he keep putting them off? I tell you, he will grant justice to them quickly! But when I, the Son of Man, return, how many will I find who have faith?" (Luke 18:1–8, NLT)

Notice Jesus' words, *they must never give up.* It's not just a good idea; more importantly, it's God's will for you to never quit.

In the story the woman is so relentless in her request that she wears out the unjust judge. Simply put, she drives him crazy with her persistence. The ungodly ruler moves on her behalf just to be rid of her. What's amazing to me is that Jesus uses this example as an illustration of how we are to petition God, for He says, "Learn a lesson from this." Then He speaks of His people pleading day and night and asks, "Will he [God] keep putting them off?" God is not unjust; He is *for* us. Therefore, He will grant our requests quickly when we are *determined,* as the woman was in Jesus' story.

At this point a clarification needs to be made. A misapplication of this parable could cause one to slip into a routine of praying day and night by rote or repetition. Jesus actually warns against this: "When you pray, do not heap up phrases (multiply words, repeating the same ones over and over) as the Gentiles do, for they think they will be heard for their much speaking" (Matthew 6:7, AMP). The objective is not frequent, thoughtless recitations or repetitions of prayer. The focus is *a relentless, fervent,* and *sure attitude* as we place our requests before God. We approach Him confidently because we know our request is according to His will, and consequently we will not be denied. Elijah wouldn't take no for an answer. He was determined to see change according to what he prayed. He stayed with it until he knew he was heard.

ARDENT SEEKING AND KNOCKING

Jesus not only instructs us to keep asking but also to keep seeking and keep knocking. Fervent prayer isn't limited to speaking in our closet; it includes follow-through—earnest seeking and knocking. In other words, we live out what we've asked for. This is a crucial factor in seeing results.

There are numerous stories from my experience I could share in regard to this aspect of prayer. Here are some recent examples:

Lisa and I had the opportunity to spend two and a half days alone in Maui, Hawaii, prior to speaking at a conference. The timing was great because we had not had a refreshing break together in quite some time, and also her dad had just passed away. I'd carefully planned for this special time alone.

Each day as our departure for the trip approached, the weather report remained unchanged: nonstop heavy rain! Bad weather would definitely put a damper on our plans, so I prayed passionately that it wouldn't rain, commanded the weather system to avoid our location, and spoke to heaven's angels to carry out what I'd prayed.

"It's going to rain. It's going to rain," Lisa kept saying,

I kept replying, "We will have great weather. All will be fine."

We arrived in Hawaii in the evening and were greeted by dark, gloomy weather. The reports still indicated that the rain would not let up. I happened to catch a weather report on television in the hotel. A massive weather system had rolled in and covered not only all the Hawaiian Islands but also a huge region of the surrounding Pacific Ocean.

In the morning I opened our drapes to behold dark clouds and pouring rain. I couldn't see a break in the dark clouds anywhere. It was exactly as predicted. But I refused to say anything contrary to what I'd requested. I shouted out, "Thank You, Father, for a beautiful, sunny day. I want to see my wife in a bathing suit, lying in the sun and resting."

Lisa laughed at my silly behavior. I played along with her, but I really was serious. I would not relent. We made our way to breakfast. Because of the heavy rain, the restaurant staff was forced to move half the tables from the outside patio into the hotel hallway.

Once our food arrived, I glanced at the rainy, dark clouds and purposefully prayed, "Lord, thank You for this food, we sanctify it in the name of Jesus. And thank You for a beautiful day in the sunshine."

Lisa smiled and, in jest, teased, "John, why don't you pray something we know can be answered?" We both laughed. She often comes up with the funniest lines.

"Honey, I'm actually serious," I told her. "It will be beautiful today."

Our server came to the table to check on us. "Can I get you two anything else?"

"Yes, can you please shut off the rain?" I responded.

We all laughed. However, before we completed breakfast, the rain had stopped, the dark clouds left, blue sky appeared, and the sun was shining brightly. For the rest of our time in Maui, we never saw rain or even a cloud blocking the sun.

Later we traveled to another part of Hawaii—Oahu—for the conference. Once there, several locals told us that they had been drenched with rain the same days we had sunshine in Maui. In fact, we were on the dry side of Oahu, but the beaches were closed because the excessive rain had washed dangerous waste into the ocean. The locals were surprised at our report of beautiful weather in Maui.

I believe that our amazing God answered my persistent petitions and formed a hole in the weather system.

BOOKS FOR THOSE IN NEED

I shared the previous story with you to eradicate the fallacy that God is interested in fulfilling only "big requests." He truly cares for every detail of our lives. He's our Father! But now let me testify of His response to a much more important request: prayer for benefiting those in need.

Lisa and I believe our books are God-given messages for His global church. When describing them, I often mention that the only reason my name is on a book is because I'm the first one to read it. In light of this, we've been given a serious stewardship. Lisa and I are responsible to pray for the means to get these messages out to the church around the world.

God truly cares for every detail of our lives.

At the time of this writing, my books have been translated into more than sixty languages. Our long-time, passionate prayer has been to give these books to pastors and leaders in closed or developing nations as a gift. In fact, we want to give more away than are sold.

In the last ten years we've distributed approximately 250,000 books to leaders in China, Iran, Pakistan, India, Fiji, Tanzania, Rwanda, Uganda, and other nations. We're still far behind our goal of giving more than we sell, as multiple millions of copies have been sold.

At the beginning of 2011, as our leadership team was strategizing for the future, I discovered that we had only given away 33,000 books in 2010. After much discussion I announced, "This year, our goal will be to give 250,000 books to leaders overseas."

The room became quiet. One team member spoke up, "I think that might be setting the bar a little high. The increase will be too significant from last year. We need to introduce this large of an outreach to our financial partners on an incremental basis. We need time. Could we set it at 100,000 and maybe move higher in the years to come?"

"No, we need to believe God and step out to help these needy pastors and churches worldwide," I said. "Two hundred and fifty thousand is not too much to shoot for."

The debate intensified. This team member provided additional reasons why my goal was too large. Ultimately, he flat-out identified it as an unreasonable goal. He was accurate and logical in his assessment, but he wasn't considering the grace of God.

I became more firm. "Guys, no other ministry holds these books; God has entrusted them to us. We are the only ones who can give *The Bait of Satan*, *Under Cover*, *Lioness Arising*, *Driven by Eternity*, *Extraordinary*, and our other titles. We are responsible to believe God for this. We must set our sights high."

The resistance continued. At this point I became loud and adamant: "I don't want us to stand before Jesus at His judgment seat and have to explain why we asked for so little. I don't want pastors questioning us at the judgment, 'Why didn't you give us these books that God entrusted to you?' Other ministries will not have to give an accounting for this—only us!"

The atmosphere was charged, and our meeting ended on a stressed and conflicted note. I was sorry it had escalated to the degree it did and for speaking with such intensity. Our department heads are sincere, godly people, just trying to look out for the good of the ministry. But deep in my heart I knew I couldn't back down. It was important to stand in the gap for the hungry pastors and needy churches located in developing regions of the world.

A few days later our head of administration approached me. "John, we will do what is in your heart. We are here to serve your and Lisa's vision. Please tell me if you still believe we are to give away 250,000 books. If you pray and believe this, then we are 100 percent with you in this endeavor. We will pray and work diligently toward it."

I again sought God, and I still believed the goal should be set for 250,000 books. Doors had already opened for us to give books to leaders in Vietnam, Liberia, China, Iran, Turkey, Ghana, Tajikistan, Lebanon, Burma, and other nations. We also knew many more requests would come in. To print and distribute this number of books worldwide would cost somewhere in the range of $600,000 to $700,000 (U.S.). This was a huge sum of money for us, but not for God.

Two weeks later our team members called me in a hotel room in Florida. They reported with excitement in their voices, "John, we've just received a check for $300,000 to print books for leaders overseas." On the balcony of my hotel room, I literally screamed for joy.

It turns out that one of our employees had shared the vision with a Texas businessman. He wrote the check. The largest single donation our ministry had received in the previous twenty years had been $50,000. This was truly a miracle! This money would print close to 150,000 books. The astounding fact was that we were now more than halfway to our goal for 2011—and it was only February! The phone call turned into a celebration—we were all energized and full of joy.

Before hanging up I asked, "Guys, do you now understand why I was so strong and adamant in the meeting two weeks ago?"

Our head of administration, who had been my biggest challenger in the meeting, laughed and said, "I thought you were going to say, 'Get behind me, Satan.'" We all laughed.

Later that day Lisa commented, "God didn't want us to believe Him for the possible; He wanted us to believe for the impossible. If we didn't stick to the goal, I don't believe the check for $300,000 would have come into our hands." I have to agree with her. Lisa's wisdom was spot on.

By the close of the year, over 250,000 books were distributed to the hands of leaders in forty-one nations. None of this could have happened without the support and prayers of our partners and diligent efforts of those involved. The testimonies of these outreaches would take volumes to record.

This was a great faith-building event for our entire team. It had taken persistent asking, seeking, and knocking to see this door open to impact countless lives. We must always remember that God "is able to do exceedingly abundantly above all that we ask or think, according to the power that works in us" (Ephesians 3:20). We cannot allow our finite human minds to limit Him in our thinking and believing. If we really believe, we'll ask persistently and keep knocking until we see His glory revealed.

WHAT ARE YOU WAITING FOR?

Kingdom progress doesn't happen in the natural realm until it's first secured in the spiritual realm. Paul instructs Timothy, "Run hard and fast in the faith. *Seize the eternal life,* the life you were called to, the life you so fervently embraced" (1 Timothy 6:12, MSG). To seize eternal life is to lay hold of Jesus' provision, and we certainly cannot do it halfheartedly. When God sees this kind of determination on the part of His children, it moves Him.

"Without faith it is impossible to please Him," we're told in Hebrews 11:6, "for he who comes to God must believe that He is, and that *He is a rewarder of those who diligently seek Him.*" We aren't told that God rewards those who *casually* seek Him but that He rewards those who *diligently* seek Him. He's drawn to earnest, heartfelt, relentless passion.

In the same light, God speaks through the prophet Jeremiah:

For I know the thoughts that I think toward you, says the LORD, thoughts of peace and not of evil, to give you a future and a hope. Then you will call upon Me and go and pray to Me, and I will listen to you. And you will seek Me and find *Me,* when you search for Me with *all your heart.* I will be found by you, says the LORD. (Jeremiah 29:11–14)

God's plans for your life are only good. However, to receive this abundant provision takes passionate and persistent pursuit. This is true faith.

Do you remember Jesus' final words in the parable of the woman and the unjust judge? "When the Son of Man comes, will He really find faith on the earth?" What a question! Will He find mundane, halfhearted, cautious faith— or real faith? The Message translation reads, "How much of that kind of *persistent faith* will the Son of Man find on the earth when he returns?" The kind He speaks of is compared to the woman who wears out the judge with her relentless pursuit.

So don't be shy in approaching God. Don't be timid with your requests. Be bold, strong, adamant, and specific. Our persistence with God does not come from desperation but from firm confidence that He is our loving Father and will give us what we adamantly ask for in His name.

> Don't be shy in approaching God.

What are you waiting for? The needs around you are great. There are so many people in your world who need you to approach God boldly in prayer on their behalf. Be a light to them! Approach God with relentless persistence now!

16

Run for the Prize

So run [your race] that you may lay hold [of the prize]
and make it yours.

1 Corinthians 9:24 (amp)

As we've learned throughout this book, you and I are in a challenging race. And as the passage above from 1 Corinthians reveals, the race is personal. It's your race. It's my race.

Our competition is not with each other but with forces that do not want us to finish well. You and I live in a fallen world, which inevitably brings opposition. We are contending. The New King James version of this verse reads, "Run *in such a way* that you may obtain it."

Note the apostle Paul's phrase, *in such a way.* In what way are we to run? We must run relentlessly. The writer of Hebrews spells it out: "Let us run with patient *endurance* and steady and active *persistence* the appointed course of the race that is set before us" (12:1, amp).

I've been an athlete all my life, so many of my friends are amateur or professional athletes. The serious ones practice hard, persevere through adversity, and endure grueling training. Paul writes, "Every athlete in training submits to strict discipline" (1 Corinthians 9:25, tev). Why do athletes do this? The apostle answers, "They do it to win a prize."

For the professional football player, the prize is winning the Super Bowl. For the professional golfer, it may be winning a PGA event, the Masters, or another Major. For the hockey player, it's the Stanley Cup, and for an Olympic athlete, it's the gold medal. Their vision for the prize is their motivation. Those who firmly fix their vision on the prize will train more relentlessly and endure extreme adversity—more so than those who do not have vision and are not motivated to win the prize.

I've seen a hockey player sustain a broken ankle but plead with his trainer to tape up the injury so he can continue battling for the Stanley Cup. He keeps skating with pain that most human beings wouldn't even walk on. I've seen a football player shatter his nose but tape it so he can continue competing; his vision of winning the Super Bowl overrides the excruciating pain. We've all witnessed this at one point or another, whether in sports or other endeavors. Vision is the great motivator. It's what makes people stand out from all the others. It's what makes them champions. Only those who have their sights firmly set on the prize will endure such adversity.

> **Starting well is important, but...how we finish bears far greater significance.**

As kingdom people contending daily against the powerful, destructive legions of Satan, we must know what it is we're competing for. What's our motivation to finish well? Why is it so important that we remain faithful? What do our individual lives as God's people add up to? Why is the course God has placed before us so important to the big, kingdom picture?

Paul tells us that the answer to each of these questions is the same as for the athlete. We labor for the prize or reward: "So run [your race] that you may lay hold [of the prize] and make it yours." In his later years, the apostle John recorded a similar command of God:

> Watch out, so that you do not lose *the prize* for which we have been working so hard. Be diligent so that you will receive your *full reward*.
> (2 John 8, NLT)

Solomon disqualified himself from the highest prize due to not finishing strong. The goal wasn't fixed in his focus.

Starting well is important, but in God's economy how we finish bears far greater significance. Finishing well and receiving the prize require our relentless persistence and endurance, both of which must be fueled by motivation. So this is a good place to address a very important question: *What is the reward we are working for—the prize we are warned not to lose?*

The reward can be considered on two levels. We'll explore the first here and the second in the next chapter.

THE FIRST REWARD

The first reward or prize revolves around the fact that our life's course is directly involved in the building of God's house—the home in which He will dwell for eternity.[1]

God is building Himself a house—a glorious, custom home. It's the home He's longed to dwell in, and it's been the focus of His plans for thousands of years. And He's very excited about it!

Lisa and I had the privilege of building a custom home. In the late 1980s when we lived in Orlando, Florida, a well-known custom homebuilder named Robert approached us. "I love your ministry," he declared, and then added, "I want to build you a custom home." At the time we were living in a small, modest house and thought his prices would be far too expensive for us. But when we hedged, Robert blurted out, "I'll do it for a 'God price.'" As it turned out, he didn't take one cent in profit from the house.

Prior to this, Lisa and I had owned two homes. They were both tiny tract houses, and we'd had nothing to do with their layouts or blueprints. So we were accustomed to simply choosing a standard floor plan along with a limited selection of colors and materials; we had never been allowed to make major decisions. So the process of building a custom home was foreign to us.

I'll never forget when Robert came to our tract house a few days later, sat down with us at our kitchen table, laid out a blank piece of paper, and enthusiastically said, "Draw your dream house!"

We were stunned. We didn't realize you could do such a thing. Immediately Lisa went to work. She started drawing away as if she had been thinking

---

1. For more in-depth discussion of God's house, see my book *Driven By Eternity* (New York: Faith Words, 2006).

about it for quite some time. (Fact is, she had!) I was a bit slower on the draw, proposing ideas for my study and the garage while my wife did most everything else. It was exhilarating, and the excitement grew more and more as we discovered we could actually design our new house however we desired. There were no limitations.

Then our dream, scribbled so roughly on that big piece of paper, went to the architects and designers and several days later Bob showed us the blueprints. It was so exciting. Soon they broke ground and started building.

My wife and I went to the job site every day during the entire construction process. Sometimes we went twice a day. We were so eager; we couldn't wait for the next facet of the house to be built. Those few months seemed to last years, and days seemed to last weeks, because of the anticipation of something new being added to our custom house and the ultimate expectation of one day moving in. We were amazed to watch the dream we'd sketched on a blank piece of paper come to life before our very eyes!

Well, I believe the joyful anticipation we felt closely resembles God's emotions and anticipation for His dream home. But He's been waiting a lot longer than a few months. In fact, God has been looking forward to its completion since the foundation of the world.

On earth, we frequently give names to special homes. For example, the queen of England's home is Buckingham Palace. In America our president lives in the White House. Actor Michael Douglas's home in Bermuda is Longlands. The home of the late George Harrison, the former Beatle, is Friar Park. Actor Nicolas Cage's home is Midford Castle. What most people don't realize is that God started this house-naming trend long before any of us did. He refers to His eternal house, which is still under construction, as Zion. As the psalmist writes,

For the LORD has chosen *Zion*;
He has desired it for His dwelling place;
"This is My resting place forever;
Here I will dwell, for *I have desired it*." (Psalm 132:13–14)

Notice that God desires this house. In other words, He's eagerly anticipating it, just as Lisa and I so eagerly anticipated our new custom home. Other scriptures tell us that the house called Zion has been in God's heart for untold generations: "For the LORD shall build up Zion" (Psalm 102:16); "The LORD, who dwells in Zion" (Psalm 9:11); and "Out of Zion, the perfection of beauty, God will shine forth" (Psalm 50:2).

When you build a house, you begin with the foundation. Hear Isaiah's words: "See, I lay a stone *in Zion,* a tested stone, a precious cornerstone for a sure *foundation*" (Isaiah 28:16, NIV). What (or more accurately, who) is that foundational cornerstone? None other than God's beloved Son, Jesus Christ. According to Isaiah, Jesus is part of the building material of God's eternal house, Zion. In fact, as the cornerstone, He is the most important part.

Then God's Word declares, "You also, as living stones, are being built up a spiritual house" (1 Peter 2:5). The house Peter refers to, of course, is Zion. Jesus is figuratively referred to as *a stone,* and so are we. We are "living stones," and He is the cornerstone. Along with Jesus, Christians are the building materials making up the house God is going to dwell in forever!

> God is building a home. He's using us all—irrespective of how we got here—in what he is building. He used the apostles and prophets for the foundation. Now he's using you, fitting you in brick by brick, stone by stone, with Christ Jesus as the cornerstone that holds all the parts together. We see it taking shape day after day—a holy temple built by God, all of us built into it, a temple in which God is quite at home. (Ephesians 2:19–22, MSG)

THE SUBCONTRACTORS

Not only do we make up the building material of the house, but we're also referred to as fellow workers (see 1 Corinthians 3:9). A more contemporary term would be "subcontractors" (or in builders' slang, "subs"). Who are the subs? They are the plumbers, electricians, framers, drywall installers, roofers, tile layers, bricklayers, carpet layers—the list goes on. These are the people who really build the house. When Robert built our house, he didn't nail a single nail into the house, didn't lay one brick, didn't cut one piece of wood or drywall. No, the subs did all this work.

So if the subs are the ones who really build the house, what is the builder's job? The answer is threefold. First, the builder designs the house. God, as the builder of His own house, designed His master plan in the distant past. The apostle Paul writes, "Long before he laid down earth's foundations, he had us in mind" (Ephesians 1:4, MSG). Hebrews tells us, "The works were finished from the foundation of the world" (4:3). God's house was completely planned before Adam was created. Amazing!

Second, the builder orders the materials used in the construction of the house. Aren't you glad God ordered us up? This is why He says, "I chose you before I gave you life, and before you were born I selected you" (Jeremiah 1:5, TEV). Paul tells us, "He chose us in Him before the foundation of the world" (Ephesians 1:4).

The third responsibility of the builder is to schedule the subs. This is a very critical aspect of the project because you don't want to bring in the sheetrock installer before the plumber or electrician. You don't want the carpet layer coming in before the roofers or the painters. If the subs are not scheduled to work in the proper sequence, chaos is inevitable.

Modern-day houses do not usually have a "chief subcontractor," but God's house does. Who do you think is the chief subcontractor building God's custom home? You got it: Jesus Christ. Galatians 4:4 (TEV) says, "When the right time finally came, God sent his own Son." God the builder scheduled Jesus, the cornerstone and chief sub, at the "right time" in the construction of Zion.

In regard to His work as chief sub, Jesus fulfilled His assignment perfectly. He most definitely finished well! At the Last Supper, He was able to say to His Father humbly and confidently, "I have finished the work which You have given Me to do" (John 17:4). Jesus finished His work as the main subcontractor building Zion.

What about you and me? What does God's Word say about our role as subcontractors building God's house?

We are told, "For we are God's workmanship, created in Christ Jesus to do good works, which God prepared in advance for us to do" (Ephesians 2:10, NIV). Notice that we were created in Christ "to do good works." In other words, we were not created just *to be* someone, but we were also created in Christ *to do* something. Pay close attention now: In recent years there's been an imbalance of teaching in the body of Christ about this. We've strongly emphasized *who we are* in Christ, which is important, but we've emphasized it to the neglect of *what we were created to do* in Christ. This imbalance has created two major problems.

First, it has produced a very lethargic church in the Western world. The majority of believers attend church once a week, and many not even that often. We get wrapped up in moving ahead in our jobs, pursuing a good social life, buying the latest gizmos, paying off the home, raising the kids, saving for their education, and having a nest egg for retirement. All of this becomes our motivation rather than the fulfillment of our personal commission from God. Too many of us are ignorant to the fact that we have an eternal "work" to finish.

Think about this: how could Paul say, "I have finished the race" (2 Timothy 4:7) if he didn't know his path? Let me explain. If you ran cross-country (long-distance) track in high school, you'd know that all the participants view a map of the course prior to the race. If you run in a long-distance race and don't know the planned course, you could run and run until you collapse and your teammates carry you home. But you still won't know if you finished the race. The only way you can honestly and accurately say you finished the race is if you knew and completed the preplanned course. Like Jesus, Paul was saying, "I've finished the work You gave me to accomplish."

How can we finish our race when we're solely focused on, and consumed by, everyday affairs? How can we know God's work for us when our major connection with Him is a single, short Sunday service each week? How can we possibly know His plan if we fail to seek Him daily and diligently?

The second problem created by our imbalanced emphasis on *being* over *doing* is that it gives many Christians the impression that only those in full-time ministry have a genuine calling on their lives. This is baloney! Every child of God, man or woman, young or old, has a heavenly calling, and that calling is to be a faithful subcontractor building God's custom home. The Amplified translation of the Bible brings this out beautifully, asserting that we were created in Christ Jesus "that we may do those good works which God predestined (planned beforehand) for us [taking paths which He prepared ahead of time], that we should walk in them [living the good life which He prearranged and made ready for us to live]" (Ephesians 2:10).

God gave you the privilege of serving as one of the subcontractors building Zion, His eternal home. It's not a house made with bricks and mortar or lumber and stucco. It's a house made without hands, a living home made up of royal sons and daughters. Like many subcontractors today, you may not be able to see (yet) how your life's calling complements the overall design of His home, for only He sees that as the master builder. Our contribution will make complete sense someday in the future when God's house is completed and, together with Him, we enjoy His presence there for all of eternity.

When Robert scheduled the subs to build our house, he gave each one a customized portion of the blueprints and schematics. He laid out for them exactly what he wanted them to do. He knew the overall plan; they knew only their part and were expected to do only their part. They didn't come to the site and just do whatever they felt was needed or looked good. They followed the plan that had been prearranged by the builder.

God planned beforehand the best path for you, for me, for everyone who trusts in Christ Jesus as Savior and Lord (Ephesians 2:10). As with the subs who built our house, each of us has a specific, important role in the construction of God's eternal home. No assignment is more or less important than another. God wants His house to end up exactly as He preplanned it, and that takes each of us doing our part—and doing it well.

THE BUILDER'S REWARD OR LOSS

Now you can better understand why in the Scriptures we are often referred to as builders. The psalmist writes, "The stone which the *builders* rejected has become the chief cornerstone" (118:22). Peter, as noted earlier, states that all believers are stones in God's house, but then he shifts from *who we are* to *what we are called to do* in Christ—figuratively referring to us as builders (or subcontractors) of the house of God: "You also, as living stones, are being built up a spiritual house.... Therefore, to you who believe, He is precious; but to those who are disobedient, 'The stone which the *builders* rejected has become the chief cornerstone'" (1 Peter 2:5, 7).

In Peter's words we see that the obedient are the faithful and true subcontractors building the house of God, while those who don't obey the Word (God's design and blueprint) are actually working against the end goal.

With this in mind, we're ready to examine the apostle Paul's description of the process and the reward:

> God will *reward* each one according to the work each has done. For we are partners working together for God.... You are also God's building [Zion]. Using the gift that God gave me, I did the work of an expert *builder* [subcontractor] and laid the foundation, and *someone else* [another subcontractor] is building on it. But *each of you* must be careful how you build [all of us are referred to as subcontractors]. For God has already placed Jesus Christ as the one and only foundation, and no other foundation can be laid. (1 Corinthians 3:8–11, TEV)

First and foremost, notice in the first sentence that God is talking to us about a reward or prize. Keep this in mind as we continue delving into this 1 Corinthians passage.

Paul has built the foundation. His letters were written almost two thousand years ago and are still used today as the trustworthy basis for how we are to live in Christ. The first subcontractors who built our home in Florida were the foundation layers. Once their work was done, all the other subcontractors came and built on top of the concrete slab that these original subs established.

Paul continues: "Some will use gold or silver or precious stones in building on the foundation; others will use wood or grass or straw" (3:12, TEV). The gold, silver, and precious stones refer to the eternal, while wood, grass, or straw refer to the temporal. In every moment of life we have a choice: we can build either for the eternal or for the temporal. When our motives are to make money, become popular, help people solely for our personal advantage, move up the ladder of success in order to be important, and other self-seeking focuses, we are building for the temporal. But when our focus is on building God's kingdom and His house by bringing the eternal Word and provision of God to those in need, we are building for the eternal.

Paul continues, "And the quality of each person's work will be seen when the Day of Christ exposes it. For on that Day fire will reveal everyone's work; the fire will test it and show its real quality" (3:13, TEV).

Fire will test our work, but it will also test the motives and intentions behind our work (see 1 Corinthians 4:5). When you put fire under wood, grass, and straw, the fire devours them. However, place the same fire under gold, silver, or precious stones, and they become purer and more beautiful. They are tested and refined. So now comes the payoff: "If what was built on the foundation survives the fire, the builder will receive a reward. But if your work is burnt up, then you will lose *it*; but you yourself will be saved, as if you had escaped through the fire" (3:14–15, TEV).

Notice that you, the builder, will receive a reward if you finish well! However, if you do work that is out of line with God's Word—if your motives are selfish, disobedient, or prideful—then your work will burn up. As a believer in Christ you will make heaven, but there will be no reward of lasting labor. Strong words of warning to all of us!

As we continue unpacking this great passage, remember that Paul is not addressing an individual but the whole church:

> Surely you know that you are God's temple [custom home] and that
> God's Spirit lives in you! God will destroy anyone who destroys God's
> temple. For God's temple is holy, and you yourselves are his temple. You
> should not fool yourself. (3:16–18, TEV)

Again, strong words! This should arouse holy fear in anyone who would think of mistreating or misleading God's house or Christ's bride, the church. Consider this a strong caution against mistreating anyone, even the least little "brick" of God's house or what we would call "the least of the saints."

THE SUBCONTRACTOR'S REWARD

Paul concludes, "Let no one deceive himself" (3:18). Unfortunately, some Christians have not finished strong because they veered off course to follow the allure of self-seeking. They turned from building God's house for His glory and went after glory that fades—pursuing the fleeting approval of man or the riches of this world that will one day burn up.

Don't be fooled! Stay focused; you have a task to do in Christ. Your work must be finished as God originally designed it, or else the work you were intended to do will be replaced. The Message strongly underscores this crucial point:

> Let each carpenter who comes on the job take care to build on the foundation! Remember, there is only one foundation, the one already laid: Jesus Christ. Take particular care in picking out your building materials. Eventually there is going to be an inspection. If you use cheap or inferior materials, you'll be found out. The inspection will be thorough and rigorous. You won't get by with a thing. If your work passes inspection, fine; *if it doesn't, your part of the building will be torn out and started over.* But *you* won't be torn out; you'll survive—but just barely. (1 Corinthians 3:10–15)

If our work doesn't pass God's standard of inspection, then our "part of the building will be torn out and started over." No one wants to have his or her work redone—especially when it's work we've done for the Creator of the universe!

I remember when one subcontractor didn't do a good job on our house. He didn't perform his work according to the blueprints Robert had given him. Since Lisa and I were on the job site every day, we were the first to notice the problem. I called Robert, and he and I met at the homesite. He was furious. This particular subcontractor wasn't one of his normal subs, so Robert immediately fired him. That man lost his reward. Not only did he lose pay, but he also lost the good credentials of being among those involved in the construction of our beautiful home.

I watched Robert tear out the work this man had done. He then hired another sub who came in and did the job exactly as Robert had specified in the blueprints. This man received the reward—both in his pay and in his satisfaction of knowing that he had contributed positively to building such a beautiful home.

The Scriptures tell us that this principle is even more true in the construction of God's house. There will be those whose seasonal labor (or even their life's labor) will not endure. It will be torn out and will not be a part of the eternal home.

Let me help you envision the gravity of this. Since I went to my homesite daily, the subs came to know me quite well. They called me "the preacher." When I drove up each day, their acid-rock music was blaring away. Upon seeing me, one of the subs would dash over to the boom box and shut it off. I'd smile inside because of the reverence they held for the things of God. Then we would all chat for a while. I had some great conversations with those guys—even some great ministry opportunities.

I recall one day when the subs talked with me about some of the magnificent homes they'd played a part in building. They'd light up as they spoke about their contributions. You could see the enormous satisfaction they treasured from being part of such glorious works.

Let's take this a step further. Can you now imagine how the subs felt who built the White House in Washington, D.C.? Imagine the day their own children came home from school and enthusiastically announced a scheduled field trip to see the most famous house in the entire nation. Can you imagine the enormous pleasure and satisfaction Dad experienced when he told his excited child of his personal involvement in building that very house? Can you imagine Dad's feelings when he accompanied his child's class to the White House? How it felt to see the pride in his child's countenance as the other children discovered their classmate's dad helped build the regal house where the President of the United States resides? Can you imagine?

The same is true for us with God's house! However, we are not working on a house that will be torn down and replaced in a few hundred years. We are working on the house that will be the central focus of the entire universe forever and ever. Oh, yes, hear the words of Micah the prophet:

> Now it shall come to pass in the latter days that the mountain of the
> LORD's *house* shall be established on the top of the mountains, and shall
> be exalted above the hills; and peoples shall flow to it. Many nations shall
> come and say, "Come, and let us go up to the mountain of the LORD, to
> the *house* of the God of Jacob; He will teach us His ways, and we shall
> walk in His paths." For out of *Zion* the law shall go forth. (Micah 4:1–2)

The affairs of the universe will all revolve around this house. The wisdom and laws governing all creation will flow from the leadership in this house. And perhaps the most amazing fact: God's house, Zion, will be just as beautiful ten trillion years from now as it will be on the first day of its completion.

There's a great minister of the gospel who was faithful to the end. He ministered effectively for more than sixty years and entered his reward close to the turn of the millennium. A year or so after his departure, I traveled to a large church in the Midwest, where the worship leader told me that God had given him a vivid dream. In this dream he was in heaven and saw this great minister who had finished well. With a large smile the minister said to the worship leader, "It's much better than I'd ever imagined." They conversed for a few minutes, then the minister turned and pointed out the work that he was a part of on Zion. It was massive. The impact of this man's faithfulness went so much farther and wider than he had dreamed while on earth, and it was right there before him. He was able to show his work, just as those construction subs were telling me of their work on the homes they'd helped build. What a reward! What a prize!

> We are working on the house that will be the central focus of the entire universe forever.

Can you imagine, throughout all eternity, being able to show your descendants and the nations and the myriad of people that come to behold the glorious house of God *your part* in the construction of His home?

It's a glorious thought, isn't it? What an incredible reward to look forward to! What a motivator to make sure we finish well!

Now consider the flip side. Can you imagine not having any representation of your work in the house called Zion because you failed to finish well? Can you imagine your ancestors and descendants and nations coming to behold what you did, but you have nothing to show throughout all eternity because your portion was torn out and replaced by another who was faithful? What an eternal loss, just as Paul spoke of in 1 Corinthians 3.

Oh, dear saint, I don't want that for you. God doesn't want that for you. The sad fact is, this will happen to many believers. But you can determine right now that you will *not* be one it happens to. Heed carefully John's words:

Watch out, so that you do not lose the prize for which we have been working so hard. Be diligent so that you will receive your full reward. (2 John 8, NLT)

The Lord himself has designed a way for every one of His children to have the opportunity to receive the full reward of taking part in the construction of

God's eternal home. Your labor will never fade, never grow old, never need to be replaced. It will be admired by billions of people and angels forever and ever.

And this is only the first reward or prize we'll receive for relentless faithfulness and obedience to our Lord. As magnificent as this motivation is, there's another prize that's even greater. We'll discover it in the next chapter.

17

CLOSE TO THE KING

Watch out, so that you do not lose the prize for which
we have been working so hard. Be diligent so that you
will receive your full reward.

2 JOHN 8, NLT

Adversity is inevitable. The right incentive will keep us running our
race relentlessly while others lacking motivation will falter—or
even quit. Motivation is crucial to finishing well.

The first prize is the reward of witnessing your labor on God's custom home
throughout eternity and knowing that your work was worthy of His "Well
done." The second reward is a bit more obvious and entails how closely we'll be
associated with Jesus throughout eternity.

A CLOSER RELATIONSHIP WITH THE KING

Throughout my years of traveling and communicating with believers around the
world, I sometimes wonder if most Western Christians believe that God is a Social-
ist. Many believers' perception is that He will reward everyone equally and that
we'll all have the same authority, responsibility, and honor in the new heaven and
new earth. Erroneously, they fail to grasp this truth: although God's redemption is
equal to all, and not based on our works or performance, He rewards our faithfulness according to how we've obeyed, persevered, and stayed true to His Word.

Our greatest reward for finishing well—a prize even greater than the one
we explored in the previous chapter—is how closely we will be associated with
Jesus throughout eternity. There's nothing more magnificent than being near

and intimate with the One we love and adore. The Scriptures offer conclusive evidence of this. One such reference is to a group of overcomers who will be privileged to "follow the Lamb wherever He goes" (Revelation 14:4). What a privilege and honor—to follow Jesus wherever He goes throughout all of eternity!

This truth is also clearly seen in the Gospels. Toward the end of Jesus' earthly ministry, the mother of two of His disciples approached with a request: "Give your word," she demanded of Jesus, "that these two sons of mine will be awarded the highest places of honor in your kingdom, one at your right hand, one at your left hand." (Matthew 20:21, MSG).

Of course the highest place of honor would be right next to Jesus, who is seated next to the Father. There could be no better place to be! The Bible identifies mighty angels, called seraphim, who are very close to the throne of God (see Isaiah 6:1–6). They continually cry out to each other, "Holy, holy, holy is the Lord!" Christians sing a hymn taken from their words. However, they are not singing a song in order to make God feel good about Himself. No, they are responding to what they see! Every moment another facet of His greatness is revealed, and all they can do is shout, "Holy!" In fact, so passionate are their cries that the doorposts of an auditorium that seats billions of angels and saints in heaven is shaken by their voices.

These mighty angels don't resent their longstanding place. They're not secretly thinking, *We've been doing this for ten trillion years now. We're getting a little bored. You'd think God would get someone in here to take our place so we'd get a break and possibly explore other parts of heaven or the universe.*

No way! Heaven's angels don't want to be anywhere else. There is no place in the entire universe better than by God's side, beholding His greatness and hearing His wisdom. To put it simply, there is nothing in all creation more spectacular than the Creator. We must remember that nothing is hidden from His sight, so when you are near Him you see all things from His vantage point. For an admittedly weak example, imagine gazing through a telescope into outer space while sitting next to Albert Einstein, Neil Armstrong, and Sir Isaac Newton. Wow, what insight you would get! I realize this doesn't hold a candle to seeing things from God's perspective, but I'm sure you get the point.

A minister I know was taken to heaven. He shared that while there he felt an insatiable yearning to be in the throne room. And everyone in heaven felt the same—they all wanted to be as close to God as possible. My friend exclaimed that heaven was far more beautiful than anything he had ever imagined, but nothing in heaven was more desirable than the Lord Himself.

Back to the request from the mother of James and John. Jesus responded, "As to awarding places of honor, that's not my business. My Father is taking care of that" (Matthew 20:23, MSG). Now we must ask, Are there truly places of honor awarded in heaven? Or was Jesus more or less saying, "Hey, don't consider places of honor. Why would you even consider who's going to be closer to Me and My Father? You and your sons should just live your life for God. One day it will all sort itself out and God will give every Christian equal places of honor. It's all based on what I do, not what you do, so don't let it be a concern."

To answer this question we must look at another question posed to Jesus regarding the next life. One day the Sadducees came to Him, wanting to see if they could back Him into a theological corner. There were seven brothers, the Sadducees began. The oldest married a woman and died childless. The second brother married her, but he also died childless. And so it went, one after the other, until each of the seven brothers had her as wife. The Sadducees then asked, "So tell us, whose wife will she be in the resurrection?"

Jesus' response was different from His reply to the disciples' mother. "Marriage is for people here on earth," He said.

> But that is not the way it will be in the age to come. For those worthy of
> being raised from the dead won't be married then. And they will never
> die again. In these respects they are like angels. They are children of God
> raised up to new life. (Luke 20:35–36, NLT)

So Jesus corrected the Sadducees, then told them exactly how marriage would be regarded in heaven. However, He didn't correct the mother of James and John in regard to the accuracy of what she asked. In fact, He asserted that there would be greater positions of honor in heaven and those would be the ones nearest Him. These positions are awarded by God the Father at the Judgment.

Other scriptures show that positions of honor will be awarded to those who finish the race well—to the relentless believers.

A Type of Things to Come

This truth is also seen in the book of Ezekiel. Even though Old Testament priests are referenced here, Ezekiel provides a prophetic insight—a foreshadowing—of how life will be in the great temple of Zion, the eternal house of God.

Through Ezekiel the prophet, God discusses the Levites—the Old Testament priests. How does this relate to us? We are told by the apostle John,

> To Him who loved us and washed us from our sins in His own blood,
> and has made us kings and *priests* to His God and Father, to Him be
> glory and dominion forever and ever. Amen. (Revelation 1:5–6)

See how I emphasized the word *priests*? Christians, who are born of the Spirit, are now priests unto our God forever and ever. Hear God's words:

> The Levites (priests) who walked off and left me, along with everyone
> else—all Israel—who took up with all the no-god idols, will pay for
> everything they did wrong. From now on they'll do only the menial
> work in the Sanctuary: guard the gates and help out with the Temple
> chores. (Ezekiel 44:10–11, MSG)

The "no-god idols" is a reference to Israel's idolatry. Idolatry in our society most often doesn't take the form it did in their day, but it is just as horrible in God's sight. We are told, "Don't be greedy for the good things of this life, for that is idolatry" (Colossians 3:5, NLT). Idolatry happens when we lust intensely for the attractive things of this life. In our Western culture today, idolatry is the prioritization and pursuit of promotion, money, material things, status, popularity, pleasure, fame, or any other manifestation of envy or selfish ambition. An idol is anything we love or desire more than we love or desire God. It is something or someone we give our strength to or draw our strength from.

Idolatry can show up in practically any area of life—even in something as basic as eating. There are numerous Christians who are greedy for food. When sad, they eat; when happy, they eat; if it tastes good, they eat—no matter what the nutritional value is. They'll ingest pure junk in their bodies because they covet the fleeting pleasure of taste. They would never put used oil or dirty gas in their car, but they've abandoned reason when it comes to the quality and quantity of food they in-gest. They've made food an idol. Because they draw their strength from the temporary sensation of taste and a full stomach, they give their strength to that sensation.

> Idolatry can show up in practically any area of life.

Idolatry can also be found in a person's desire to be known. There are those who will do anything to gain a position of "honor" in the church, at their job, or in society. They'll gossip, slander, deceive, lie, or compromise integrity to get a place of recognition, position, or authority. Even if they do not engage in such underhanded practices, they make a god of their quest for position. They draw their strength from popularity, status, and fame; consequently they give their strength to it.

An idol will rob you of relentless faithfulness. It will steal the strength you need to run the race faithfully to the end.

In the Ezekiel passage above, God is speaking of those believers who left their pursuit of Him for things that do not give enduring satisfaction. Those idols may please us in the short run, but they can never fulfill us in the long run. God states that the idolaters will pay for everything they did wrong. They will pay by seeing their reward burned up. They'll be saved, but just barely. They'll belong in His house, but as servants doing menial work and helping with house-hold chores.

We must remember that God is speaking to us as well, in the here and now. He doesn't want you or me to miss out on all the riches He has in store for us. Heaven is going to be so much better than anything we can imagine; nothing on earth compares to its splendor. However, there will be status in heaven—places of greater honor and those of far less honor. Any position in the household of God is much better than anything here on earth, for even David affirms, "I would rather be a doorkeeper and stand at the threshold in the house of my God than to dwell [at ease] in the tents of wickedness" (Psalm 84:10, AMP). The Message Bible paraphrases this verse beautifully:

> One day spent in your house, this beautiful place of worship, beats thousands spent on Greek island beaches. I'd rather scrub floors in the house of my God than be honored as a guest in the palace of sin.

David is saying, "I'd rather be a mere servant in the house of God than be anywhere else!" There is no place more desirable in the entire universe than God's custom home, the residence of His very tangible presence. Any position in Zion is better than anything or anywhere else.

But do not miss the point God is making here. Because He loves us so much, He is trying to alert us to the potential sorrow we could experience if we fall short of the very best: the reward of being nearer to, and working closer with, God Himself throughout eternity. There will be tears at the believer's judgment, and we're assured that "God will wipe away every tear from their eyes" (Revelation 21:4). But the realization that we misused our short lifetime, which positioned us for all eternity, will not go away. We'll always know what we missed because of our pursuit of that which didn't last. This is the eternal loss I discussed at length in the previous chapter (see 1 Corinthians 3:12–15).

On the other hand, hear what God goes on to say: "But the Levitical priests who descend from Zadok, who faithfully took care of my Sanctuary when everyone else went off and left me, *are going to come into my presence and serve me*" (Ezekiel 44:15, MSG).

Even though God is referring specifically to the Old Testament priests in this verse, we are told that these are "a shadow of things to come" (Colossians 2:17) and that "All these events happened to them as examples for us" (1 Corinthians 10:11, NLT). In many situations the events of the Old Testament are types, shadows, or illustrations of things to come in future ages. Notice the words *serve me*. It is one thing to be a servant in the house, scrubbing floors as David was willing to do. But it is an entirely different thing to serve God!

I was a member of an 8,000-member church when I began full-time ministry in 1983. This church was known not just in my city but globally. We had up to 450 staff members at one time. I was hired to be the executive assistant to the pastor and his wife. It was an honor just to serve them. I was more privileged than other team members because my office was located right next to theirs, I was in their home frequently, and often I joined them at lunch or dinner with some of the greatest ministers in the world. There were times I sat in awe. Tears would well up as I pondered how fortunate I was to be so close to these great leaders.

I heard wisdom, thoughts, and ideas that the other staff members were not privileged to hear. I gleaned insights that still guide me today. My position was the most coveted job in the entire church. Staff members frequently would tell me, "You are so fortunate to serve in the position you hold." Some asked, in envy, "How come you got this position? What did you do to get it?" Others frequently discussed who would get to take my place if I left someday. I knew they were right: it was the best position on the staff.

Now can you imagine this kind of privileged status with God Himself? Relentless believers, those who do their work well and endure the race to the end are the ones who will be close to the presence of God in the ages to come. They will be the ones who sit in the places of honor. As God says in Ezekiel 44:28, "It shall be, in regard to their inheritance, that I am their inheritance."

Wow! Could there be any better reward or prize? The ones who will be near Him, hearing His ideas, visions, and insights, assisting Him in planning the future and in other matters of leadership, are those who endure diligently and faithfully. We will sit and rule with Him forever. We will serve Him directly. What an amazing promise!

So hear Paul's exhortation again:

All athletes practice strict self-control. They do it to win a prize that will fade away, but we do it for an eternal prize. So I run straight to the goal with purpose in every step. (1 Corinthians 9:25–26, NLT)

Professional athletes rigorously train and persist toward the prize of the Super Bowl trophy, the Masters' green jacket, the Stanley Cup, and the Olympic gold medal, but all of these pale in comparison to what we are running for! This is why we are exhorted, "Let us run with *patient endurance* and *steady and active persistence* the *appointed* course of the race that is set before us" (Hebrews 12:1, AMP). The Message bottom-lines it this way: "Strip down, start running—and never quit!" Another contemporary paraphrase says straightforwardly, "Run, then, in such a way as to win the prize" (1 Corinthians 9:24, TEV).

Now ask yourself: *Are these words more significant now that I've heard about the prizes that await me?*

I think I know your answer.

18

NEVER GIVE UP!

Don't quit. Don't cave in. It is all well worth it
in the end.

MATTHEW 10:22 (MSG)

N o one can force you to quit; you are the only one who can make that
decision.

So don't.

The reward for overcoming, both in this life and the next, is so far greater
than the adversity or hardship you face. As Jesus said, "It is all well worth it in
the end."

Our Savior foretells a very sad fact that will occur in these latter days. "Many
will give up," He says in Matthew 24:10 (CEV). To even utter these words must
have broken His heart. People He loves so dearly, those He's given His life for to
purchase their freedom and success, will give up.

The sad fact is, they don't need to. God has given us His powerful grace to
not only pull us through hardship but come out far stronger, wiser, and more
fruitful than before we entered into suffering. Many will quit because they don't
have the right perspective. They are not armed.

Quitting takes on different forms. Most often it's rooted in compromise—
an antonym of *relentless*. From the vision I recounted for you in the first chapter,
we need to imitate the man rowing against the current. To walk with God,
manifest His kingdom, and distinguish ourselves for His renown involves moving against the flow of the world's system.

We must be relentless in adhering to God's wisdom. Compromise is not an
option.

Hard to Be a Christian

Just before his martyrdom, the apostle Paul foresaw the rough currents of the last days. "In the last days it is going to be very difficult to be a Christian," he wrote to Timothy (2 Timothy 3:1, TLB). Paul had received thirty-nine stripes five different times, was beaten with rods three times, was once stoned, and suffered years in prison. He had faced hostility and persecution everywhere he went. Yet he prophesies that in *our* time period it will be more difficult to live for God! How could he say this after experiencing such extreme hardship in his life? He proceeds to spell it out:

> People will be selfish, greedy, boastful, and conceited; they will be
> insulting, disobedient to their parents, ungrateful, and irreligious; they
> will be unkind, merciless, slanderers, violent, and fierce; they will hate
> the good; they will be treacherous, reckless, and swollen with pride; they
> will love pleasure rather than God. (2 Timothy 3:2–4, TEV)

At first glance we may question, "What's his point? How does this list of behavioral patterns foretold for our time differ from Paul's era?" Indeed, these character traits were also found in his society. People loved themselves and money, were unholy and unforgiving, the whole list. Peter had even said on the day of Pentecost, "Be saved from this crooked (perverse, wicked, unjust) generation" (Acts 2:40, AMP).

So why does Paul single out our generation? Why does he target these traits in describing the most difficult time in history to walk with God? The next verse provides the answer: "They will act as if they are religious, but they will reject the power that could make them godly" (2 Timothy 3:5, NLT).

The great difficulty, Paul says, stems from "believers" compromising truth. Along with other writers of the New Testament, the apostle forewarns that, in our time, a large percentage of professing "born-again Christians" will not stand strong in God's grace. They'll cling to the fact that they are saved by grace, yet they'll reject the power of grace that could set them apart as relentless warriors of the kingdom.

These are the ones who've put up the oars. They may be pointed upstream, but they flow with the current of this world's system. To make matters worse, my vision contained large party boats filled with these people. Their unified belief makes the deception even stronger and more convincing. They're not only self-deceived but are also misleading others and causing many sincere ones to stumble. This is the difficulty Paul addresses.

As I look back over history, I believe the greatest battle the early church fathers fought was *legalism*. Legalism attempted to get new believers back under the law to be saved, rather than trusting in God's grace.

We fight a different battle now. I believe the greatest battle we face in these latter days is *lawlessness*. Lawlessness communicates a salvation without expectation of a changed lifestyle. We live no differently as Christians than before we were saved, but now we're part of a club, we wear the label, we speak our club's language as our party boat heads downstream with the current. We're no longer relentless in our trust in God and our obedience to His way.

Jesus warns that in the latter days "Sin will be rampant everywhere, and the love of many will grow cold. But those who *endure* to the end will be saved" (Matthew 24:12–13, NLT). But wait—sin was rampant when Jesus spoke these words. What makes our day different? The shocking reality: Jesus isn't talking about society in general; He's talking about those who claim to follow Him. He testifies that sin will be rampant amongst professing Christians in our day. Why else would He finish His statement with "but those who *endure* to the end will be saved"? You don't say to a nonbeliever, "If you finish the race you'll be saved," for he or she isn't even in the race. However, you would say to one who is already in the faith, who has already started the race, "If you finish…"

> I believe the greatest battle we face in these latter days is lawlessness.

The key word Jesus uses is *endure*. To *endure* means there will be opposition, resistance, or hardship in adhering to truth. We must be relentless to finish well.

The Time Has Come

In light of this, Paul's second letter to Timothy deserves some more of our attention. After he spells out the difficulty, Paul gives the antidote: "Impostors will keep on going from bad to worse, deceiving others and being deceived themselves. But as for you, continue in the truths that you were taught and firmly believe" (2 Timothy 3:13–14, TEV).

Truth is not trendy; it remains constant through time and unaffected by opinion or culture. Notice that Paul both urges and warns his apprentice to "continue in the truths you were taught and firmly believe." Steadfastness to the truth is the antidote.

The alluring enticement is to follow the world's trends, but they lead only to deception. For this reason Paul continues:

> You have been taught *the holy Scriptures from childhood,* and they have
> given you the wisdom to receive the salvation that comes by trusting in
> Christ Jesus. All Scripture is inspired by God and is useful to teach
> us what is true and to make us realize what is wrong in our lives. It
> straightens us out and teaches us to do what is right. It is God's way of
> preparing us in every way, fully equipped for every good thing God wants
> us to do. (2 Timothy 3:15–17, NLT)

I've highlighted two key terms in this passage: *the holy Scriptures* and *from childhood.* God inspires all Scripture. It's His truth that transcends time and culture. It's the foundation upon which we build our lives; it equips us with the knowledge and power to please God in every way.

As 2 Timothy 3 draws to an end, most of us assume Paul is finished with this particular thought. However, it wasn't until AD 1227 that the church added chapter and verse divisions to the Bible. As Paul penned it, Second Timothy is one letter. And he definitely is not finished with his thought. Paul's very next words continue along the same lines:

> I charge *you* therefore before God and the Lord Jesus Christ, who will
> judge the living and the dead at His appearing and His kingdom: Preach

the word! Be ready in season and out of season. Convince, rebuke, exhort, with all longsuffering and teaching. For the time will come when they will not *endure* sound doctrine, but according to their own desires, because they have itching ears, they will heap up for themselves teachers; and they will turn their ears away from the truth. (2 Timothy 4:1–4)

"I charge you before God and the Lord Jesus Christ." Paul can give his student no stronger command. What is the charge? To proclaim and teach the Word of God. It's not to teach philosophy, secular leadership principles, life-coaching techniques, or any other material relevant to the times. No, the charge is to preach the timeless Scripture.

Paul has just established all Scripture to be inspired by God and useful for directing our lives. Then he charges Timothy to proclaim and teach it. Why? Because the time will come (and I believe it has now arrived) when those who are deceiving and being deceived will not endure sound doctrine. What is doctrine? It's not merely teaching, but rather foundational or backbone teaching of the Scripture. It's the teaching that holds everything together.

Sadly, I have witnessed our spiritual (scriptural) foundations shifting to accommodate the trends and times. It's gotten so out of control that a minister of a large church can stand before his congregation, declare he's a homosexual, and receive a standing ovation. Another can declare it's no longer God's will to heal, and his people will believe him instead of God's Word. Another can author a book declaring that all humanity is going to eventually enter heaven—that no person will burn in eternal fire—and he remains a "rock star" in Christendom. Another can challenge the virgin birth and the return of Jesus Christ and still be celebrated as a leader of the Christian faith. More and more sad scenarios such as these play out among "Christians" each day.

Some recent surveys may help us understand these ludicrous shifts. According to one national survey, only 46 percent of "born-again Christians" believe in absolute moral truth. More than 50 percent of "evangelical Christians" believe people can attain heaven through avenues other than the sacrifice of Jesus Christ. Only 40 percent of "born-again Christians" believe Satan is a real force.[1]

---

1. www.barna.org/transformation-articles/252-barna-survey-examines-changes-in-worldview-among-christians-over-the-past-13-years.

How can this be? The answer is found in Paul's words to Timothy: "They will not *endure* sound doctrine"—we are not remaining *relentless* in truth.

More and more we're hearing and declaring a nontransformational gospel. Its core message is unfaithful to the core doctrine of God's Word, as in "Jesus died for our sins to get us to heaven, but we are human, and God understands our different vices and sexual preferences." A popular teaching of late is the removal of the need for repentance from sin. Multitudes of believers are gleefully told that there's no need to embrace godly sorrow over disobedience or to confess it to God because sin has already been covered by grace. I've heard men and women who embrace this teaching boast of how simple, fresh, and liberating the message is. But if simple, fresh, and liberating were the real indicators of truth, then any doctrine that gratifies the flesh would be truth! If it's an accurate teaching that Christians no longer need to repent, then Jesus Christ was way off base when He told five of the seven churches to "repent" in the book of Revelation (see Revelation 2:5, 16, 21, 22; 3:3, 19).

Truth does not change to accommodate those who want to sin. Truth does not conform itself to human desire, convenience, or so-called "political correctness." On the contrary the Son of God declares, "Difficult is the way which leads to life" (Matthew 7:14).

We've now heaped up for ourselves teachers who've veered away from sound doctrine. These crafty communicators have contrived a gospel that accommodates our culture's moral disintegration. Truth no longer shapes the life of a believer, but instead truth is reshaped and interpreted through cultural trends. Why? Because our ears itch to hear words that will allow us to jump in bed with the world rather than "come out from among them and be separate" (2 Corinthians 6:17).

Many believers do feel the tug of the Holy Spirit when they first begin to flirt with compromise. Yet, because of the mass numbers floating with the current on large party boats, the majority eventually quench the voice of the Spirit, close their ears, and become dull of hearing the truth.

A GENERATION OF CHAMPIONS

And why should this surprise us? We have been told of a great apostasy that would occur in the latter days (see 2 Thessalonians 2:3).

On the other hand, we've also been told of a generation of champions that would arise in the same time period. These great ones include men and women, both young and old (see Acts 2:17–18). The prophets and apostles of old described these heroes as relentless in truth. The adversity of darkness and deception would set the stage for these warriors. They'll not draw back, but through their tenacious beliefs and actions will make great advancements for the kingdom of God. They will truly distinguish themselves as strong lights amid the darkness. They will excel in all aspects of life—not through compromise, but just as Daniel did through the wisdom of God that is found only in godly fear and empowering grace.

Dear reader, I'm hopeful that you will be one of these champions. I pray that you will establish your greatness by girding your loins with truth and arming yourself with the breastplate of righteousness. I hope you will hold up the shield of faith and run relentlessly the race set before you, confidently fighting any opposition to the end. You are an overcomer. You possess the seed of the one who endured the greatest hostility ever encountered. His strength is in you! His nature is yours. You were not made to quit, draw back, falter, or compromise. You've been blessed with the amazing grace of God.

No matter how great the adversity against you, view it as a steppingstone to the next level of rulership. Learn from adversity as Paul did:

> It was so bad we didn't think we were going to make it. We felt like we'd been sent to death row, that it was all over for us. As it turned out, it was the best thing that could have happened. Instead of trusting in our own strength or wits to get out of it, we were forced to trust God totally—not a bad idea since he's the God who raises the dead! And he did it, rescued us from certain doom. *And* he'll do it again, rescuing us as many times as we need rescuing. (2 Corinthians 1:8–10, MSG)

Paul's hardship was so severe it appeared that he and his team wouldn't live through it. Yet he states that "it was the best thing that could have happened." Through opposition, Paul ascended to a higher level of authority and power. God's grace (power) is always sufficient. God will pull us through again and again.

All we have to do is stay with it, to not let go of our faith, for on the other side is great victory, satisfaction, and fulfillment. As James writes, "God will bless you, *if you don't give up* when your faith is being tested. He will reward you with a glorious life" (James 1:12, CEV).

You have God's empowering grace, nature, essential characteristics, and fullness implanted in you. You are one with Him; you are the body of Christ. The head (Jesus) never failed, so neither should His body. "We are pressed on every side by troubles," Paul writes, "but we are not crushed and broken. We are perplexed, *but we don't give up and quit*" (2 Corinthians 4:8, NLT).

We are the body of Christ; we don't give up. We don't quit! Paul repeats these words over and over, "We never give up" (2 Corinthians 4:1, CEV), and again, "So we're not giving up. How could we!" (2 Corinthians 4:16, MSG), and the list continues. You were made to succeed in a magnificent way.

And don't ever think God has given up on you. He will never do that. Hear His ironclad promise: "God, who got you started in this spiritual adventure, shares with us the life of his Son and our Master Jesus. *He will never give up on you. Never forget that*" (1 Corinthians 1:9, MSG).

> Don't ever think God has given up on you.

Isn't that a remarkable promise? God will never give up on you. He's relentless about that.

And if He won't give up on you, how could you ever give up on Him or on yourself? Stay relentless.

What is the reward for sticking it out? Here it is, right from the Lord's mouth:

> Here's the reward I have for every conqueror, everyone who keeps at it, refusing to give up: *You'll rule the nations.* (Revelation 2:26, MSG)

What a reward! Paul confirms Jesus' promise: "If we don't give up, we will rule with him" (2 Timothy 2:12, CEV). And remember, it's not only in the age to come but also in the here and now. "All who receive God's abundant grace and are freely put right with him will *rule in life* through Christ" (Romans 5:17, TEV).

So, my dear fellow brother or sister in Christ, you positively possess the power to be relentless. You have what it takes to finish well: the grace of God, and it cannot fail. So run with confidence to your prize. Whether it's for a divine assignment, a key position, or a kingdom relationship; whether it's for the short-term, long-term, or even a lifetime, you are destined to conquer and reign. You have the privilege of experiencing the rich fulfillment and abundant life that comes from sticking it out. Rulership awaits. You'll be distinguished for the glory of your King. Indeed, a sweet reward. So always remember:

Stay with GOD!
    Take heart. Don't quit.
I'll say it again:
    Stay with GOD. (Psalm 27:14, MSG)

Prayer to Become a Child of God

How do we become a child of God? First and foremost it has nothing to do with you, but what was done for you by Jesus Christ. He gave His royal life, in perfect innocence, for you to be brought back to your Creator, God the Father. His death on the cross is the only price able to purchase for you eternal life.

No matter your social class, race, background, religion, or anything else favorable or unfavorable in the eyes of men, you are eligible to become a child of God. He desires and longs for you to come into His family. This occurs by simply renouncing your sin of living independently of Him and committing your life to the Lordship of Jesus Christ; once you do, you'll literally be reborn. You're no longer a slave to darkness; you're born-again as a brand new son or daughter of God. Scripture declares,

> For if you confess with your mouth that Jesus is Lord and believe in your heart that God raised him from the dead, you will be saved. For it is by believing in your heart that you are made right with God, and it is by confessing with your mouth that you are saved. (Romans 10:9–10, NLT)

So if you believe Jesus Christ died for you and you're willing to give Him your life—no longer to live for yourself—confess this prayer from a sincere heart, and you will become a child of God:

> *God in Heaven, I acknowledge that I am a sinner and have fallen short of Your righteous standard. I deserve to be judged for eternity for my sin. Thank You for not leaving me in this state, for I believe You sent Jesus Christ, Your only begotten Son, who was born of the virgin Mary, to die for me and carry my judgment on the Cross. I believe He was raised again on the third day and is now seated at Your right hand as my Lord and Savior. So on this day of _____, 20__ I give my life entirely to the Lordship of Jesus.*
>
> *Jesus, I confess you as my Lord, Savior, and King. Come into my life through Your Spirit and change me into a child of God. I renounce the things of darkness which I once held on to and from this day forward I will no longer live for myself, but for You who gave Yourself for me that I may live forever.*
>
> *Thank You Lord; my life is now completely in Your hands, and according to Your Word I shall never be ashamed.*

Now, you're saved; you're a child of God. All heaven is rejoicing with you at this very moment! Welcome to the family! I'd like to suggest three beneficial steps to immediately take:

1. Share what you've done with someone who is already a believer. Scripture informs us one of the ways we defeat darkness is by our testimony (see Revelation 12:11). I invite you to contact our ministry, Messenger International, at www.messengerinternational.org. We'd love to hear from you.

2. Join a good church that teaches the Word of God. Become a member and get involved. Parents do not put babies on the street the day they're born saying, "Survive." You are now a babe in Christ; God your Father has provided a family to help you grow. It's called the local New Testament Church.

3. Get water baptized. Though you are already a child of God, baptism is a public profession to both the spiritual world as well as the natural world that you've given your life to God through Jesus Christ. It is also an act

of obedience, for Jesus says we are to baptize new believers "in the name of the Father and of the Son and of the Holy Spirit" (Matthew 28:19).

I wish you the very best in your new life in Christ. Our ministry will pray for you on a regular basis. Now start living relentlessly in truth!

WHY I USE SO MANY DIFFERENT BIBLE TRANSLATIONS

The question sometimes arises why I use so many translations and, second, why I use only portions of verses of Scripture? Allow me to answer these questions.

1. The Bible was originally written with over 11,000 Hebrew, Aramaic, and Greek words. However, the average English translation uses approximately 6,000 words. From this statistic alone we could safely conclude various shades of meanings could slip through and be lost in the translations. Drawing from several English sources helps to recover the full riches of what God is communicating.

2. In using only a single translation, if the reader recognizes a verse, it is easy to skim over it due to familiarity. Using different translations decreases the probability of this occurring and keeps the reader focused on the Scripture.

3. In writing, I carefully read the selected portion of Scripture from at least five to eight different translations and determine which one communicates the point being highlighted the best. I also make sure if I'm using a paraphrase, that the portion I'm using is not out of sync with a well-respected translation.

4. The reason I don't always use full verses is that chapter and verse were added to the Bible in AD 1227. The Bible was not originally written with these divisions. Jesus in the Gospels many times only quoted portions of verses from the Old Testament.

For Further Reflection and Discussion

1. Do you agree or disagree that how we finish in life is more important than how we begin? Explain your answer.

2. How would you define a "relentless spirit"?

3. What would you say is the meaning of God's grace? How has your understanding of grace been enhanced by reading this book?

4. What are the implications for you of the truth that Christians are to "rule in life" (see Romans 5:17, TEV)? How does this truth affect your family? Your work? Your response to any challenge in life?

5. Many Christians do not appear to rule in life. Why do you think this is the case?

6. What are some of the basic attitudes and actions that make it possible for a believer to become a ruler in every challenge life presents?

7. What is Satan's game plan of opposition to you (see John 10:10)? In the past days or weeks, how have you seen Satan at work to "steal, and to kill, and to destroy" in your life?

8. Jesus said that we would have trouble in this world but that He had "overcome the world" (see John 16:33). What is it that helps us actually be overcomers and conquerors?

9. What are the characteristics of someone who is proud? What are the characteristics of someone who is humble?

10. The apostle Peter urged followers of Jesus to be "clothed with humility" (1 Peter 5:5). In practical life terms, what do you think he meant?

11. What are some of the tactics we can use to resist the devil?

12. Why is hardship such an important reality in a Christian's life?

13. What is the role of prayer in the life of a relentless Christian?

14. How would you describe "earnest" prayer?

15. Why will there be different types and levels of rewards in heaven?

16. As you reflect on the major themes of this book, in what areas of your walk with God do you want help from the Holy Spirit to increase your "relentless spirit"?

It's time to pursue your *extraordinary* life!

In *Extraordinary*, best-selling author and internationally known speaker John Bevere reveals how all of us were "meant for more," extraordinarily created and intended for a life that is anything but ordinary. In this book you'll find the roadmap for your journey of transformation, because you are marked for a life that far surpasses the usual definitions of success or fulfillment.

EXPERIENCE GRACE.

USE YOUR GOD-GIVEN POWER.

FULFILL YOUR DESTINY.

LIVE EXTRAORDINARILY.

Read an excerpt at WaterBrookMultnomah.com